THE ROMANIAN COOK BOOK

The ROMANIAN COOK BOOK

BY ANISOARA STAN

Decorations by John Teppich

TO

OUR DEAR GRANDMOTHERS AND MOTHERS
WHOSE COOKING WAS ONE OF THE GREAT JOYS
OF OUR YOUTH

Contents

Introduction	ix
Important Tips and Suggestions	xv
EGGPLANTS	1
APPETIZERS AND HORS D'ŒUVRES	7
SOUPS	13
CIORBAS: THE SOUR SOUPS	23
VEGETABLE DISHES	33
MUSHROOMS	71
FISH DISHES	79
CHICKEN AND FOWL	87
MEAT DISHES	97
STEWS	139
OMELETS	153
MAMALIGA DISHES	159
DUMPLINGS	165
SAUCES	171
SALADS	187
DESSERTS AND PRESERVES	193
Index	221

Introduction

WHY ANOTHER COOKBOOK, and one with recipes from such a little known country as Romania at that? I believe more people should know Romanian cookery, especially in these days of rising food costs.

By the artful use of herbs and flavorings truly gourmet dishes may be prepared from the cheaper cuts of meats like beef, lamb and veal . . . from extras like tripe, heart and sweetbreads . . . and from leftovers. A cheap and most delicious dish is the chicken stew made out of wings, liver and gizzards.

Even vegetable dishes can be made delectable this way. Very many novel ones are given here, like the eggplant and ghivetch, which will make the Lenten season more enjoyable . . . for fast days, which in the Balkans come on Wednesdays and Fridays, these recipes will make a greater choice of dishes available. And the great variety of vegetable dishes should be of particular interest for vegetarians.

Very many of the recipes are for one meal dishes. They supply all the needed nourishment, cost little and are easy to prepare.

I think the cooking of my native land is exquisite. It is impossible for one not to love the food that was first prepared by Mother and that always brings forth memories of one's youth. But, fortunately, the Americans love Romanian dishes, too. Those who have traveled in that far-off country have come back enthusiasts, and even those who had eaten at the Romanian Pavilion of the New York World's Fair. This need not surprise

X : INTRODUCTION

us. Bigness does not make for goodness, often it is the other way around. Romanian cooking is famous among gourmets around the world.

The Romanians love good food. They love to prepare it and they love to eat it. If this book will show how gourmet dishes can be made from the materials available to everyone, and sometimes even cheaper than before, I will be happy, indeed. Pâté de foie gras (fat goose liver paste) was at first a delicacy reserved only for aristocrats, but after the French Revolution the chef who invented it opened a restaurant where he served his creation to all who came in. It immediately became popular. That is the way it should be. Excellent cooking need not be exclusive.

It is more than ever important in our troubled world for peoples of different countries to understand and know each other. And what better way is there to bring people together than through food? Since it is impossible for a whole nation to take a vacation to another country to sit down with their hosts and partake of their food, its place will have to be taken by a cookbook. Since America is unique in that so many of its citizens have a foreign heritage, it is fitting that the American people who have extended their hands in welcome to the immigrants and who have accorded them all the privileges of living in this democratic nation should have the opportunity to know the culture of their fellow citizens; and cooking is an important part of folk culture.

We all know food is essential to life but it is really more than that. Cooking is essential to living. No one objects to sitting in a railroad coach next to a stranger, but you prefer eating at the same table with a friend. Why should this be so? Because friendship is the unseen guest at any table where food is being served. Eating together unites people and many a romance has flowered at a table for two in a quiet little restaurant.

Traditionally it is woman's role to feed the race and it is a role that gives most of them a real joy. In Romania, where the women look up to the men, they put their hearts into cooking in order to excel, to become true artists of the kitchen. It is not a chore with them but an accomplishment of which they are proud. And like true artists, they need an audience, people who

INTRODUCTION : xi

will recognize their work and derive pleasure from it. This need of an appreciative audience explains why people who are great cooks are also very friendly and hospitable.

Whether the kind of food a nation eats changes its personality or whether the temperament of a people decides what they will eat has always puzzled me. But we all know that those people who eat interesting, spicy and flavorful food are invariably interesting, impulsive and colorful themselves. The American people are becoming more spontaneous and emotional with the years. Could it be due to the great amount of foreign type food which is consumed here?

Cooking is primarily an art. You must sing at it, love it, hope it will turn out to be a masterpiece and that your loved ones will love it too. It is an art when one can combine the good things of the earth to bring out the ultimate in flavor. The truly great cook uses her materials as the composer combines notes to form a symphony. It is interesting, but certainly not surprising, to learn that a nation of great cooks should also produce a beautiful folk art. Cooking and folk art go hand in hand because each demands imagination and a love of the materials and forms of nature. Romania, France and China are good examples of this fact.

Romanian cooking has a character all its own. It is savory, light, not greasy, very flavorful and stimulating to the appetite. In the old country it is done with simple equipment, often even primitive, but effective nonetheless. The Romanian housewife, even when she follows a recipe, adds a pinch of this or that to make her dish personal and exciting . . . she refuses to cook by a rigid formula.

Romanian cooking is very healthful because it is full of flavor. Many books in discussing food talk about proteins, fats and vitamins. But something just as important is left out. It is flavor, the vitamin of the soul. The human body consists of more than the stomach. It consists of eyes to see, a nose to smell, palate to taste and a mind to become overjoyed at a good thing to eat. Tasty food enlivens the appetite, so one not only eats more but gets more good out of what one eats.

The secret of flavor lies in the proper use of herbs. Many, like parsley and dill, are natives of southeastern Europe. These xii : INTRODUCTION

fragrant and aromatic plants from ancient times on have been used as medicines. All people close to the soil have used herbs, roots and vegetables to heal as well as for food. Even now very many consider garlic to be an excellent blood germicide, not only in the old country, but right here in America. In Romania every peasant home is aromatic with basil and mint and other herbs and flowers in season. They pluck these mirositoare, good smelling herbs, on their return from field work or on holidays and consider them a blessing sent by God for the poor. I have watched them caress these herbs with gentleness and love, these plain people of the earth.

With such tasty food it is little wonder that the Romanian peasants are so healthy, in fact one of the healthiest in the world. Good food puts one in a happy state of mind, the body becomes relaxed and the digestion improved. But equally important is their attitude towards life, a love of the soil and of nature's work, their songs and dances, their fairy tales related to the children, their anecdotes, proverbs and riddles, their famous spinning evenings where work and fun are so intermingled that the spinning and weaving takes on a festive air, their embroidery and carpet weaving, the making of the peasant costumes, the painting on pottery and even the painstaking carvings on their wooden household utensils. All this gives them no time to feel bored. They are busy and happy.

It is a tradition from olden times in Romania to look with reverence not only upon God, but also upon the earthly goods He gave us, like bread, water and the fruits of the fields. And this respect applies also to cooking. It is considered a sin to change in any way the patriarchal dishes and drinks which their beloved ancestors had created and passed on to them.

It is our good fortune in this country that we can learn the cooking arts of our grandparents, which have been brought to our shores by the immigrants from every corner of the world. With our new methods and ready availability of all kinds of food at every season of the year we can change any recipe to suit our needs and form a bridge between the past and the present.

It is well to keep in mind that we must never, absolutely never, prepare food when we are angry or dejected. Be cheerful

INTRODUCTION : xiii

while preparing your food and joyful and thankful while eating it. Keep bad news away from the dinner table. Do not read while eating, as then you cannot do justice to either.

The Romanians, like all Europeans, are a wine-drinking people and their wines are famous for their variety and bouquet. Good food becomes better with a good wine to drink. Let wines be served in beautiful glasses to excite the eye. Take the glass in your hands and inhale its good aroma. With delicious pork, fried, boiled or roasted, or a suckling pig, serve only good old red wine. Please do not interrupt the drinking of it, but continue on to the cheese, as it certainly is no sin to enjoy it. But it is a sin if you use anything but white wine for fish, eggs, lobster, oysters or clams. If the white wine is a little sweet, do please cool it a little, but if it is a little sour, then serve it as it comes out of the bottle. If you can afford more than one kind of wine, you should first serve the sour ones and end with the sweet wines. And finally, do not drink brandy or whiskey just before starting the meal (ugly habit), as your palate will not be capable of feeling the deliciousness of the food and wine.

Some of the ingredients in the recipes in this book, like grape vine leaves, black olives or sharp little red peppers, may not be obtainable in your neighborhood store. But do not despair. They can be bought at a Greek or oriental grocery, or in New York in the lower East Side or on Ninth Avenue below 42nd Street.

I couldn't end these few words without expressing my gratitude to the good Romanian housewife, whose love and genius have created the delicious dishes in this book, and many thousands more. I leave you with a wish. May you derive only pleasure when you prepare them and eat them.

Important Tips and Suggestions

To PREPARE FOOD so as to get the most value and the greatest flavor out of the ingredients and so that our bodies should be well fed is properly a part of science. Yet it is surprising how much has been discovered about food and its preparation by the simple peoples of the earth, to whom it was an art. In fact, in many respects, especially in the art of making food more palatable, we can learn much from these simple people.

The enjoyment of food is partly a matter of training; training which should begin very early. In Romania an infusion is made of herbs by boiling them in a little earthen pot and made a trifle sour by adding a little lemon juice, sour cherries, raspberries or grapes. No sugar is used. The lips of babies are moistened with this infusion. At this early stage they become acquainted with beautiful aromas in their nostrils and good taste on their lips. After the fourth month the babies are given some of the infusion. After the fifth month strictly fresh strained vegetables are given the babies. To have fresh vegetables for the winter they cover them with leaves and straw in a deep hole in the ground and when the snow covers the ground they are preserved in a fresh state. They prefer this method to canning. The vegetables given to babies and children are changed from meal to meal to give variety and increase appetites. I have never seen Romanian children refuse to eat spinach. The spinach is flavored with lemon juice, sorrel and various sour berries to make it more tasty.

When the children are a little older, they start to help in the kitchen. They do their chores happily, in the meantime having had explained to them how to prepare food, to know the qualities of all food materials, those which make them strong

xvi : IMPORTANT TIPS AND SUGGESTIONS

and brave if boys or beautiful if girls, and to recognize fine flavors and tastes. They are taught about the sweet-smelling herbs, the legends about them, their curative powers and what they do to food. The girls and women use herbs to make their linens aromatic. The girls tuck basil, mint or sweet marjoram in their bosoms as a substitute for perfume, which they cannot afford. They believe that basil will bring good luck in love and that when taken to church with them their wishes will be fulfilled. The liking for herbs and their aroma grows with continued use. Thus they develop a love of flavor, taste and good food, which never leaves them.

Here is a list of some herbs and flavorings and where best to use them in foods:

GARLIC—A well-known blood germicide and purifier. Also when used in food has the property of preserving it, so that leftovers can keep longer. Wonderful for lamb, to mask the lamb taste. Used in nearly everything. Before adding to food crush together with a drop of water. The garlic greens make salads most delicious.

GREEN PARSLEY—Also a blood purifier. Use in nearly all kinds of food.

HORSE-RADISH ROOT—Grated. Use for roasts, game and fish. You may also color the grated root under a high flame for a short time.

TABASCO PEPPERS—Dried. Use in stews, marinated fish, meats and brown sauce.

CELERY—Use stalk and leaves in soups, ciorbas, stews and nearly all kinds of dishes.

BLACK PEPPER—Use only in food that you want to give a sharp taste to.

WHITE PEPPER—Used generally in nearly everything.

DILL—Use the green dill, finely chopped or in sprigs, in soups and ciorbas, sweet and sour cabbage, pickles, salads and nearly everything. Even when dry, dill is gathered, tied with a string and kept in the attic or pantry.

THYME—Dried and crushed. Use in sweet and sour cabbage, stews, soups, sauces, salads and in pickling cucumbers.

LAUREL (BAY) LEAVES—Use in herrings, marinated fish, meats and game.

SWEET MARJORAM—Use in sausages, stews, sauces and liqueurs.

IMPORTANT TIPS AND SUGGESTIONS : xvii

CORIANDER—Use in marinated fish, pork and sauces.

ANISE—Use in pastry, biscuits, tea and liqueurs.

CARAWAY SEEDS—Use in bread, soups and marinated fish and meats. When roasted, then finely powdered, it is used in making liqueur. It is slightly laxative and is even given to babies.

SCALLIONS—Never throw away the green part. Use in salads, stews and soups. Flavorful and slightly laxative.

ONIONS—Do not be afraid to use large quantities. To make onions melt quickly in your food, slice as thin as you can. When you have to fry them, first sprinkle with salt, cover tightly and simmer for a few minutes. They will then just melt away.

LOVAGE—Its flavor is so pronounced, use a pinch of a pinch for soups, ciorbas, sauces and marinades.

CHIVES—Use for stews, sauces, chicken and omelets.

FENNEL—Use for sauces, vegetables, salads and tea.

PINE CONES—Whole or powdered. Use for game sauces, marinated fish and meats and especially smoked pork.

NUTMEG—Use in minute quantities (pinches) for cakes, salads, fish and piquant sauces.

CINNAMON—Bark or powdered. Use in compotes, cakes and some sauces. When added to hot wine, it is a fine remedy for colds.

CLOVES—Whole or ground. Use in cakes, also stick in hams, game, meats with sauces, onions, apples or turnips, but sparingly as it is very strong.

VANILLA—Use in cakes, biscuits, pancakes and in home-prepared liqueurs, but use sparingly, drop by drop.

The parsley, chives, leek, shallot, dill, celery and green garlic are a must in every kitchen. It is essential to use the right fat for blending each particular herb but this comes with experiment and experience. Pork has such a delicious flavor by itself, care must be used in adding herbs to it, so as to enhance it, not to mask it.

The use of herbs to flavor food should be more widespread than it is. I read recently that tarragon can only be obtained in fancy groceries, but this fact should not prevent you from obtaining this delightful herb and many others. They can be grown in your garden or in window boxes. With tarragon you must experiment a little to get a sunny spot, but much detailed

xviii : IMPORTANT TIPS AND SUGGESTIONS

information can be gotten from your nurseryman or your Agricultural Experiment Station. Green garlic shoots can easily be grown right on your window sill and when added to your salads and other dishes will improve them immeasurably.

MEAT NOTES

Never use meat from fresh-killed animals, keep it for a few days. If meat should develop an odor, wash with a mixture of equal quantities of wine vinegar and water, dry and then prepare. Pound all meats with a mallet to tenderize them; you will get a better taste. Never wash meats in water; wipe well with a damp cloth. When you have large pieces of meat to fry or bake, start with a low flame until the heat penetrates through, then increase the heat until done. Finally use a high flame for a few seconds to brown. With small pieces of meat or for chicken or duck start with a high flame, being careful not to burn. For broiling use a quick high flame. To keep meats fresh trim of all fat and bones and keep in paper in a cool place. Chicken must never be frozen, only kept cold. Liver, veal and other meats can be kept fresh for a longer period by keeping in a large covered earthenware dish and topped with sour cream or sour milk, which is renewed daily. The cheapest and toughest cuts of meat may be made tender, soft and tasty by cooking with sour cream, the quantity used depending on the amount of meat and its degree of toughness. Another way to make the cheap cuts of meat soft and flavorful is by using the delicious sauces described in this book. Meat should always be served on heated plates.

GENERAL NOTES

Be sure to prepare the very best of stock. Use it in sauces and nearly all dishes. Naturally, good stock demands only the finest of ingredients. Give much care and patience to its preparation; it is one of the secrets of fine cooking. It is always advisable to have on hand a week's supply. I have found by long experience in cooking that the stock may be replaced successfully by bouillon soup (beef broth) or a solution of bouillon cubes.

IMPORTANT TIPS AND SUGGESTIONS : xix

Eggs should be kept in the bottom of the refrigerator, in stoneware containers, or if not available, then in a double brown paper bag. They must be kept cold to be better for beating and to give more foam. To obtain a stiff foam, always separate well the whites from the yolks and beat quickly with a fork, always in one direction and without interruption. Once beaten, they must not be allowed to stand, but must be used immediately.

Vegetables should be sprinkled with cold water, placed in a double brown paper bag and kept in the refrigerator. Do not wash until ready to use. Clean only about 10 or 15 minutes before use by placing the vegetables in a sieve, strainer or wire basket and rinsing through with cold water. To obtain the maximum goodness from your vegetables, be they cooked, boiled or fried, please always cut them into thin slices, crosswise or lengthwise. The heat will penetrate them sooner, thus preserving the strength and flavor by the quicker cooking.

Leftover stews must be reheated in a double boiler, adding finely chopped parsley, chives or leeks fried in butter or bacon drippings. When topped with sour cream, it will be as fresh as newly made. Other leftovers can be refreshed in the same way.

In cooking soups and stews it is well to shield the dish from the direct flame by using an iron or clay plate or asbestos pad. The secret of making good stews and soups often is a fine brown sauce.

The making of good sauces is the mark of a good cook. So, if you do not succeed immediately, do not be discouraged. Such an accomplishment in the art of cooking does not come without experience. The secret of a good sauce lies in the use of a rich stock and a slow and careful preparation. Your labor will be fully repaid when you have produced your first wonderful sauce.

Do not hesitate to use brandy, rums, wines and even ale and beer in your recipes.

The herbs, besides their known property of adding flavor to food, are important for the minerals and vitamins they contain. The flavor oils in herbs have medicinal and healing qualities. The herbs (and some vegetables) can mask cooking odors from cabbage, fish, fats, etc. They add vigor and life to freshly made dishes and refresh the leftovers. All herbs should be kept in tightly closed containers.

XX : IMPORTANT TIPS AND SUGGESTIONS

A good housekeeper will prepare her menus for a whole week or at least for two days. Then, before starting to cook, she will surround herself with all the necessary utensils, herbs, spices and the needed ingredients. Now she will arrange her food in the order in which it has to be prepared.

No one can prescribe the exact time for cooking, baking or roasting. It can only be given approximately. The size of the dish used, the condition and thickness of the ingredients and the degree of heat are some of the variables that affect the time needed. But a little practice is the best teacher and soon you will learn to recognize when the dish is done to your liking.

For the more experienced cooks (and this applies also to young women just starting to cook) I suggest they experiment in the making of a dish by using first small quantities in the correct proportions. This will give them an opportunity to correct errors and to get experience. Also, by adding various herbs you will make a dish that will be distinctive and your own creation. In these experiments invite your young daughter into the kitchen with you. Explain to her what you are doing, or better still, have her work together with you in the perfection of a known dish or the creation of an entirely new one. Your child will thus be stimulated to love the art of cooking, and the excitement of doing something that is not routine will add joy to the hours you will spend in the kitchen.

Always arrange the table artistically. Good food will taste even better when served nicely. Have serving plates heated and ready for use.

You may use a pressure cooker in making many of the dishes described here. The greater degree of heat which results from the pressure blends the herbs and flavorings into the food to a great depth and gives truly wonderful results.

And now please follow the recipes as given. Your adventures in Romanian cooking are about to begin.

The recipes in this book are generally proportioned to serve from 4 to 6 persons

EGGPLANTS
Patlagele Vinete

THE EGGPLANT is most popular in Romania and many are the ways in which it is prepared, each with its own distinctive flavor and charm. Even the poorest peasant has a patch near the corn where he grows this colorful vegetable. Despite its cheapness, it is also relished by the rich, and the visitors from foreign lands invariably love it. The eggplant paste (*vinete tocate*, as it is called) is a real favorite, one of the most delicious of appetizers. In the old country it is prepared by broiling in the ashes of an open fire or in the baking oven, but here it can be made over the open flame of the stove. Before serving, it is customary for one to accept one or two glasses or *tzuica*, or plum brandy, which the country people quaintly call *apa chiora* or "cross-eyed water."

EGGPLANT PASTE
Patlagele Vinete Tocate

Choose a large eggplant, firm and with a smooth skin. Broil it under the open flame of the broiler, or over the flame of a top burner, turning constantly until tender. After the skin is burned, let cool a little, then with fingers dipped in cold water, peel the burned skin until the pulp is very clean. Now place on a wooden board and begin to chop it while still warm with a wooden knife (or the edge of any wooden utensil or board),

2 : EGGPLANTS

at the same time adding a few drops of olive oil. Transfer the paste to a wooden bowl, using a wooden spoon. (Wooden utensils only must be used, as metal blackens the eggplant.) Stir constantly the eggplant paste with the spoon, adding at the same time about ½ cup of olive oil, drop by drop, and also enough lemon juice, added drop by drop, and salt and pepper to suit your taste. The stirring must continue until the seeds have disappeared and the paste is firm. Keep in a dry, cool place.

Just before serving, chop some onions very fine, place at the side of the plate holding the paste, and garnish with ripe black olives. Or serve it on crackers or small pieces of bread.

FRIED EGGPLANT
Vinete Prajite

Wash one eggplant, cut crosswise into ¼-inch slices, sprinkle with salt, place on napkins and let stand until the juice is absorbed. When ready to prepare, season and dip in flour. Flavor butter by adding a sprig of green leek well chopped and simmering for a few seconds. Now add the eggplant slices to the butter and fry until crisp. Serve garnished with parsley and black olives.

STUFFED LENTEN EGGPLANT
Vinete Umplute de Post

Wash and cut one large eggplant in half lengthwise. Scoop out the seeds with a little of the center pulp and chop well. Now rub salt into the eggplant halves and place them on a napkin. Let stand one hour. Finely chop 2 onions, a few cloves of garlic, a sprig each of dill, parsley and leek. Combine with the chopped pulp and fry in hot olive oil.

Scald the eggplant halves and fill the scooped out centers with the fried ingredients. Place in a saucepan with a little olive oil. Pour over the stuffed eggplant a little tomato sauce, cover with sliced tomatoes, a little chopped parsley, cubed green peppers and chopped spring onions. Over this sprinkle some olive oil, salt and pepper and a little finely chopped leek. Simmer on a very low fire until tender.

EGGPLANTS : 3

BAKED EGGPLANT IN BUTTER
Vinete Copt In Unt

Wash one large eggplant, cut lengthwise into 6 slices, sprinkle with salt and place on a towel. Let stand until the juice is absorbed. Dip in flour and brown in butter.

Butter well an earthen or a glazed baking dish (never use iron). On each piece of eggplant put a layer of sliced tomatoes. Sprinkle with finely chopped green parsley, leek and thyme, then season with a little pepper and salt and dot with butter.

Place in the baking dish, cover well with bread crumbs and dot liberally with butter. On top place a layer of sliced tomatoes previously fried in butter, sprinkle with finely chopped parsley and bake in a moderate oven until tender.

LENTEN EGGPLANT WITH TOMATOES AND OLIVES
Vinete Cu Rosii Si Masline (De Post)

Wash one large or 2 to 3 smaller eggplants. Cut lengthwise into slices or into small cubes or any desired shape. Add finely chopped onions, a sprig each of green leek and dill also finely chopped, slices of tomato and pepper and salt to taste and fry in oil. Now sprinkle over with a level teaspoonful of flour and some finely chopped parsley. Add a few ripe olives and a little water. Slowly bring to a boil, then cook slowly until tender. Serve with slices of cold or hot mamaliga (see MAMALIGA).

STUFFED EGGPLANT WITH MEAT
Vinete Cu Carne

2 to 4 eggplants	1 or 2 slices bread soaked in
2 onions	milk
1 clove of garlic	½ lb. chopped meat
green leek	sliced tomatoes
1 tbs. chopped parsley	bread crumbs
thyme	butter
olive oil	

Wash 2 to 4 eggplants, cut lengthwise in halves, scoop out the seeds with some of the pulp and chop. Salt the halves, place

4 : EGGPLANTS

on a towel and keep there until the juice is absorbed. Chop finely 2 medium-sized onions, one clove of garlic, a sprig of green leek and enough parsley to make a tablespoonful when chopped, add a little thyme, and fry in olive oil for 3 minutes. Now add the chopped pulp, one or two slices of bread soaked in milk, and heat for 2 minutes more. Add ½ pound of chopped meat (pork and beef mixed) and cook for another one to two minutes.

Fill the eggplants with this stuffing, place in a buttered or oiled baking dish, cover with sliced tomatoes, sprinkle with bread crumbs, dot with butter and bake in a moderate oven. Baste now and then. Bake until tender.

EGGPLANT ALA BUCHAREST
Vinete Ala Bucuresti

Wash 2 eggplants and cut lengthwise in halves. Scoop out and chop the seeds with some of the pulp. Simmer the halves in olive oil. Make a white sauce of about the same amount as the pulp. Mix with the pulp, add salt and pepper, 2½ table-spoonfuls of grated cheese and 3 egg yolks well-beaten. Now beat the egg whites to stiffness, add to the above mixture and mix. Fill the cavities and place the eggplant halves in a well-buttered baking dish. Bake slowly in a moderate oven until tender, but not overdone. Serve as soon as it comes out of the oven.

EGGPLANT MASHED FOR GARNISHING
Vinete Frecate Pentru Garnituri

Prepare eggplant paste (see EGGPLANT PASTE). Mix in very well some butter, beef juice and finely chopped parsley and leek. Serve hot with roast beef or any roast meat.

EGGPLANT CUBED FOR GARNISHING
Vinete Cuburi Pentru Garnisit

Wash one eggplant and cut into cubes or dice. Fry in very hot butter until it is crisp or to your liking. Serve with plain rice, or rice cooked in butter or with butter and cheese.

EGGPLANTS : 5

CHEESE EGGPLANT
Vinete Cu Brinza

Wash one large eggplant. Cut lengthwise into rather thick slices. Sprinkle with a little salt and pepper to taste, then dip in flour and pat in well. Sear quickly in hot butter (do not fry) and remove to a plate. Place the slices adjacent to each other, do not pile one on top of the other. Let stand while you prepare a thick paste out of two eggs yolks and grated Parmesan cheese. Spread this thickly on the eggplant slices, then join two slices together to form sandwiches. Let stand until you are ready to serve, then dip both sides in hot butter, place quickly into a frying pan and fry in deep, very hot lard. Remove the eggplant sandwiches with a spatula and let drain. Sauté very quickly 2 tablespoonfuls of finely chopped green parsley in a little fat and sprinkle over the eggplant. Serve very hot.

BAKED EGGPLANT STEW WITH MEAT
Tocana De Vinete (Copt)

1 lb. beef	1 tbs. chopped parsley
lard	salt and pepper
2 to 4 eggplants	bouillon
3 onions	sliced tomatoes
1 tbs. flour	2 or 3 cloves of garlic

Cut into small cubes one pound of beef, place in a pan and brown in very hot lard. Add slowly a little cold water, bring to a boil, then continue at a slow heat. Wash and peel 2 to 4 eggplants, cut into cubes or dice, sprinkle with salt and keep on a towel until the juice has been absorbed. Put into a saucepan with a little lard or oil and brown.

Prepare a sauce as follows: Fry 3 finely chopped onions in very hot lard in a frying pan until golden brown. Add one tablespoonful of flour and brown it a little, then put in a level tablespoonful of finely chopped parsley and salt and pepper to taste. Now add slowly enough bouillon to make a medium thick sauce. Pour this sauce over the eggplant.

Before the meat is completely tender combine it with the eggplant in a baking dish. Cover the top with slices of tomatoes,

6 : EGGPLANTS

add 2 or 3 cloves of garlic, then sprinkle with finely chopped parsley and salt and pepper. Cover and bake in a moderate oven until tender. Serve hot.

EGGPLANT ALA GARLIC
Vinete Cu Usturoi

4 eggplants
olive oil
3 onions
2 cups diced mixed
vegetables (celery, car-
rots, turnips, parsley,
green leek)
sliced tomatoes
tomato sauce
garlic

Wash 4 eggplants and cut lengthwise into halves. Scoop out the seeds and the pulp. Prepare a vegetable mixture as follows: Fry in hot olive oil in a pan 3 medium-sized sliced onions until soft. Add two cups of diced mixed vegetables (celery, carrots, turnips, parsley and green leek). Scald and chop the pulp, then combine with the vegetables and fried onions. Fry until brown.

Stuff this mixture into the eggplant cavities, arrange the eggplant halves nicely in a baking dish, cover with tomato slices and sprinkle with hot olive oil. Bake in a moderate oven. During the baking baste with tomato sauce, in which a few crushed cloves of garlic have been placed to soak. When done, remove from the oven and sprinkle with finely chopped parsley. Cover and let cool. Serve with small sharp red peppers.

APPETIZERS and HORS D'OEUVRES

PASTE OF OLIVES
Masline Frecate

½ lb. large ripe olives
½ lb. sweet butter
pepper
chives
fennel
parsley

Pit ½ pound of large ripe olives, chop fine and press through a sieve. Mix well with ½ pound of sweet butter, a little pepper, finely minced chives (or if you prefer minced onions) and fennel and parsley to taste. Serve cold on pumpernickel bread with radishes and sour pickles.

WHITE GOAT CHEESE PASTE OF BRAILA
Brinza De Braila Frecata

½ lb. white goat cheese
½ lb. sweet butter
1 tsp. caraway seeds
½ tsp. sweet paprika
1 tbs. minced chives
1 tbs. each chopped parsley and fennel

Mix ½ pound (or more) of white goat cheese with ½ pound of sweet butter to a smooth paste. Add a teaspoonful of caraway seeds, a little pepper to taste, ½ teaspoonful of sweet red paprika, one tablespoonful of very finely minced chives, one tablespoonful of chopped parsley and one tablespoonful of chopped fennel. Mix again. Arrange in a mound on a service plate, decorate with

8 : APPETIZERS AND HORS D'OEUVRES

sprigs of parsley and garnish with red radishes, green scallions, black olives and hard sliced tomatoes.

PASTE OF CARP ROE
Icre De Crap

Carefully remove the roe from the carp, do not wash it, but clean away the small blood vessels. Salt it and let stand for 1 to 2 days in a cold place. When ready to make the paste, transfer the roe to a bowl which is to be kept in a pan of hot water while working. Start to beat lightly with a fork, adding at the same time drop by drop 3 to 6 tablespoons of olive oil (vary according to taste), the juice of one lemon (or more if you wish) and a few drops of cold water. Continue beating constantly until the roe becomes firm and fluffy, and each small grain can be distinguished.

Soak a little bread in water, press out excess liquid, then add to the paste and mix. Add more olive oil, a little at a time, beating very well with a fork or an egg beater. Then put in one grated onion, a little more olive oil and lemon juice and beat until you get a nice thick foam.

Serve on a platter, surrounded with sliced tomatoes and black olives. Or serve on small pieces of bread.

PASTE OF PIKE ROE
Icre De Stiuca

Carefully remove the roe from a pike, clean away the small blood vessels, salt and let stand in a cool place for 7 hours. Do not wash. Place in a bowl, beat lightly with a fork, adding slowly at the same time 2 to 6 tablespoons of olive oil, drop by drop, the juice of one lemon and a few drops of cold water. Continue the beating constantly, until the pike roe becomes firm and fluffy and each small grain can be distinguished in the white froth.

Serve on a platter with finely chopped onion, sliced tomatoes and black olives, or on small pieces of bread or crackers.

APPETIZERS AND HORS D'OEUVRES : 9

FISH ROE IN JELLY
Icre De Peste Piftii

Prepare a fish roe paste (see PASTE OF CARP ROE and PASTE OF PIKE ROE above). Make a jelly of unflavored gelatin and while still warm and fluid, pour half on a platter. When it starts to become solid, gently lay the fish roe paste on top, then cover with rest of gelatin. Let cool. Serve cold with black olives and sour pickles.

MARINATED HERRING
Hirinca Scrumbie Marinata

2 or 3 herrings	ripe olives
olive oil	hot peppers
vinegar	laurel leaves
1 carrot	dry mustard
3 onions	salt and pepper

Soak 2 or 3 herrings overnight in cold water. Press the herring milk out of the herring into a bowl. Mix in a little olive oil, added drop by drop, and a little vinegar. Beat well to make a sauce. Clean and cut the herring into small pieces. Clean and slice one carrot and 3 onions crosswise. Into a glass jar place first a layer of onions, a layer of herring and then a layer of carrots. Put between the layers a few ripe olives, small dry sharp hot peppers, a few laurel leaves, salt and pepper and a little dry mustard (on the point of a knife). Repeat this until the jar is filled. Now pour on the milk sauce, then cover with olive oil.

Cover the jar tightly and keep in a cool place. In about a week it is ready to eat. It will keep for a long time.

CREAMED HERRING
Hirinca Scrumbie In Smantana

Clean one large salt herring and soak it in cold water until only enough salt remains to be just right to eat. Press out the milk from the herring, mix with the yolk of one egg, adding slowly lemon juice and olive oil, and a little pepper. Beat to make a sauce.

10 : APPETIZERS AND HORS D'OEUVRES

Cut the herring into small pieces, place on a plate, then pour on the milk sauce. Garnish with ripe or green olives and lemon slices.

PASTE OF HERRING
Hirinca Macinata

Clean one large herring, soak in cold water overnight, then remove the bones. Do not press out the milk, let it remain in the herring. Cut into small pieces, then run through a chopper a few times or until you get a fine paste. Soak 1 or 2 slices of dry white bread in milk and mix thoroughly with the paste.

Into a bowl put one very finely chopped small onion, some olive oil, lemon juice, black pepper and a pinch of red paprika. Mix them well. Now add the herring paste and mix all together thoroughly. Serve with black olives and slices of tomatoes.

HERRING IN VINEGAR
Hirinca In Otet

Clean one herring as above, but cut it into larger pieces. Bring to a boil one cup of vinegar, then add one carrot and one onion (both sliced crosswise), one or two laurel leaves, a few grains of pepper, a little mustard (use grains if possible) and a little thyme. Now add the herring pieces, together with ½ cup of olive oil and continue to boil for 1 to 2 minutes. Keep in a cool, dry place. Serve cold. It will last for a week.

HERRING WITH VEGETABLES
Hirinca Cu Zarzavaturi

2 or 3 herrings	salt and pepper
carrots, celery, turnips,	olive oil
onion	5 or 6 tbs. white wine
parsley and fennel	

Wash and clean 2 or 3 medium-sized fresh herrings. Cut through the gills and thoroughly clean the insides, through the gills, then salt and stuff the gills with the following fried

APPETIZERS AND HORS D'OEUVRES : 11

vegetables: carrots, celery, turnips, all cut into cubes, parsley, fennel, one tablespoonful of finely chopped onion and salt and pepper to taste, all of these fried in olive oil. Stuff the herring with this mixture through the open gills.

Put the leftover fried vegetables in the bottom of a baking dish, cover with the stuffed herring, pour on 3 tablespoonfuls of olive oil and add 5 or 6 tablespoonfuls of white wine. Bake in a moderate oven. Keep in a cool, dry place. Serve cold.

GOURMET HERRING
Hirinca Gourmet

1 or 2 herrings	1 cup ripe olives
2 tomatoes	1 tsp. capers
sugar	celery, leek
salt	vinegar
dill, tarragon, parsley	3 to 4 tbs. olive oil

Soak one or two herrings overnight in cold water. Cook until soft 2 sliced tomatoes in a small cupful of water to which has been added some salt and a level tablespoonful of sugar. Let cool. Now boil a little water containing some dill, a sprig of tarragon and parsley, one cup of ripe olives, a teaspoonful of capers, a stalk of celery, a sprig of green leek, vinegar and 3 to 4 tablespoonfuls of olive oil. When done, mix with the tomatoes.

Cut the herring into small pieces, arrange on a deep dish, pour on the cooked mixture and sprinkle with finely chopped parsley. Keep in a cool, dry place. Serve cold.

See also EGGPLANT PASTE (*Eggplants*).

Soups

CHICKEN SOUP
Supa De Pui

4 to 5 lb. chicken	1 small parsnip
3 or 4 carrots	1 celery knob
celery leaves, parsley	1 parsley root
1 small onion	salt and pepper

Choose a good, fat 4 to 5 pound chicken, clean very well and place in a large pot of cold water. (If you want to make a good soup always cook your meats in cold water, but if you want the meat to be better, place it in boiling water.) Bring to a boil and continue the boiling for one hour on a low fire. Now add at short intervals 3 or 4 cleaned carrots, one bunch of celery leaves and one bunch of parsley leaves, each bunch being tied together with white thread. After a few minutes remove the celery and parsley leaves. Continue to add at short intervals one small onion, a small parsnip, a knob of celery cut in half and one parsley root. Season to taste and continue to boil for 2 to 3 hours more until the chicken is tender.

Strain from the chicken stock enough liquid into a pot to make the right amount of soup for one meal. Bring to a boil and add thin noodles or rice. But if you add farina dumplings (see FARINA DUMPLINGS) the soup tastes wonderfully delicious. If not done correctly, they turn out hard and that is a great disappointment.

14 : SOUPS

Keep the pot containing the chicken warm until ready to serve. Serve the chicken on a heated plate with mashed potatoes, garnished with the soup vegetables, and sprinkled over with finely chopped parsley. As a side dish serve compote in small saucers.

In Romania this is a Sunday or holiday dish, and is also used when important guests are entertained. They also make the same soup for a young mother, but with a little delicious difference. They mix the yolk of one egg and 2 to 3 tablespoonfuls of heavy sweet cream, then pour the hot soup on this mixture, stirring gently. Sometimes sour cream is substituted for the sweet cream. A little lemon juice is then added, and this results in a captivating flavor.

It is also the custom to bring nourishing soups as a gift to a new mother, so she may have good milk to feed her baby. Usually it is chicken soup, with tender chicken parts in it. Friends or neighbors are not ashamed to inquire if the new mother has already gotten the soup they mean to bring. If this is the case, they will make changes in it, perhaps straining the soup and adding lemon juice and sour cream sauce, putting on top a few diced bread pieces toasted in butter.

MEAT SOUP
Supa De Carne

This is made in the same way as the chicken soup. Instead of the chicken, get 2 to 3 pounds of shank or breast of beef, place in a large soup kettle of cold water with some marrow bones and boil very slowly until the meat is tender. Put noodles, barley or rice into the soup.

Serve the meat on a heated plate with tomato sauce (see TOMATO SAUCE), boiled potatoes, radishes, rice, etc., according to your wish. Sprinkle with a little finely chopped parsley.

SOUP OMELET
Supa De Omlete

You can make a delicious meal the next day from the left-over chicken or meat soup, which should be kept in the refrigera-

SOUPS : 15

tor. Beat the whites of eggs (use 2 eggs per person) until stiff, then beat the yolks together with one teaspoonful of flour for each two eggs and a pinch of salt. Mix both together well. In the meantime bring the soup to a boil, adding some lemon rind to taste (or finely chopped dill or tarragon). Pour the egg mixture into the soup, cover the pot and boil gently for a few minutes or until firm. When ready, turn into a warm soup bowl. Cut the omelet into individual portions and serve immediately on heated plates. Sprinkle with chopped parsley.

BEEF STOCK
Prepararea Supei De Carne

10 to 12 lbs. beef and veal	1 large potato
large marrow bone	1 large parsnip root
1 lb. liver	20 to 24 peppercorns
lard	nutmeg
1 large red onion	4 or 5 slices of lemon
1 tbs. salt	1 tbs. brown sugar
1 large celery knob	2 tomatoes
2 or 3 large parsley roots	1 leek
1 turnip	saffron
3 or 4 carrots	

Ask your butcher for 10 to 12 pounds of the middle cut of shin beef, mixed with some veal. Have him give you a large marrow bone and cut the meat and the bones into small pieces. Wipe the meat with a cloth which has been wetted and squeezed dry, then score the meat in a few places with a sharp pointed knife. Cut one pound of beef liver into slices and sauté in a little lard. Now place the meat, bones and sautéed liver in a very large enameled soup pot. Add one large red onion, one tablespoonful of salt and enough cold water to cover the meat deeply. If you want to measure the water, use one quart per pound. Cover tightly and boil slowly with a low flame.

After one hour of boiling add one large celery knob, 2 or 3 large parsley roots, one young turnip, 3 or 4 large carrots, one large potato and one large parsnip root. All of these vegetables should be well washed and cut lengthwise in two. Now add 20 to 24 peppercorns, a little nutmeg, 4 or 5 slices of lemon, one tablespoonful of brown sugar and 2 whole tomatoes. Cover

16 : soups

and let boil slowly. Skim the scum now and then. Do not add more water, nor must you interrupt the boiling once started. After the vegetables have been boiling for two hours add one stalk of leek and some saffron. Boil for one hour more or a total of 4 hours. If the beef is not yet soft, cook until it is. If needed, add more salt. When finished, cover and let stand for 4 or 5 hours. Strain through a fine sieve and keep the beef stock covered and in a cool place. Use when needed for meats, sauces, soups, ciorbas, etc.

POTATO SOUP
Supa De Cartofi

4 potatoes	salt and pepper
3 onions	¼ lb. lean bacon
2 tomatoes	2 tbs. flour
1 carrot	paprika
1 tbs. chopped parsley	1 egg yolk
1 tbs. chopped green leek	4 tbs. sweet or sour cream
green (or clove of) garlic	chopped dill

Many are the varieties of potato soups and always they are served as a whole meal in the old country with good homemade bread. Here you can use pumpernickel or rye bread.

Wash, peel and cut lengthwise into 4 parts four or more medium-sized potatoes, place in a pot with 2 quarts of cold water and bring to a boil. Then add 2 finely chopped onions, 2 tomatoes, one carrot sliced in halves, one tablespoonful of finely chopped parsley, one tablespoonful of chopped green leek and a little chopped green garlic (or a clove of garlic) to taste. If you cannot get green garlic, and it probably is hard to obtain here, it is simple to grow it yourself. If you have a garden, fine! If not, plant a garlic clove in good earth in a window box or an earthenware pot and let it sprout. The green blades will shoot up quickly and you will have the pleasure of using this delightful green. It can be used in nearly everything, but it is simply wonderful in salads.

Returning to the potato soup after this flavorful interruption; when the added vegetables in the pot are half-cooked, season with salt and pepper to taste.

SOUPS : 17

Now fry in a deep iron pan ¼ pound of lean bacon, cut into small pieces. Leave in the pan. Add a finely chopped small onion and fry until soft. Add 2 tablespoonfuls of flour and stir constantly so as not to burn, and season with a little salt, black pepper and red paprika. Pour in slowly enough liquid from the boiling soup to make a paste, stirring constantly. Now turn this mixture into the soup, stir well and let cook. Beat the yolk of one egg with about 4 tablespoonfuls of heavy sweet or sour cream, add a little chopped dill, mix well and pour this into the potato soup, stirring constantly.

When the mixed ingredients have become tender, the soup is ready. Serve in large soup plates, with a teaspoonful of sour cream on top, and eat with fresh pumpernickel, corn or rye bread. Oh, how I wish I had a plate of it right now, I would gulp it down!

POTATO SOUP WITH SMOKED PORK
Supa De Cartofi Cu Carne De Pork Afumata

This soup is prepared the same as above, but with the addition of smoked pork knuckles or smoked pork ribs, which are put into the pot of cold water with the potatoes, adding at the same time 3 or 4 cloves of garlic. When ready to serve, sprinkle with a little finely chopped dill or parsley.

STRING BEAN SOUP
Supa De Fasole Verde

Prepare the same as the potato soup, but replace the potatoes with fresh string beans.

GREEN LETTUCE SOUP
Supa De Salate Verde

1 large head of lettuce	salt and pepper
juice of 1 large lemon	1 tbs. flour
(or 2 tbs. vinegar)	5 or 6 eggs
4 large cloves of garlic	3 tbs. sour cream
2 tbs. chopped parsley	¼ lb. bacon
1 tbs. butter	green garlic

18 : SOUPS

Bring to a boil 2 quarts of water to which has been added the juice of a large lemon (or 2 tablespoonfuls of vinegar), 4 large crushed cloves of garlic, one tablespoonful of finely chopped parsley, one large tablespoonful of butter or lard and salt and pepper to taste. Cover tightly and boil gently. Now put into a bowl one heaping tablespoonful of flour and mix into it very well the yolks of 2 eggs and 3 tablespoonfuls of heavy sour cream. Thin with some of the boiling water, added slowly, little by little, and in the meantime stirring constantly and quickly so you will not scald the eggs. Pour this thinned mixture into the boiling pot, stirring constantly. Bring to a boil, reduce the fire and let simmer slowly.

Wash thoroughly one large crisp head of lettuce (Boston is preferable), break into large pieces with the hands and place the pieces in a pot. Bring the soup to a boil again, turn off the flame, and pour the soup over the lettuce. Let stand on the warm stove.

In a heated iron pan fry ¼ pound of bacon cut into small pieces until crisp. Add a few sprigs of green garlic, finely chopped (or one clove of crushed garlic) and one tablespoonful of chopped green parsley and sear quickly. Scramble 3 or 4 well-beaten eggs in the pan, mix well and then put into the soup. Cover and let stand for 3 to 4 minutes, then serve at once in heated soup bowls, topped with sour cream. If you desire it more sour, add more lemon juice or vinegar.

This soup is very nourishing and with bread makes a satisfactory one meal dish. Yet it is so light and simply delicious. It is fine for late suppers. Children all love it and so do women who want to reduce.

GOOSEBERRY SOUP
Supa De Agrisa

1 cup gooseberries	1 tsp. chopped chives
small chicken	1 large tomato
2 large carrots	salt and pepper
2 stalks celery	2 eggs
1 onion	1 cup sour cream
1 parsley root	1 tbs. chopped parsley

SOUPS : 19

Cut a small spring chicken into pieces, place in a pot of cold water and bring to a boil. Add 2 large cubed carrots, 2 stalks of celery, one chopped onion, one parsley root, a teaspoonful of chopped chives, one large fresh tomato, one cup of gooseberries, and salt and pepper to taste. Cook until all the vegetables are tender, then remove from the fire.

Beat together 2 eggs and one cup of sour cream in a serving soup bowl. Add the hot soup slowly to the cream mixture, stirring constantly. Sprinkle the soup with one tablespoonful of very finely chopped parsley.

DRIED BEAN SOUP
Supa De Fasole Uscata

1 lb. dried white beans	2 stalks celery
pork butts	2 parsley roots
sausage	garlic greens
fresh short ribs	1 tsp. flour
salt and pepper	½ to 1 cup sour cream
3 cloves garlic	¼ lb. bacon
5 onions	parsley
2 stalks leeks	red paprika
1 carrot	

This is a great favorite in Romania. It is extremely nourishing, with as much proteins as in a steak, and it is flavorful too, being full of herbs. Oh, how good it tastes with some smoked ham butts and smoked sausage!

Soak overnight one pound of dried white beans. The first thing in the morning put into your soup kettle the beans and the water they were soaked in, some pork butts, sausage, fresh short ribs with salt and pepper to taste, add enough cold water to come 4 or 5 inches above the top of the ingredients and cook slowly. Later, add 3 crushed cloves of garlic. From time to time add some hot water.

After boiling about half an hour add 4 chopped onions, 2 stalks of chopped leek, a carrot sliced lengthwise in two, 2 stalks of celery chopped up, 2 parsley roots sliced in halves, and if obtainable, the greens of garlic chopped fine.

After the beans and the meat are cooked, strain, leaving only

20 : SOUPS

a few tablespoonfuls of beans in the strained soup. Now add a mixture of a teaspoonful of flour and from one half to a full cup of sour cream (depending on the amount of soup). In a pan fry ¼ pound of bacon cut up into small pieces, together with a finely chopped onion, some parsley and red paprika. Pour this over the bean soup and serve hot.

GARLIC SOUP
Supa De Usturoi

The garlic soup is made exactly like the caraway seed soup above, naturally substituting for the caraway seeds a whole cluster of garlic, cut into very small pieces. After the soup is finished and strained, sprinkle with chopped dill. Serve hot, without dumplings, but with small pieces of toasted buttered bread tossed into the soup.

It is well-known that garlic has medicinal virtues, that it is an excellent blood disinfectant and its use can ease pain. Nearly all peoples living close to the land eat garlic. They know from experience that it is good for them, besides adding to food a distinctive flavor that makes any dish much more appetizing.

CARAWAY SEED SOUP WITH DUMPLINGS
Supa De Chimen

¼ cup caraway seeds	sprig of parsley
2 large onions	1 tbs. flour
salt and pepper	Dumplings:
2 tbs. bacon drippings	1 egg
1 tbs. chopped green	cold water
scallions	1 tbs. olive oil
	salt and flour

Add to 2 quarts of cold water ¼ cup of caraway seeds, 2 large onions, washed and with the peel left on, and salt and pepper to taste. Boil until tender.

Now fry in a deep iron pan with 2 tablespoonfuls of bacon drippings, one tablespoonful of finely chopped green scallions

SOUPS : 21

(or leek or chives). Add a sprig of parsley finely chopped, cover and simmer until soft, then put in one tablespoonful of flour, stirring constantly until it becomes a nice dark brown. Add some of the boiling water slowly, with constant stirring, until you get a thick sauce. Cook slowly for 10 minutes, then pour it over the boiling caraway seeds and again cook on a slow fire for about 10 minutes.

Strain the soup into another pot, pressing the ingredients through a sieve, and bring to a boil.

The dumplings are made by beating together quickly with a spoon one egg, half an eggshell full of cold water, one tablespoonful of pure olive oil, salt and enough flour to make a soft dough. Place the dough on a flat wooden board and with a knife wetted in the soup, cut off small pieces and drop into the soup. Boil until done. Cover and let stand on the warm stove. Serve quite hot.

This soup is an aid to good digestion and is usually prepared once each week. For children the soup is strained only, none of the ingredients being pressed through a sieve. Even babies of a few months are given a little of it, without dumplings.

BEAN PUREE
Fasole Frecata

From the beans obtained above prepare the puree as follows: Put the beans through a sieve or strainer, then beat vigorously with a wooden spoon for 4 to 6 minutes, adding if necessary a little soup to obtain a nice, soft puree.

Now put into the frying pan a few slices of bacon cut into small pieces and fry together with one onion chopped coarsely, chopped green parsley, a little chopped leek and some paprika.

Pour the bean puree on a heated platter, garnish with pieces of ham butts and sausage, then, when you are ready to serve, sprinkle the puree with the hot onion mixture from the pan.

As a side dish serve sauerkraut, a glass of sauerkraut juice or sour pickles. Although it is considered a real man's dish, women and children relish it, too. Serve with mamaliga (see MAMALIGA).

22 : SOUPS

BEER SOUP
Supa De Bere

1 qt. beer
½ piece of cinnamon bark
4 cloves
sugar

1 tbs. butter
4 egg yolks
½ pint of sweet cream

Put into a pot one quart of beer, ½ piece of cinnamon bark, 4 cloves and sugar to your taste. Cover tightly and boil slowly. Beat in a serving soup bowl one tablespoonful of sweet fresh butter to a foam with a fork. Combine with 4 egg yolks and beat together very well. Add ½ pint of strictly fresh heavy sweet cream and beat with an egg beater to a foam. Now remove the cinnamon bark and the cloves from the beer. Holding the pot in one hand, pour the beer a little at a time into the foamy mixture, while at the same time stirring constantly with your other hand without interruption until you have poured in all the beer. Serve with toasted slices of roll.

CIORBAS:
The Sour Soups

ROMANIA is famous for the rich variety of her sour soups, which are called ciorbas. They are very healthful and all have their own distinctive piquant aroma and flavor. To smell a steaming bowl is enough to give one an appetite. Vegetables, greens, meats and fish of all kinds have been used in the making of ciorbas.

The traditional sour base for these soups throughout the Balkans has been the sour juice of wheat bran, which goes through a fermentation process. As there is much work required to produce this, it is being used less and less. The young generation is not willing to devote much time to the kitchen and the understanding and love of food and its preparation seems to be dying out. Besides the soured wheat bran, there are many other souring agents used by the Romanians. These are unripened green grapes, green plums, green sorrel leaves, sour grape vine leaves, sour apple juice, lemons (which are rarely used as they must be imported into the country) and primarily sauerkraut juice. As sauerkraut juice and lemons are easily obtainable here, they will be used as the sour bases in all the recipes for ciorbas that follow.

Since the flavor of the ciorbas improves with time, a quantity to last the family a number of days is always prepared. And as they are practically a meal by themselves, the housewife saves much time in making a large quantity at one time. When working people come home from their labors, or peasants from the

24 : CIORBAS

fields, they buy fresh bread (unless they baked some at home), and so they are able to get up a wholesome meal in no time at all.

After dinner, the Romanian mother gathers her children around her and discusses with them the next day's meal. If they decide on a ciorba, every one gets busy. I wish you could watch the little hands of the youngsters peeling and cutting the vegetables, preparing the meat, bringing in water, getting wood, making the fire, and all this done happily, with smiling eyes, and do believe me, with singing. Once they start to work they concentrate on what they are doing, having pride in their work, and so all their chores which mother or grandmother has delegated to them are done well and speedily, too. As mothers sometimes work in the fields, the grandmother runs the kitchen. She is treated with great respect and love, as befits her years and experience.

After the children have completed their tasks, they can go out to play, to visit or work on whatever they love to do. They feel a responsibility to their parents and help them always cheerfully, not with grumbling. The parents, in turn, know how important it is to teach the girls the art of cooking, so that they in time will be fitted to run their own households.

CIORBA WITH MEAT BALLS
Ciorba De Perisoare Cu Carne

veal shank bone	lovage, hot pepper seeds
fresh pork bones	½ lb. chopped veal
2 large carrots, 1 onion	½ lb. chopped pork
2 parsley roots	1 egg plus 2 egg yolks
1 celery knob, 1 tomato	4 tbs. uncooked rice
1 qt. sauerkraut juice	1 cup sour cream
celery, leek, fennel, thyme	1 tbs. flour
parsley, tarragon, dill	salt and pepper

Into a large pot (if you want to have enough ciorba for a few days or a week) put 3 quarts of cold water, add a veal shank bone and some fresh pork bones and bring to a boil. Now add 2 large carrots, cut in half lengthwise, 2 whole parsley roots, one large celery knob cut in half or a stalk of celery, one whole

CIORBAS : 25

tomato and 2 sprigs of green parsley. Cover and boil until vegetables are tender. Now pour in one quart of sauerkraut juice and bring to a boil, cover and let stand, while you are preparing the meat balls as follows:

Mix ½ pound of veal and ½ pound of pork (not too fat nor too lean) chopped together with one whole egg, salt and pepper to taste, one tablespoonful of finely chopped parsley, one finely chopped small onion, a little thyme and 2 large tablespoonfuls of rice (well rinsed in cold water). Mix very well all the ingredients with the hands. Form small balls the size of a walnut in the palms of your hands. Roll the meat balls in flour and let stand on the meat board.

Strain the soup into another pot. (If it is too sour, add a little water. If you wish to make it more sour, add some sauerkraut juice.) Bring to a boil and add 2 more tablespoonfuls of rice well-rinsed in cold water. Wait until the boiling starts again, then drop in the meat balls. Add celery, leek, fennel, parsley, tarragon and lovage (all coarsely chopped) and a few seeds from a sharp pepper. Mix in a bowl one cup of sour cream, 2 egg yolks and one tablespoonful of flour, adding slowly cold water until you get a thin paste. Pour this paste into the ciorba, stirring constantly. Let boil slowly for 20 minutes. Cover the pot and throw over the cover a large towel to preserve the exquisite bouquet.

Serve hot with a tablespoonful of sour cream and sprinkle with chopped fresh green dill, tarragon or parsley. On the side serve a small red or green sharp pepper.

The ciorbas improve with time. They taste better the following day after being made, and even more so the third, fourth and even the fifth day. The flavor keeps reacting and penetrating into the ciobra ingredients, which explains this interesting phenomenon. Of course, you must keep the ciorba very tightly covered and in the refrigerator. With a few slices of bread, a plateful of this ciorba makes a wholesome meal. The vegetables and herbs used are a good source of minerals and vitamins, and its tastiness creates a joy in eating, the healthful effects of which cannot be measured.

For twenty-five years I have served these ciorbas and especially the one with the meat balls. All over America they have made good friends. Children or adults, factory workers or dignitaries,

26 : CIORBAS

they all loved it. I even received grateful appreciation from some Indians in Minnesota. Please try making it. I know you will enjoy it like all the rest.

SPRING LAMB CIORBA
Ciorba De Miel

lamb (or lamb kidneys, head, heart and lungs)	1 tbs. chopped dill
	2 tbs. uncooked rice
3 carrots, 1 onion	2 eggs
2 or 3 tomatoes, celery	lemon juice
thyme, lovage, fennel	salt and pepper
1 tbs. green tarragon	

To obtain a most savory and delicious ciorba, you must use a very young milk-fed spring lamb (about 2 weeks old). Even the poorest family in Romania makes this dish, but instead of using lamb meat, they use the liver, kidneys, head, heart and lungs of the lamb, which are much cheaper, but give a flavorful ciorba nonetheless.

Cut the lamb meat (or the lamb liver, kidneys, head, heart and lungs) into small pieces, place in 2½ quarts of cold water, add pepper and salt to taste, and boil slowly. Add 3 medium-sized carrots, one or two stalks of celery and one onion all cut into small cubes. Boil slowly 15 to 20 minutes. Now add 2 or 3 sliced tomatoes, one tablespoonful of coarsely cut green tarragon (or if not obtainable, some tarragon leaves which are preserved in vinegar and kept in tightly covered glass jars) and a little thyme and lovage. Boil another 5 minutes, then add 2 tablespoonfuls of well-washed rice. Continue boiling until the rice and meat are done. Remove from the fire, cover tightly and place a towel over the cover to prevent the evaporation of the aroma.

Place 2 eggs in a serving soup bowl, add one or two drops of cold water and beat well. Then pour the soup into the eggs, stirring all the time. Now add a little pepper to taste, a tablespoonful of chopped dill (or chopped parsley), a little fennel and one teaspoonful of lovage. Add enough lemon juice to suit your

CIORBAS : 27

taste. Let stand a few minutes. Serve hot. Place sour cream on the ciorba of those who relish it.

CIORBA OF VEAL
Ciorba De Carne De Vitel

1 veal shank (or breast or neck)	1 cup diced celery
	shallot, dill or parsley
¼ lb. butter	lemon juice
3 onions and 3 carrots	salt
2 parsley roots	sour cream
1 cup diced potatoes	

Take one veal shank, breast or part of the neck meat (these are cheap cuts but just as nourishing and tasteful as the more expensive cuts of veal), cut into 3 or 4 pieces and boil slowly in a tightly covered soup pot with 2 quarts of cold water. Add salt to taste.

In the meantime put ¼ pound of salt butter into a frying pan and sauté 3 large onions, diced, until they have turned golden in color, then add the following vegetables, all diced, and sauté until tender: 3 carrots, 2 parsley roots, one cup of potatoes, one cup of celery, and a little finely chopped shallot.

When the veal is nearly done, add the vegetables and continue boiling until well done. Remove from the fire, add the juice of one or more lemons to taste, and sprinkle with finely chopped dill or parsley. Keep tightly covered. Serve the meat with the ciorba in individual soup bowls and add a tablespoonful of sour cream.

If prepared a day before, it will be more delicious. This ciorba with the veal is a one-course dinner and costs very little. It should be eaten with pumpernickel or rye bread, It is fine for growing children and those already grown up, too.

RABBIT CIORBA
Ciorba De Iepure

Prepare exactly like any other ciorba. Cut the rabbit meat into small cubes, also cube the mixed vegetables. Combine and

28 : CIORBAS

place in a pot to boil. Season to taste. Boil until done. Add the sour ciorba stock (see CIORBA WITH MEAT BALLS), then boil a little longer.

Beat well in a serving bowl 3 egg yolks and ¼ cup of sour cream. Pour the soup over this mixture slowly and stir constantly. Sprinkle with finely chopped fresh dill or tarragon. Cover, let stand for a few minutes, then serve hot. It is a delicious meal by itself.

TRIPE CIORBA
Ciorba De Burta

honeycomb tripe	laurel leaf, lovage and
veal knuckle	thyme
1 potato and 1 onion	1 egg yolk
2 tomatoes	green hot pepper
salt and pepper	butter
1 bunch assorted herbs	4 to 6 tsp. lemon juice

Wash well a nice piece of honeycomb tripe, let stand in salt water for ½ hour, then wash again.

Now put it into a pot with 2 quarts of water and add one onion sliced, one laurel leaf, a bunch of assorted herbs, salt and pepper to taste, 2 sliced tomatoes, a veal knuckle, one potato and a little thyme and lovage. Cook slowly for 4 hours or until the tripe is tender.

Lift out the tripe and place it on a board. With a sharp knife cut it into thin strips. Let stand ½ hour, then remove the vegetables from the liquid.

Place the strips of tripe back into the pot and continue the boiling in the clear liquid a little longer. Put into a large serving soup bowl one egg yolk and one teaspoonful of lemon juice or vinegar for each person you expect to serve. Beat with a fork until light. Now pour the boiling ciorba with the tripe slowly into the egg mixture and stir constantly.

Serve very hot with a green sharp pepper. If you like a sharper flavor in the ciorba, add to it a few pepper seeds. Dab with butter.

CIORBAS : 29

FISH CIORBA
Ciorba De Peste

8 cups ciorba stock
salt and pepper
scallions
1 tomato
2 small green peppers
1 bunch parsley

1 bunch fennel
sturgeon, carp or salmon
  slices
sharp red peppers
lovage

The sour stock for fish ciorba can be made from sauerkraut juice, dry vine leaves, dill pickle juice, green tomatoes or lemon. Any one of these can produce a fine ciorba. If you have none on hand, prepare fresh (see CIORBA WITH MEAT BALLS).

Add to 8 cups of ciorba stock, salt and pepper, finely chopped scallions, one peeled and sliced tomato, 2 small sweet green peppers cut lengthwise into a few strips, a bunch of parsley and a small bunch of fennel, both chopped. When the vegetables are nearly done, add slices of sturgeon, carp or salmon. Cook for ½ hour longer very gently over a low fire.

Season again before serving with very sharp tiny red peppers and add some minced lovage. Serve with mamaliga (see MAMA-LIGA). It is customary to serve a drink of tzuica (plum brandy) before you start to eat.

FISH CIORBA WITH SOUR CREAM
Ciorba De Peste Cu Smantana

2 to 3 lbs. fish
1½ qts. ciorba stock
2 carrots
1 large potato
2 tomatoes
1 stalk celery

fennel, parsley, leek
salt and pepper
lovage and tarragon
2 egg yolks
½ cup sour cream
butter

Add to 1½ quarts of sour ciorba stock (see CIORBA WITH MEAT BALLS), 2 medium-sized carrots sliced lengthwise into halves, one large potato cut in half, a stalk of celery, a sprig of fennel, one bunch of parsley, one whole stalk of leek and salt and pepper to taste. Boil until the vegetables are tender. Put in 2 to 3 pounds

30 : CIORBAS

of any fish you desire cut into pieces, and add 2 tomatoes sliced. Continue to boil until the fish is tender to your taste. Remove the bunch of parsley, add finely chopped lovage and tarragon (or dill). If you like it more sour add some more ciorba stock, sauerkraut juice or lemon juice.

Beat together 2 egg yolks and ½ cup sour cream in a serving bowl and pour over this slowly the ciorba and the fish. Place dabs of butter in the ciorba, if you wish, and sprinkle with a little freshly chopped parsley.

Serve either hot or cold with little sharp peppers. A glass of cold white wine to wash the ciorba down heightens the enjoyment of this marvelous dish.

FISH CIORBA FOR HANGOVER
Ciorba De Peste Pentru Betie

This ciorba is prepared the same as the one above, but it is made much more sour, and usually with sauerkraut juice as the sour agent. When the liquid is thick enough, strain through a fine sieve. The fish is served separately with boiled potatoes dotted with butter and sprinkled over with chopped fresh chives and parsley.

SUMMER SQUASH CIORBA
Ciorba De Dovlecei

squash	1 egg
ciorba stock	parsley, fennel and leek
¼ lb. chopped veal	tomatoes
¼ lb. chopped lean pork	1 cup sour cream
1 tbs. uncooked rice	salt and pepper

Cut a few squash lengthwise in halves, remove seeds and stuff with the following mixture: ¼ pound chopped veal, ¼ pound chopped lean pork, one tablespoonful well washed rice, one egg, chopped parsley, fennel and leek, salt and pepper to taste, all thoroughly mixed together. Let stand.

Bring to a boil some ciorba stock (see above). Pour some of this over the stuffed squash. Add a few sliced tomatoes to the

CIORBAS : 31

boiling ciorba, then put in the squash. Boil very slowly for 30 minutes. Take out the squash and place gently into a soup serving bowl. Pour one full cup of sour cream over them, then add the boiling ciorba. Serve hot in large soup bowls, sprinkled over with chopped fresh dill or parsley.

LEEK CIORBA
Ciorba De Praz

6 leeks, 3 onions	1 cup dry wine
⅔ cup butter	2 tbs. chopped chives
6 cups beef stock or	2 tbs. chopped parsley
bouillon	salt and pepper
1 potato	1 cup cream

The onion, raw or cooked, is used lavishly and in nearly everything in Romania. It is considered to have curative properties and to help regulate the stomach. They even prepare an onion juice for newborn babies. Onions, figs, caraway seeds and camomile tea leaves are boiled in water and strained, then the baby's lips are moistened with it.

For ciorba the leek (part of the onion family) is preferred and a really delightful dish results. In Romania it is made only in the summer, but here we can prepare it anytime as we have fresh leeks all year round.

Wash 6 leeks. Cut off the green parts and chop finely. Cut the remainder into thin slices, cook in ⅔ cup of butter together with 3 onions, finely chopped, until they turn golden, not brown. Now add the chopped green leek and cook a little longer. Combine with 6 cups of beef stock or bouillon, add one large potato sliced very thin, and cook together on a slow fire until done.

Strain the mixture through a very fine sieve. The soft pulp remaining on the sieve is crushed and forced through into the liquid. Add one cup of dry wine, salt and pepper to taste, and simmer for 2 minutes. Just before removing from the fire, add 2 tablespoonfuls each of finely chopped chives and parsley and one cup of cream. Beat the mixture with a rotary egg beater to give a smoothness to the ciorba.

Serve hot with toasted bread which has been spread with

32 : CIORBAS

butter and cheese and broiled under a low fire. This ciorba is just as delicious cold and served with the same toast.

CIORBA WITH MUSHROOMS
Ciorba De Ciuperci

⅔ lb. dried mushrooms
bouillon
4 cups ciorba stock

parsley, fennel, thyme
1 egg yolk
½ cup sour cream

Cut up ⅔ pound dried mushrooms into pieces and boil in bouillon until tender. Then add 4 cups of sour ciorba stock, some finely chopped parsley and fennel and a little thyme. Cook a little while longer. Beat together one egg yolk and ½ cup sour cream in a serving bowl, then pour over this the hot mushroom soup and stir well. Sprinkle with chopped fresh dill or parsley.

Vegetable Dishes

GHIVETCH

ALL THOSE who have been fortunate enough to visit Romania or any country of the Balkans must have eaten this savory and wholesome dish. It is made out of all the vegetables you can put your hands on. As here we can get our vegetables fresh all year round, we can enjoy this dish in winter as in summer.

Romania is a country that has felt the invader's iron heel many, many times. But with all the misery that any invasion brings to a conquered people, some good also came out of it. From the strangers who settled in their land the Romanians learned many things, and incorporated them into their art, their songs, and even their cooking. Needing to trade, they became friendly, observed different ways of preparing food and smelled intriguing aromas coming from the kitchen, and used this new experience to improve their national dishes.

What has all this to do with ghivetch? The Romanian country people look upon this dish as a "melting pot" and so symbolic of their country, which is full of numerous nationalities living in friendship side by side. They say that by mixing together all the vegetables and herbs that the good earth produces they obtain something truly wonderful. Instead of one vegetable clashing with another, they blend in harmony. Why then cannot people of different ways and backgrounds live together in amity and friendship? Ghivetch proves to them that it is not only possible but that each people will surely be benefited by close association with other peoples.

34 : VEGETABLE DISHES

VEGETABLE GHIVETCH
Ghiveciu Cu Zarzavaturi

1 bunch carrots	1 squash
4 large potatoes	leeks
1 eggplant	okra
1 cup green peas	8 to 10 tomatoes
1 cup green beans	1 bunch mixed herbs
1 green pepper	1 bunch grapes
1 cup green lima beans	4 clusters garlic
3 parsley roots	4 or 5 onions
2 celery roots	1½ cups olive oil
1 turnip	2 cups soup stock or
1 small head cabbage	bouillon
1 small head cauliflower	salt and pepper

Those who have seen a vegetable ghivetch as made in Romania will never forget it. First there is the baking dish as big as a wheel and filled with the white, yellow, green, purple and orange colored vegetables in a riot of color. This is then placed in the great earthen bread oven, and as the changing aromas force themselves out into the kitchen and reach your nostrils, a wonderful feeling of anticipation comes over you. In the cities they prepare their ghivetch in the largest glazed earthenware dish that they have and send it out to the neighborhood baker to be baked in his oven.

Prepare the following vegetables: One bunch of carrots sliced crosswise, 4 large potatoes diced, one eggplant which has been washed, left unpeeled and cubed, one cup of green peas, one cup of green beans sliced lengthwise, one meaty green pepper sliced lengthwise, one cup of green lima beans, 3 parsley roots, 2 celery roots, one turnip, all of these cubed, one small head of cabbage and one small head of cauliflower both cut into thick pieces, a few chopped leeks, one summer or winter squash diced, one handful of okra, 8 to 10 tomatoes sliced thick, one bunch of mixed herbs chopped, one bunch of grapes and 4 clusters of garlic separated into cloves. Mix together all the vegetables gently and place in a large earthenware baking dish.

Fry 4 or 5 sliced onions in ½ cup of olive oil or butter to a nice golden brown, add 2 cups of soup stock or bouillon and bring to a boil. Now pour over the vegetables in the casserole one

VEGETABLE DISHES : 35

cup of boiling olive oil, add about 2 teaspoonfuls of salt and some pepper to taste, and finally pour on the hot bouillon with the fried onions. Cover and bake in a moderate oven, until the juice has been absorbed. Serve hot or cold.

GHIVETCH WITH MEAT
Ghiveciu Cu Carne

Prepare the same as the VEGETABLE GHIVETCH, but ½ hour before it is done place on top of the vegetables broiled pork chops, lamb chops or pork ribs.

GHIVETCH WITH FISH
Ghiveciu Cu Peste

Prepare exactly as the above, using a deep pan instead of a pot. Lay the fish of your choice on top of the vegetables whole, not cut. When nearly done, cover the pan for 20 minutes. Then remove cover and place in hot oven to brown.

MUSACA

THIS DISH is a favorite of the Romanian people. They look upon cooking as an art and each cook an artist and a creator. Even if following a recipe exactly, no two dishes will come out the same if made by two different cooks. Variations no matter how slight, in the amounts of herbs added, in the degree of heat, the time of cooking, etc., will make noticeable changes. But in Romania each cook tries to excel and so will experiment, and this applies especially to the making of musaca. If the village housewife can make a more savory musaca, she will be envied, but there exists also a practical reason why she wants her cooking to be outstanding. She wishes her daughter, whom she starts to teach the cooking art at an early age, to be known as an excellent cook.

It is traditional for a mother to teach her young daughter the everyday and holiday dishes. First she is taught how to bake bread and then to make mamaliga, the yellow corn meal which is the staple national food. Later she learns to prepare the sweet

36 : VEGETABLE DISHES

and sour soups and the wholesome one-course dinners. When a girl can bake a good bread, make an appetizing ciorba and a savory ghivetch and musaca, her mother will be filled with pride. Naturally she will tell it to her good neighbors and also to the village "long tongues" as the gossips are called, who will broadcast the news far and wide in no time. Of course, it soon becomes known in the families having marriageable young men. It means a great deal to say of a young girl, "Her musaca is simply out of this world." Perhaps a young man will invite her to the village dance, and who can tell, in time he might even lead her to the altar.

If it is true that you can reach a man's heart through his stomach, you can see how important it is to be a good cook. And especially if the girl is not beautiful, she must make up for this shortcoming by excelling in the dishes she can turn out, thus intriguing the man and keeping him always eager for her cooking.

Here are a few of the many kinds of musaca.

MUSACA WITH EGGPLANT
Musaca Cu Patlagele Vinete

2 large eggplants	flour
6 tbs. of butter	bread crumbs
3 onions	tomatoes, green peppers
2 lbs. ground meat	pepper and salt
3 tbs. uncooked rice	1 cup bouillon or stock
parsley, thyme	

In a saucepan containing 6 tablespoonfuls of butter, drippings or olive oil, fry 3 finely chopped onions to a nice light brown. Add 2 pounds of ground meat (mixed pork and veal) and cook until brown, stirring constantly to prevent burning. Wash 3 tablespoonfuls of rice very well in cold water, mix with the meat, add a tablespoonful of finely chopped parsley and a little thyme, and cook for 2 to 3 minutes. Cut 2 large eggplants into one-third-inch slices without peeling, heat the butter (or drippings or olive oil) and fry quickly each slice on both sides, place on a plate, until all have been done. Add more butter if required while frying.

VEGETABLE DISHES : 37

Grease the bottom and the sides of a casserole with butter and sprinkle with a little flour mixed with bread crumbs. On the bottom place a layer of eggplant, a layer of the ground mixed meat and thirdly a layer of sliced tomatoes. Continue adding layers in this order and finish with a layer of tomatoes on top. Between layers place some diced green peppers, parsley, and pepper and salt to taste (and also dill, but this is optional). Pour one cup of boiling soup stock or bouillon over the ingredients and bake for one hour in a moderate oven with the casserole covered, and 20 minutes longer uncovered. If needed, add more soup stock. When baked there should remain only a little juice on the bottom.

MUSACA WITH WINE
Musaca Cu Vin

3 eggplants	2 tomatoes
4 onions	¼ cup red wine
butter	2 eggs
2 lbs. chopped veal	6 tbs. bread crumbs
salt and pepper	1 cup milk
parsley, thyme	⅓ cup grated cheese

Brown 4 chopped onions in 4 tablespoonfuls of hot butter. Add 2 pounds of chopped veal and heat until brown. Season with salt and pepper to taste, and also with parsley and thyme, and simmer together for 2 minutes. Add 2 sliced tomatoes and ¼ cup of red wine, cover the dish and simmer slowly until the liquid is absorbed.

While the meat mixture is heating, cut 3 eggplants into slices of ⅛ inch thickness, salt and let stand until the juice is all out. Rinse, drain and dry, and fry both sides in butter quickly until brown. Place the meat mixture in a bowl, add the well beaten whites of 2 eggs and 3 tablespoonfuls of bread crumbs (and more seasoning if needed). Mix well.

Grease the baking casserole with butter and sprinkle with 3 tablespoonfuls of bread crumbs. First put in a layer of eggplant, then a layer of the meat mixture and keep alternating layers until filled, finishing with a layer of eggplant on top. Sprinkle between layers some chopped parsley and a little thyme.

38 : VEGETABLE DISHES

Beat the yolks of 2 eggs with one cup of milk, add ⅓ cup of grated cheese and mix well. Pour this mixture over the top, dot with pieces of butter and sprinkle with finely chopped parsley. Bake in a hot oven until done.

MUSACA WITH NOODLES
Musaca Cu Tatei

1 lb. chopped pork	1 lb. fine noodles
1 slice bread	4 eggs, ½ cup cream
parsley, fennel, leek	butter, flour
salt and pepper	4 tbs. grated cheese

Mix one pound of finely chopped pork (or you may try this recipe with liver) and one slice of bread soaked in milk, add a sprig of parsley, a sprig of fennel, some leek and salt and pepper to taste. Boil one pound of very fine noodles, strain, place in a bowl, add 2 eggs and mix well.

Grease the bottom and the sides of a casserole with butter and sprinkle with a little flour. Arrange alternately one layer of noodles, then one layer of meat, ending with a layer of noodles on top. Sprinkle with a little finely chopped parsley and fennel and dot with butter between layers. Place in a moderate oven and bake for ½ hour. In the meantime prepare a mixture of 2 eggs well beaten with ½ cup of cream, to which has been added 4 tablespoonfuls of grated cheese. Mix well and pour over the ingredients in the casserole. Return to the oven and bake slowly until nice and brown. Remove from the oven and turn contents onto a platter. Place another platter on the musaca and holding both in the hands, turn around, so that the crust is now on top. Serve very hot on heated plates.

MUSACA WITH POTATOES
Musaca Cu Cartofi

2 lbs. potatoes	2 tbs. flour
3 onions	¼ cup wine
butter	4 eggs
1 lb. chopped veal	1 cup cream
parsley, fennel, thyme	bread crumbs
salt and pepper	wine sauce or tomato sauce

VEGETABLE DISHES : 39

Fry 3 chopped onions in 2 tablespoonfuls of butter until golden in color, add one pound of finely chopped veal, cook a little, now add one tablespoonful of chopped parsley, a little thyme, fennel and salt and pepper to taste and heat a little more. Now add one tablespoonful of flour and cook for 3 minutes more, mixing constantly, and taking care it does not burn. Add slowly ¼ cup of wine and let cool. When cool, pass through a meat grinder and mix into it the yolks of 2 eggs, a little cream, some chopped parsley, and then add the stiffly beaten egg whites.

Peel and slice 2 pounds of potatoes. Fry in butter until brown. Butter a casserole and sprinkle with bread crumbs. First put in a layer of potatoes, then a layer of the meat mixture, and keep adding alternate layers until filled, ending with a layer of potatoes. Dot with butter, sprinkle with a little parsley and bake. One-half hour before it is done, remove the casserole from the oven and pour over the top a mixture of one cup of cream well beaten with 2 eggs, one tablespoonful of flour and a little salt. Place back in the oven, bake a little longer and brown the top under the flame. Serve hot with wine sauce or tomato sauce.

MUSACA WITH CELERY
Musaca Cu Telina

1 lb. celery knobs	1 tomato
3 tbs. lard	2 tbs. wine
1 onion	butter
1 lb. chopped veal	bread crumbs
1 slice bread	milk
leek	flour
3 eggs	tomato sauce
parsley, fennel, thyme	grated cheese
salt and pepper	

Peel and clean well one pound of celery knobs, slice lengthwise and brown in 2 tablespoonfuls of lard. Fry one finely chopped onion in one tablespoonful of lard, add one pound of chopped veal mixed with a piece of bread soaked in milk and a little chopped leek. Heat together until brown and let cool. Now add one egg, finely chopped parsley, fennel, a little thyme, salt and pepper to taste, one sliced tomato and 2 tablespoonfuls of wine. Mix well together.

40 : VEGETABLE DISHES

Grease a casserole with butter, sprinkle with bread crumbs, and arrange in it alternate layers of celery and meat, starting and finishing with layers of celery. Cover the top layer with tomato sauce and bake in a moderate oven for ½ hour.

Beat in a bowl 2 eggs with a large piece of butter, add enough milk and flour to make a thick sauce and salt to taste. Pour this sauce over the top, sprinkle with a little cheese and chopped parsley, place back in the hot oven and continue to bake slowly until you get a nice brown crust.

STUFFED VEGETABLES

DURING the summer when vegetables are plentiful, there is hardly one household in Romania where stuffed vegetable dishes are not prepared daily. As soon as a new vegetable is in season, it is stuffed in most interesting ways. During Lent and on Fridays no meat stuffing is used, but they know how to create delicious combinations without meat and at low cost.

CABBAGE STUFFED WITH RICE
Sarmale—Varza Umpluta Cu Orezi

cabbage leaves	1 tbs. chopped leek
1 onion	salt and pepper
oil	1 cup uncooked rice
thyme, dill	sauerkraut

Sarmale can be made either from pickled or fresh cabbage. If you have a pickled head of cabbage, select equal-sized leaves. If you do not, buy a nice head of cabbage, place in a large dish, scald with salted boiling water, let stand for 30 minutes and select equal-sized leaves from it.

Prepare the stuffing by browning one finely chopped onion in a saucepan containing 2 large tablespoonfuls of hot oil. Add a little thyme, a tablespoonful of chopped leek, fresh or dry dill and salt and pepper to taste, a cup of rice and a little more oil if needed. Heat until brown, stirring constantly.

The cabbage rolls are prepared as follows: Select a cabbage leaf and slice off with a sharp knife enough of the thickened

VEGETABLE DISHES : 41

border between segments, so that it will have about the same thickness as the rest of the leaf. Lay the leaf flat and put some stuffing in the center. Turn the right and left edges over towards the center, but not far enough that they will touch. Starting with the end in front of you, begin to roll (loosely so there will be enough room for expansion during the cooking) and continue till the end. Now tuck in the loose side edges.

Choose a glazed earthenware pot and line the bottom with some sauerkraut and sprinkle over with some oil. Now place the cabbage rolls close together until a layer is formed, leaving no empty spaces between rolls. Form layer on top of layer and between each put a little sauerkraut, some dill, thyme (green if possible, but if not handy, dry is good, too) and generously sprinkled over with oil. On the top layer place a little sauerkraut. If it is too sour, add a little sauerkraut juice diluted with water. This is the method used for both pickled and fresh cabbage leaves.

Cover the rolls to the top with sauerkraut juice. (If you use fresh cabbage leaves, an alternative method permits adding tomato juice at this point). Add 5 to 6 large tablespoonfuls of oil and let stand for a few hours. My mother always used to prepare the stuffed cabbage after supper and let the pot remain on the kitchen stove overnight to allow the aromas to permeate through the rolls. You may also prepare the sarmale in the morning and cook at night.

Heat slowly. When it starts to boil, be prepared for any possible overflowing with a bowl and a spoon and dip out some of the liquid. As the liquid in the pot is reduced by evaporation and absorption, pour back the saved liquid as needed. Now and then take hold of the pot (cover with a towel to protect you from the heat) and turn and shake gently a few times to prevent burning of the rolls. Reduce heat, cover and let cook on a slow fire for 2 hours. Place in a slow oven and bake for one hour longer. When finished, there should not remain more than one cup of liquid. Leave in pot, cover lid with thick towels and let stand until next day.

Serve hot with sour cream. Mamaliga (see MAMALIGA) goes excellently with it. It will keep for a whole week, and the last portion is the best.

42 : VEGETABLE DISHES

CABBAGE STUFFED WITH MEAT
Sarmale—Varza Umpluta Cu Carne

Prepare the same as the rice sarmale (Cabbage Stuffed with Rice) above, except that you replace the rice with meat. Also on the bottom of the pot put some bacon drippings, one or two slices of bacon, the sauerkraut and then the layer of cabbage rolls. Between layers instead of oil use slices of bacon and on the top pour 4 or 5 tablespoonfuls of bacon drippings. Buy a 1 to 1½-pound piece of fat pork tenderloin, cut in half and place one piece in the center and the other close to the top.

Make the stuffing with one pound of rather fat pork and ½ pound of beef, both chopped and mixed with 4 tablespoonfuls of well-rinsed rice. Serve hot with mamaliga.

STUFFED KOHLRABI
Calarabe Umplute

kohlrabies	parsley, thyme, dill
vinegar	leek
chopped veal or chicken	butter, flour
salt and pepper	sour cream sauce

Scoop out the insides of as many new kohlrabies as you will need and scald them in boiling water and vinegar. Make a stuffing of chopped veal or chicken to which you will add pepper and salt, finely chopped sprigs of parsley, leek and a little thyme. Mix well together and stuff into the cavities. Butter well a casserole, sprinkle with flour, put in the kohlrabies, cover with sour cream sauce, dot with a little butter, sprinkle with chopped parsley and bake. Serve with sour cream as a topping, sprinkled with dill.

LEEKS STUFFED WITH RICE
Praz Umplut Cu Orezi

4 large leeks, 2 onions	thyme, parsley
2 tbs. olive oil	flour, bread crumbs
½ lb. uncooked rice	butter, sugar
beef stock or bouillon	½ cup tomato sauce
salt and pepper	juice of ½ lemon

VEGETABLE DISHES : 43

Cut off the white part of 4 large leeks to about finger length. Scald in salted water and drain. Without tearing, slip off the shells. These leek tubes are used to hold the stuffing. Prepare the stuffing by frying 2 finely chopped onions in 2 tablespoonfuls of olive oil, adding ½ pound of rice well rinsed in cold water and frying further. Now add slowly cold water until the rice is covered. Cook until the water is absorbed. Cover again with good beef stock or bouillon, add salt and pepper to taste and sprinkle with a little thyme. Cook until done and the liquid has been absorbed. Cool, then fill the leek tubes with stuffing. Dip the ends in flour and fry in hot oil very slightly.

Grease the bottom and sides of a casserole with butter and sprinkle with bread crumbs. Place the stuffed leeks carefully inside, pour over the top a mixture of ½ cup of tomato sauce, a little sugar and the juice of ½ lemon. Sprinkle with a little finely chopped parsley, cover and bake in a moderate oven.

LEEKS STUFFED WITH MEAT
Praz Umplut Cu Carne

Prepare as above, but substitute chopped meat for the rice.

PEPPERS STUFFED WITH MEAT
Ardei Umplut Cu Carne

large green peppers	parsley, chives and fennel
2 tbs. butter	salt and pepper
onion	½ cup soup stock
½ lb. chopped meat (pork and veal)	1½ cups tomato sauce
	lovage, dill
sour cream	2 tbs. bacon drippings
2 tbs. uncooked rice	1 tbs. flour
1 egg	

Prepare the stuffing as follows: Fry in 2 tablespoonfuls of butter in a frying pan ¼ of a finely chopped onion until soft. Add a sprig of parsley chopped well and ½ pound of chopped meat (pork and veal mixed). Heat, stirring constantly until the heat has penetrated throughout, then add 2 level tablespoonfuls

44 : VEGETABLE DISHES

of rice well rinsed. Cover and let stand while you prepare the peppers.

Select large green meaty peppers, one for each person served. Wash in cold water, cut out the stem carefully and through the opening remove the membranes and seeds with the fingers. Place in a pot, cover with boiling water and keep immersed for 3 to 4 minutes. Discard the hot water, add ice-cold water and let remain for another 3 to 4 minutes. Take out the peppers and lay them on their sides for the water to drain out.

Now to finish the stuffing, put the meat and rice into a mixing bowl, add one whole egg, a little finely chopped parsley, chives, fennel, and salt and pepper to taste. Mix well together with your hands. Stuff the peppers, leaving about one inch on top unfilled to allow for the swelling of the rice.

Place the stuffed peppers in a deep saucepan standing up, top with a little sour cream and sprinkle with some chopped parsley. Now pour on a mixture of ½ cup of soup stock (or water) and ½ cup of tomato sauce. Cover and let simmer slowly.

Make a brown sauce as follows: Heat 2 tablespoonfuls of bacon drippings, add ½ of a finely chopped onion and fry to a light brown. Add a heaping tablespoonful of flour and stir constantly until it is brown. Now, stirring constantly, add one cup of tomato sauce slowly and ½ cup of cold water and then cook slowly. Add a pinch of lovage and salt and pepper to taste. Cook for 10 minutes, then pour over the simmering peppers and continue to simmer until cooked.

Use a wooden spoon in taking out the stuffed peppers and be gentle not to injure them. Serve on heated plates, top with a generous helping of sour cream, pour on some sauce in which the peppers were cooking, and sprinkle with chopped dill or parsley. As a side dish use dumplings or potatoes.

PEPPERS STUFFED WITH RICE
Ardei Umplut Cu Orez

Prepare as above, but substitute rice for the meat and pure olive oil for the butter or bacon drippings. It can be served cold also.

VEGETABLE DISHES : 45

GREEN PEPPERS STUFFED WITH VEGETABLES
Ardei Verde Umplut Cu Zarzavaturi

4 to 6 large peppers	parsley, tarragon, fennel
radishes, celery knobs	carrots, cucumbers
onions, chives	mayonnaise, sour cream

Get 4 to 6 large meaty peppers, green and red mixed. Wash, dry, cut off the stem ends and scoop out the seeds and membranes. Make the following stuffing: Mix together finely minced radishes, celery knobs, onions, parsley, carrots, chives, cucumbers, fennel, tarragon and mayonnaise. Mix slowly with a wooden spoon and fork. Stuff the peppers and sprinkle with finely chopped parsley. Top with sour cream. Serve with pumpernickel or sour rye bread.

POTATOES STUFFED WITH HAM
Cartofi Umplute Cu Sunca

1 large baking potato for each person	1 tbs. grated Swiss cheese
butter	parsley, fennel, chives
¼ lb. boiled or baked ham	pepper and salt

Select large baking potatoes, one for each person, wash very well and bake in the oven, being careful not to burn. When done, place them on a board, let cool so you can hold them in your hands, sliced off the tops with a sharp knife and scoop out the insides, leaving a not too thin shell. Put the insides of the potatoes into a mixing bowl, add one or more tablespoonfuls of butter, ¼ pound of boiled or baked ham chopped into very small pieces, one large tablespoonful of grated Swiss cheese, finely chopped parsley, fennel, chives and pepper and salt to taste. If salted butter is used, please taste before adding salt. Mix well together, stuff the potatoes not quite to the top, leaving space for a piece of butter the size of a filbert nut. Arrange the potatoes cut end up in a buttered baking dish, add butter to the top of the stuffing, sprinkle on a little parsley and chives, replace the sliced off potato tops, place in a hot oven uncovered and bake until the heat has penetrated the stuffed potatoes. Serve very hot.

46 : VEGETABLE DISHES

If any stuffing is left, form into small balls, place them around
the potatoes and bake with the potatoes.

POTATOES STUFFED WITH LIVER
Cartofi Umpluti Cu Ficat

Prepare as above, but substitute for the ham either chicken or
goose liver sautéed in butter. When done, add a little wine and
chop very fine.

POTATOES STUFFED WITH MUSHROOMS
Cartofi Umpluti Cu Ciuperci

Prepare the same as POTATOES STUFFED WITH HAM, but substitute for the ham mushrooms prepared as follows: Chop the
mushrooms very fine, sauté in butter, add a little rum or brandy,
then a little wine. After cooling a little, mix some grated Swiss
cheese with the potatoes and stuff the potato shells. All of these
one-course potato dishes are served with cooked and creamed
vegetables or mixed salads.

STUFFED SUMMER OR WINTER SQUASH
Dovlecei De Vara Or Iarna Umpluti

4 squashes	oil
¾ lb. chopped meat	tomato sauce
1 slice bread, 1 egg	parsley, fennel
onion, green pepper	butter
salt and pepper	heavy sweet cream

Peel 4 squashes, cut into halves, scoop out the pulp, scald and
fill with the following: ¾ pound of chopped meat, one slice of
bread soaked in milk, one finely chopped onion, one egg, a little
finely chopped green peppers, fennel and salt and pepper to
taste, well mixed together and fried in oil just a little bit.

Arrange the squashes in a saucepan, cover with tomato sauce,
sprinkle with chopped parsley, dot with butter, cover and cook
over a slow fire until tender. Serve with a tablespoonful of heavy
sweet cream on top.

VEGETABLE DISHES : 47

STUFFED GREEN TOMATOES
Patlagele Verzi Umplute

6 to 8 green tomatoes	parsley, chives
2 large onions	1 glass beef soup
2 tbs. butter	salt and pepper
¼ lb. uncooked rice	soup stock

Wash 6 to 8 medium-sized green tomatoes, cut a thin slice from the stem end and scoop out the seeds and pulp. Prepare a stuffing as follows: Fry 2 large onions finely minced in 2 level tablespoonfuls of hot butter. Add ¼-pound of well-washed rice, brown a little, then add a tablespoonful of finely minced parsley and stir. Add slowly with stirring one glass of beef soup and a little salt and pepper. Let cook slowly until the rice is swollen, but not cooked too soft. Cool and stuff the tomatoes.

Place the stuffed tomatoes in a casserole next to each other. Add enough soup stock to cover the tomatoes, sprinkle with a little minced chives, cover tightly and cook slowly until the liquid is absorbed. Remove the tomatoes gently with a wooden spoon, top each with a teaspoonful of sour cream and sprinkle with a little finely chopped parsley. Serve as a garnish or dish.

STUFFED RED TOMATOES
Patlagele Rosii Umplute

Prepare exactly like the above, replacing the green with red tomatoes.

STUFFED TOMATOES WITH RICE
Paradais Rosii Cu Orezi

6 tomatoes	salt and pepper
oil	raisins
1 cup uncooked rice	tomato sauce
1 onion	butter
parsley, fennel, thyme	sour cream

Select 6 firm tomatoes, wipe or rinse them, cut off the stem end, scoop out the pulp and seeds and make the following mixture for stuffing. In a pan containing heated oil put in one

48 : VEGETABLE DISHES

cup of rice, one finely chopped onion, a few sprigs of parsley and fennel chopped, a little thyme, salt and pepper and the pulp of a few raisins. Simmer slowly for a few minutes.

Place the tomatoes in a pan and fill with this mixture, replace the cut-off ends, cover with tomato sauce, dot with butter and sprinkle with finely chopped parsley. Cook until tender. Serve cold with sour cream on top.

STUFFED TOMATOES WITH HAM
Paradais Rosii Cu Sunca

6 large tomatoes	salt and pepper
butter	1 tbs. bread crumbs
chopped boiled ham	milk
1 hard-boiled egg	1 onion
parsley, fennel, thyme	tomato sauce

Select 6 or more large firm tomatoes, cut off the stem ends, scoop out the pulp and seeds and sprinkle the inside with a little warm butter. Prepare a stuffing as follows: Mix together enough chopped boiled ham, one chopped hard-boiled egg, a few sprigs of parsley and fennel finely chopped, a little thyme, salt and pepper to taste, one large tablespoonful of bread crumbs moistened with milk and one finely chopped onion. Now add the tomato pulp and mix all together well. Stuff the tomatoes with this mixture, place in a saucepan, replace the cut off ends and cover with tomato sauce. If any stuffing remains, form into balls and place in the pan around the tomatoes. Dot with butter and sprinkle with chopped parsley. Handle gently. Cover the pan and bake very slowly until tender. Serve hot or cold with sweet or sour cream.

Gauge the amount of chopped ham to use by measuring how much is required to fill one tomato.

STUFFED TOMATOES WITH CHICKEN
Paradais Rosii Umplute Cu Pui

Replace ham with the chopped white meat of chicken and prepare as above. Serve either hot or cold. Either way it is very delicious.

VEGETABLE DISHES : 49

TOMATOES STUFFED WITH EGGS
Paradais Rosii Umplute Cu Oua

Select nice large tomatoes, cut off the stem end, scoop out the pulp and seeds, sprinkle the inside with a little salt and pepper and pour in a little warmed butter. Arrange the tomatoes in a well-buttered pan. Break into each tomato one egg, sprinkle with Parmesan cheese, chopped parsley and fennel, dot with butter and replace the cut off ends. Bake in a moderate oven until tender, adding more butter if it is needed. Serve plain or with sweet or sour cream.

TOMATOES STUFFED WITH POT CHEESE
Paradais Rosii Umplute Cu Brinza

large tomatoes	paprika
pot cheese	1 apple, walnuts
parsley, leek, fennel	Roquefort cheese
salt and pepper	butter

Select nice large tomatoes (as many as you need), cut off the stem end and scoop out the inside as above. Use same amount of pot cheese as the scooped out pulp. Mix the cheese in a bowl with a little finely chopped parsley, leek and fennel, salt and pepper, a little red paprika, a finely chopped apple, a few ground walnuts, a little Roquefort cheese and a little butter. Stuff the tomatoes with this mixture, sprinkle with parsley, and replace the cut off ends. Cover with sour cream and serve cold, garnished with red radishes and black olives. It is a most delicious summer or winter dish.

FRIED ARTICHOKES
Anghinare Prajita

Remove the large outside leaves of 6 to 8 artichokes and cut off the stem close to the base. Sprinkle well with lemon juice, let stand a little, then boil in water to which have been added salt and lemon juice. When cooked, remove from the pot. When they are cool and all the water has drained off, dip in beaten eggs, dredge in roll crumbs and fry quickly in deep hot lard or butter. Use to garnish game meats with sauce, or for other meats.

50 : VEGETABLE DISHES

ASPARAGUS IN CREAM
Sparangel Cu Smantana

Buy a large bunch of young and tender asparagus. Cut off the
white base and use the green stalk. Then prepare exactly like
CAULIFLOWER IN CREAM.

BRAISED ASPARAGUS
Sparangel In Pesmet

Prepare exactly like BRAISED CAULIFLOWER. Use for garnishing boiled and roasted meats.

BEANS WITH OIL
Fasole Cu Unt De Lemn

½ lb. dried white beans	2 tbs. tomato paste
5 tbs. oil	salt and pepper
2 onions	1 tbs. flour
parsley	vinegar

Beans hold an all important place in the diet of the Romanians.
They are prepared with or without meat. During Lent the dish
most favored is Beans with Oil.

Soak ½ pound dried white beans in cold water overnight. In
the morning boil in the same water until the beans become soft.
Strain and retain the strained water. While the beans are cooking, prepare a sauce as follows:

Heat 4 tablespoonfuls of oil in a saucepan. Add one finely
chopped onion, a few sprigs of finely chopped parsley, 2 tablespoonfuls of tomato paste and salt and pepper to taste and fry.
Add one tablespoonful of flour and stir constantly until brown.
Now add slowly enough of the water strained from the beans,
to make a sauce. Add a little vinegar, boil for a few minutes,
then pour over the beans and let simmer for 5 or 6 minutes.

Before serving fry one chopped onion in a tablespoonful of
oil until brown and sprinkle very hot over the beans. Serve hot
or cold with a glass of sauerkraut juice or the heart of a head of
sour cabbage. (Split the head of a cabbage in two and take out
the center or the heart.)

VEGETABLE DISHES : 51

BEANS WITH PORK
Fasole Cu Carne De Pork

Prepare the same as above but with this difference. While the beans are boiling, place into the pot some pork meat, preferably smoked. After straining the beans, return the pork meat to the water until it is ready to be served. Instead of oil, use pork fat for making the sauce and frying the onions.

BEANS WITH SAUSAGES
Fasole Cu Carnati

Prepare the same as BEANS WITH OIL. Garnish with fried sausages. Pour some of the hot fat from the sausage frying pan over the sausages and the beans.

MASHED BEANS
Fasole Frecata

Soak one pound of dried beans in cold water overnight. Boil, strain, mash through a sieve and add 2 boiled mashed potatoes. Place on the fire, adding at the same time one cup of hot olive oil. Keep mixing until you get a white purée, adding salt and pepper to taste and a crushed clove of garlic. If the purée is too thick add a little of the liquid strained from the beans. Remove from the fire and continue to stir until it cools. Place on a platter and garnish with fried sliced onions and sprinkled with red paprika. Serve hot with roasts or sausages or serve cold with sauerkraut.

RED BEETS
Sfecle Rosii

Get a nice bunch of red beets, cut off the leaves but leave a few inches of stem. Wash, then cook in boiling water to which has been added a little lemon juice to help the beets keep their color. Young beets become tender after about 30 minutes of boiling, older ones take a longer time. When done, peel and after cooling, slice crosswise not too thin nor too thick. Place in

52 : VEGETABLE DISHES

a glazed earthenware pot, add salt to taste, sprinkle over the beets a heaping tablespoonful of grated caraway seeds. Add a few thin slices of horseradish, then enough wine vinegar to cover the beets. Cover the pot and keep in a cool dry place. Serve as garnishing for all kinds of boiled and roasted meats.

CABBAGE ALA CLUJ
Varza Ala Cluj

2½ lbs. fresh pork tenderloin	4 large onions
1½ lbs. fresh ham	1 bunch green leeks
1 lb. beef	parsley, thyme, dill
3 lbs. sauerkraut	1 cup uncooked rice
bacon drippings	salt and pepper
bacon	cream (sweet and sour)
	½ cup milk

Do you know someone you would like to please? Are you having important guests who are also gourmets? Then delight and surprise them with this utterly delectable entree. It is named after the city of Cluj where it originated, God only knows when. It is here that I was born and where I spent my childhood. Cluj is the capital of Transylvania (meaning "land beyond the mountains"), which is a province of Romania. It is a quiet university town of great charm, nestling in a valley, surrounded on all sides by high hills, which is the characteristic landscape of this part of Transylvania. The people in this region are very hospitable and marvelous cooks. Here is how they make this dish.

Put 2 tablespoonfuls of bacon drippings in a deep iron frying pan. Heat and fry in it 4 large chopped onions to a golden color, but do not brown. Add the greens of half a bunch of leeks (chopped fine) and a half bunch of finely chopped parsley and simmer slowly for 10 minutes. Then add one cup of uncooked rice and fry for another 5 minutes, stirring constantly. Sprinkle with salt and pepper to taste, then cover and let stand until ready to use.

Chop 2½ pounds of fresh pork tenderloin, 1½ pounds of fresh ham and one pound of beef (round steak or other cut

VEGETABLE DISHES : 53

which you like). In another deep pan containing one table-spoonful of bacon drippings fry one-half bunch of chopped leeks and one-half bunch of chopped green parsley and then simmer for 2 to 3 minutes. Add the chopped meat, fry with constant stirring until the heat has permeated throughout the meat. Add salt and pepper to taste and about ½ teaspoonful of dry thyme rubbed between the palms of your hands.

Take 3 pounds of fresh sauerkraut (half sour). If not obtain-able, buy 3 pounds of sauerkraut (not canned), place in a pot, pour on enough cold water to cover well, rinse thoroughly and squeeze out the excess water between your hands. However, if you like it quite sour, do not rinse with the water.

In the bottom of your baking dish place 1 or 2 slices of lean bacon, cover with a layer of sauerkraut, a layer of the rice pre-pared above spread evenly on the sauerkraut by hand, and then a layer of the chopped mixed meat. Between layers sprinkle with cream. Continue forming layers in this order and end with a layer of sauerkraut. Over each layer of sauerkraut, sprinkle only a very little pepper, some thyme rubbed between your palms and spread evenly, and some fresh or dried dill.

Over the top layer which is sauerkraut pour ½ cup of milk, then 5 cups of sweet cream and sprinkle with fresh or dry dill. Let stand to settle for one hour, or you may prepare it after supper and let it stand overnight.

Place the baking dish on the stove, protected from the direct flame by an asbestos mat. Cook slowly. To prevent burning, shake the pot with a circular motion now and then. During the cooking or baking watch to see that the cream does not boil over. When done, there must remain a little liquid in the bottom. If needed, add a little more milk during the cooking or baking. Taste to see when the rice is well cooked and the dish done. When ready, place in the oven under the flame for a few minutes till nicely browned on top.

Serve very hot on heated plates with a tablespoonful of sour cream on top. Keep the pot tightly covered at all times with a heavy towel over the cover to preserve the aroma. With each passing day it becomes more delicious. It is really funny, but this is one of those things you just can't stop eating. Will you please let me know how you enjoyed Cabbage ala Cluj?

54 : VEGETABLE DISHES

SHEPHERD'S SAUERKRAUT STEW
Tocana Ciobanului Cu Varza

4 or 5 large onions	1 cup sour cream
bacon drippings	red paprika, thyme, dill
2 lbs. sauerkraut	1 bunch scallions
2 lbs. pork or spareribs	pepper and salt

Chop 4 or 5 large onions and fry in an iron pan with 3 table-spoonfuls of bacon drippings until the onions are soft. Add pepper and salt to taste. Take 2 pounds of sauerkraut, rinse in cold water and squeeze out the excess liquid. If you prefer it more sour, do not wash the sauerkraut. Add to the pan and mix with the fried onions. Fry for 10 minutes. Stir a few times to prevent burning. Cut into cubes 2 pounds of pork meat or spareribs, place in a separate pan and sear quickly until nicely colored but not enough to dry the meat.

In a deep pot put one tablespoonful of bacon drippings, add the chopped greens of a bunch of scallions and fry them a little. Now add the sauerkraut and onion mixture and the meat. Mix well together, place tightly covered pot on a low fire, add a cup of cold water and cook slowly. (If necessary add a little more cold water to have just a little sauce when finished.) Before the sauerkraut is completely cooked, add one cup of sour cream and sprinkle with a little red paprika to taste, some thyme and fresh or dry dill, mix well and cook a little longer until the sauerkraut is done. Cover and let stand for at least an hour to allow the herbs to penetrate throughout the mixture. Heat again just before serving and place a heaping tablespoonful of sauerkraut on each plate. Garnish with boiled potatoes and sprinkle with chopped parsley.

All these cabbage dishes are one-course dinners, very palatable, and they get better by standing. Therefore it is always advisable to prepare a few days' supply, especially when you know you'll be too busy to cook, when you are engaged in club or church work. If you are a business girl you can prepare enough over a week end to last you for a whole week of suppers. I mix into the sauerkraut my boiled potatoes and it is just delicious. Serve with hot or cold mamaliga (see MAMALIGA).

VEGETABLE DISHES : 55

FRIED SAUERKRAUT
Varza Acra Calita

If you have pickled sour cabbage, take a head and cut into
very thin strips (like noodles). If you haven't, buy one or more
pounds of sauerkraut, then proceed as with the raw cabbage
above. Serve very hot with suckling pig, pork in any form,
roasted or fried, and also with duck and goose.

RAW RED CABBAGE
Varza Rosie Cruda

Cut one head of red cabbage into very thin strips (like
noodles), place in a large pan or vegetable dish, salt and let
stand for 15 or 20 minutes. Squeeze the cabbage quite dry
between your hands, put into a bowl, add one tablespoonful of
powdered sugar and mix well. Add wine or apple vinegar a
little at a time, mixing in well, until it suits your taste. Serve raw
as garnishing for beef steak schnitzel, steaks or roasts.

NEW TURNIP CABBAGE WITH CREAM
Gulie Cu Smantana

Cook 3 new turnip cabbages in boiling salted water and strain.
During the boiling prepare a white sauce with one cup of milk
(see SAUCES). Butter a pan, put in the boiled turnip cabbages,
pour on the white sauce and cook a little longer, adding chopped
chives and salt and pepper to taste. When done, sprinkle with
a little grated cheese and finely chopped parsley. Serve with sour
cream. Use a little lemon juice if you like.

SHREDDED CABBAGE
Varza Tacata Tatei

Fry one sliced onion in 2 large tablespoonfuls of lard or bacon
drippings, add one half of a small head of cabbage finely
shredded, salt and pepper to taste, and a little thyme. Mix and
continue to heat until brown. Serve with roast pork, frankfurters
or sausages.

56 : VEGETABLE DISHES

SAVOY CABBAGE WITH MEAT
Curechiu Verde Cup Carne

Cut the cabbage crosswise into ½-inch slices and cut 2 or 3 potatoes into 4 slices. Substitute the cabbage and the potatoes for the sauerkraut in the above recipe, and substitute a white sauce (made with sour cream and with some caraway seeds cooked in it) for the sour cream used above. Otherwise prepare exactly as SAUERKRAUT AND PORK STEW.

FRIED SWEET CABBAGE
Varza Dulce Calita

Cut one small head of cabbage into very thin strips (like noodles), place in a large pan or dish, salt and let stand for 15 to 20 minutes. Put 3 tablespoonfuls of lard or bacon drippings into a pan or casserole and when very hot, squeeze the cabbage quite dry between your hands, place it on the hot fat, stir well and add one tablespoonful of powdered (or granulated) sugar, which helps give a delicious taste. Cover the casserole tightly and fry slowly, stirring from time to time to prevent burning. When the cabbage is fried, add a few drops of water and 1 or 2 tablespoonfuls of wine vinegar (vary according to how sour you like it). Mix, then add a little salt and pepper to taste. When ready to serve sprinkle with a little finely chopped dill or thyme. Serve with roast chicken, pork or veal.

ROASTED CARROTS
Morcovi Prajiti

Clean and wash 5 or 6 large carrots and cut into long very thin strips. Put 2 tablespoonfuls of lard or butter in a small casserole. When very hot, add the carrots. Stir while cooking. Add one tablespoonful of powdered sugar, 2 to 3 tablespoonfuls of beef stock poured on a little at a time, and a little salt. Cover the casserole tightly and cook slowly until tender. If necessary, add more beef stock from time to time. When done, serve sprinkled over with a little finely chopped parsley. Use as a garnishing for beef steaks and boiled and roasted meats.

VEGETABLE DISHES : 57

CAULIFLOWER IN CREAM
Conopida Cu Smantana

Get one or two heads of cauliflower, remove the hard core and the green leaves, separate each bunch of flowers, boil them in salt water and when half done, remove from the water and let cool a little. Butter a casserole generously and put in it 2 or 3 level tablespoonfuls of heavy sour cream, sprinkle over with roll or bread crumbs, then cover with a layer of cauliflower flowers. Sprinkle with a little salt, add dabs of butter (or sprinkle with warm butter). Continue to alternate layers of butter, cream, crumbs and cauliflower until the cauliflower is used up. Cover the top with crumbs on which spread little dabs of butter. Place in hot oven and bake for 30 to 35 minutes. When done, cut portions of the baked cauliflower and use for garnishing roasted meats or alone as a dish.

BRAISED CAULIFLOWER
Conopida In Pesmet

Get one or two heads of cauliflower, remove the core and leaves, separate each bundle of flowers, boil them in salt water until they are done, but not overcooked. Remove from the water, and when cold, dip the cauliflower in beaten eggs, then dredge in fine roll crumbs (grating a dry roll gives a tastier result). Fry in very hot lard or hot butter until well browned. Use to garnish roasted meats.

KOHLRABI WITH NOODLES
Calarabe Cu Tatei

kohlrabies	1 tbs. flour
butter	noodles
salt and pepper	sour cream
1 onion	dill
parsley, dill, fennel, thyme	

Choose as many kohlrabies as you'll need, brown in butter, cover with water and season with pepper and salt. Heat 3 tablespoonfuls of butter in a frying pan, add one finely chopped

58 : VEGETABLE DISHES

onion and fry to a golden color. Add one small bunch of parsley
and a small bunch of fennel both finely chopped and a little
thyme. Fry a little, then add one tablespoonful of flour, and
with constant stirring heat until nice and brown. Add a little
water to make a thin sauce. Add this sauce to the kohlrabi and
cook slowly. When nearly done add some fine noodles in pro-
portion to the number of kohlrabies used, 2 tablespoonfuls of
sour cream and sprinkle over with finely chopped parsley and
dill. Cook until tender. Serve hot.

KOHLRABI AS A SIDE DISH
Calarabe Ca Garnitura

Dice kohlrabies and cook in boiling salted water, together
with a bunch of mixed greens tied together. When the kohlrabi
is tender, remove the mixed greens, drain the kohlrabi. Add a
little butter to the kohlrabi and pour over all a white sauce made
with milk. Cook a little longer with the sauce if needed, and
add a little salt and pepper. Serve hot, topped with sour cream.

LEEK STEW WITH MEAT
Tocana De Praz Cu Carne

1½ lbs. breast of beef	parsley and thyme
1 small bunch vegetable	1 tbs. flour
greens	1 tbs. sugar
6 leeks	juice of 1 lemon
oil	4 tbs. tomato sauce
1 small onion	salt and pepper
2 tbs. butter	

Boil in a little water 1½ pounds of breast of beef cut into small
pieces. Add a small bunch of mixed vegetable greens tied together, and remove it from the pot before the meat is tender.

While the meat is cooking, cut 6 leeks into one-inch lengths,
scald in salted water, drain and brown in oil. In a separate
saucepan fry one small finely chopped onion in 2 tablespoonfuls
of butter together with a little parsley and thyme. Add about

one tablespoonful of flour, stir constantly until well browned. Add a little water, one tablespoonful of sugar, the juice of one lemon, 4 tablespoonfuls of tomato sauce and salt and pepper to taste. Cook slowly for 5 minutes. Add the leeks and the brown sauce to the meat and continue the cooking until tender.

OKRA

OKRA is a delicate and very tasty vegetable. It is used in many ways, as a salad, as a side dish or cooked with meats. Okra is slightly gelatinous, and when used as a salad extract the gelatine in the following way: Cut off the stems, place in salted cold water and vinegar and let stand for ½ hour. Then rinse in cold water several times.

OKRA WITH YOUNG LAMB
Bame Cu Carne De Oaie

1 lb. okra	1 cup broth or water
garlic clove	2 or 3 tomatoes
olive oil or bacon drippings	juice of 1 lemon
4 onions	salt and pepper
1 lb. lamb	parsley, thyme, dill

Rub the bottom of a frying pan with a clove of garlic, add 2 tablespoonfuls of olive oil or bacon drippings and fry in the hot oil 4 sliced onions until very soft. Add one pound of lamb meat cut into small pieces and simmer on a slow fire until the meat is half done. Remove to a pot or a deep baking dish, adding a little more oil or bacon drippings, if needed.

Cut off the stems of one pound of fresh okra, wash well and add to the meat with one cup of broth or water. Cook together for 15 to 20 minutes. Add 2 or 3 sliced peeled tomatoes or one small can of tomatoes strained, the juice of one lemon, salt and pepper to taste, some thyme, dill, a few sprigs of parsley chopped, and more oil or bacon drippings if needed. Cover and cook slowly until done on top of the stove or bake in the oven.

60 : VEGETABLE DISHES

OKRA WITH VEAL
Bame Cu Carne De Vitel

Prepare exactly as above using veal instead of lamb. Serve with dumplings sprinkled with butter and cheese.

OKRA WITH CHICKEN
Bame Cu Carne De Pui

Prepare the same as OKRA WITH LAMB, only cook in butter instead of olive oil or bacon drippings. As a side dish serve dumplings with sour cream, or rice or potatoes.

OKRA WITH OIL
Bame Cu Unt De Lemn

Cut off the stems of one pound of okra, wash, place in salted cold water and vinegar and let stand for 30 minutes. Then wash in cold water several times. While the okra is soaking, prepare a tomato sauce with pure oil (see SAUCES). After the okra has been washed put into the tomato sauce, add a little lemon juice and cook. Serve cold or hot.

GREEN PEAS
Boabe De Mazere Verde

Sauté 1 to 2 pounds of tender green peas in 2 tablespoonfuls of hot butter. Add one tablespoonful of finely chopped parsley, one tablespoonful of powdered sugar, salt to taste and ½ to ⅔ cup of soup stock or bouillon added slowly. When the liquid is absorbed add 1 to 2 tablespoonfuls more of beef stock. Cook slowly for about ½ hour, with occasional stirring. When done, there must be no liquid left, but neither should the peas be dry.

Beat 2 egg yolks with ½ cup of sweet milk in a casserole and add the peas slowly. Continue to stir while it is coming to a boil, then remove from the fire. Use as garnishing for any kind of meat.

VEGETABLE DISHES : 61

PEPPERS

THE WELL-KNOWN green peppers need no introduction nor recommendation from me as they are loved, cooked and eaten in many ways; raw, boiled, baked, fried, in soups, as appetizers and in the oh, so delicious cold salads.

PEPPERS IN OIL
Ardei Cu Unt De Lemn

6 to 12 green or red
  peppers
salt and pepper
¼ cup olive oil

3 or 4 tbs. vinegar
½ cup water
red paprika

This is a delectable meatless-day dish. Choose 6 to 12 meaty and firm green or red peppers of fairly large size. Broil them over the flame on the range (or if possible over charcoal). Burn them quickly, turning on all sides. If you use the range, you can broil two on each burner at the same time.

When done, place them on a tray, sprinkle all over with salt from a shaker and let cool off. With fingers dipped in cold water peel off the burned skin. Leave the stems on the peppers. When finished cleaning, place peppers in a large glass or glazed earthenware bowl close to each other. In another bowl mix well ¼ cup of olive oil, 3 to 4 tablespoonfuls of vinegar, ½ cup of water, salt and pepper to taste and a little red paprika. Vary the amount of vinegar, as some prefer it less sour. Pour this liquid over the peppers and turn them a few times in the liquid on all sides. Let stand and repeat the turning. Cover and place the bowl in the refrigerator. Serve cool the next day with black olives. If you wish to serve them the same day, prepare at least a few hours earlier. Before serving, turn again on all sides in the sauce.

Serve on a plate wetted with some added sauce. Garnish with black olives, scallions or green garlic and white goat cheese, cut into small cubes, in each of which you stick toothpicks. These peppers can be eaten with the fingers, holding on to the stem, or you can slice them and dip in the sauce.

62 : VEGETABLE DISHES

BAKED ROMANIAN PEPPERS
Ardei Copt Romanesc

1 lb. cubed veal	4 or 5 large tomatoes
½ lb. cubed pork meat	salt and pepper
bacon drippings	chives
4 large onions	garlic greens (or garlic)
parsley, thyme, fennel	cream
12 green peppers	

Cut into cubes one pound of veal and ½ pound of pork meat and sear quickly (2 minutes) in 2 tablespoonfuls of bacon drippings. Add 4 finely chopped large onions and finely chopped parsley and cook until tender. Add 12 green shredded peppers. Peel 4 or 5 large tomatoes, slice them thinly and cover the shredded peppers. Add salt and pepper, a little thyme, finely chopped parsley, chives, fennel and a little garlic greens (or garlic). Cover dish and bake in a moderate oven. When meat is tender, spread on top sour or heavy sweet cream and keep under the fire till you get a nice color. Very piquant and tasty.

PEPPERS ALA SINAIA
Ardei Ala Sinaia

6 green and red peppers	parsley, fennel, thyme
bacon drippings	4 large tomatoes
5 or 6 onions	salt and pepper
1 lb. frankfurters	3 tbs. sour cream

Every housewife is interested in getting up a nourishing meal cheaply, especially when the cost of food goes up or some important purchase strains the family budget. This dish is cheap to make and so very palatable, too. During the war, when meats were hard to get, I served it often and to some very prominent people. If they should read these lines, I am sure it will bring back pleasant memories.

No water is used in preparing this dish. In a deep iron frying pan put in 2 or 3 tablespoonfuls of bacon drippings. You may use oil also, but the drippings are preferable. Slice 5 or 6 onions crosswise and fry to a nice golden color. Add one pound of frankfurters cut into small pieces and fry together for 15 to 20 minutes. Add some finely chopped parsley and fennel and a little thyme, stirring gently now and then. Cut crosswise into slices 6 red and green meaty peppers and add to the pan. Put in some of the seeds, too. Now add 4 large sliced tomatoes, salt and pepper to taste, and continue to cook on top of the stove, uncovered, until tender, but not overdone. Add 3 tablespoonfuls of sour cream. Cook a little while longer until the cream has become blended. Cover and let stand while you are getting ready the hot serving plates. Serve very hot, dividing the sauce evenly for each service, topped with sour cream. Garnish with french fried potatoes.

PEASANT STYLE POTATOES
Cartofi Stil Taranese

·Fry one large onion finely chopped in 2 tablespoonfuls of lard or bacon drippings in a deep iron pan to a golden brown. Boil 6 to 8 potatoes, peel, add to the fried onions and break up into coarse pieces with a spoon. Add salt and pepper and mix. Cover and heat over a very low fire. Sprinkle with chopped green parsley.

POTATOES WITH EGGS
Cartofi Cu Oua

2 lbs. potatoes	sweet cream
8 hard-boiled eggs	butter
2 tbs. chopped chives	flour
parsley	pepper

Wash 2 pounds of potatoes, boil in their jackets, cool and peel. Make 8 hard-boiled eggs and let cool. Cut the potatoes into not too thick slices and slice the eggs in an egg slicer. Get an enameled baking dish, grease the bottom with butter and sprinkle with a little flour. Cover evenly with 2 tablespoonfuls of chopped chives. Arrange a layer of potatoes on the bottom, dot with small pieces of butter. (If you use salted butter, do not add any salt, just sprinkle with a very little pepper.) Add a layer of sliced eggs, dot with a little butter and sprinkle with a little

64 : VEGETABLE DISHES

chives. Continue alernating layers, finishing with potatoes on top. Cover this layer with more butter, sprinkle with finely chopped chives and parsley and pour on sweet cream to cover. Bake in a hot oven. Place under flame before serving to get a nice crust. Serve hot with asparagus or any other hot vegetable dish.

POTATOES WITH CHEESE
Cartofi Cu Brinza

Prepare exactly as above, but replace the eggs with slices of Swiss cheese. Between layers sprinkle finely chopped fennel, chives and parsley and add small pieces of bacon which have been prepared by frying ¼ pound of lean bacon, removing from fat and cutting into pieces. Place also pieces of fried bacon on top layer. Dot with butter between layers as above.

POTATO STEW
Tocana De Cartofi

2 lbs. potatoes	paprika
2 onions	parsley, fennel and celery
2 tbs. bacon drippings	2 cups tomato juice
1 tbs. flour	1 green or red pepper
salt and pepper	sour cream

Peel 2 pounds of potatoes, cut each lengthwise into 4 slices and keep in cold water in a bowl. Fry 2 finely chopped onions in 2 tablespoonfuls of bacon drippings or lard in a deep frying pan to a light brown. Add one tablespoonful of flour and mix constantly until brown. Be careful not to burn. Add slowly a little water to make a thin sauce, add salt and pepper, a dash of red paprika and let simmer slowly. Chop some parsley, fennel and celery and add to the sauce. Let cook for a little while on a slow fire. Now add the potatoes, over which you will pour 2 cups of tomato juice, and cook until the potatoes are done. If necessary, add more tomato juice. When the potatoes are done, add one diced green pepper (or a red one if obtainable) and cook 5 minutes more. About ½ cup of liquid should remain

VEGETABLE DISHES : 65

at the end. Serve hot. Add 2 tablespoonfuls of sour cream for each serving and sprinkle with chopped parsley.

POTATOES WITH SAUSAGE
Cartofi Cu Carnati

Select medium-sized oval-shaped potatoes, peel and with a potato corer cut a hole lengthwise in each potato and insert a small link sausage. Arrange the potatoes in a shallow baking pan previously buttered, coat each with butter and bake in a hot oven until done. Sprinkle with chopped parsley.

ROASTED POTATOES
Cartofi Prajiti

Wash, peel 4 to 6 large potatoes, cut into ½-inch slices and rinse. Spread out on a napkin, let dry, salt and fry in very hot lard or butter until nicely browned. Keep turning and moving the potatoes around with the end of a knife. Do not use a spoon or a fork, as they might break the potato slices. Serve hot with roasted or fried meats.

POTATOES FRIED WITH ONIONS
Cartofi Prajiti Cu Ciapa

Wash and boil 2 pounds of unpeeled potatoes. When done, peel, break into pieces and salt. Chop 3 onions into small pieces and fry to a light brown in 2 tablespoonfuls of very hot lard. Add the potatoes, mix and fry together till nicely browned. Prepare just before serving, as keeping it hot on the stove detracts from the taste. Serve as a garnish or dish.

BREADED POTATOES
Cartofi Prajiti In Pesmet

Wash 6 to 8 large potatoes and boil. When done, peel, let cool, cut into ½-inch slices and salt. Dip in beaten eggs, dredge

66 : VEGETABLE DISHES

in bread crumbs, then fry in hot lard or butter to a light brown. Serve hot with boiled or roasted meats.

BREADED POTATO PATTIES
Piftele De Cartofi In Pesmet

Wash 5 or 6 large potatoes and boil. When done, peel and press through a sieve into a bowl. Add to this one whole egg plus one egg yolk, a little salt and a few sprigs of parsley finely chopped. Mix, then shape small patties from the above mixture with your hands. Sprinkle the patties with flour, dip in beaten egg, dredge in bread or roll crumbs and fry in very hot lard to a light brown. Serve hot with meats and game.

FRIED NEW POTATO
Cartofi Noi Prajiti

Wash and clean with a soft cloth one pound of very small new potatoes. Place them in a clean napkin to dry, then fry in very hot deep lard or butter with one tablespoonful each of chopped parsley and chives to a light brown. Put on a hot plate, salt and serve with pot roasts.

FRIED RICE
Orez Nabusit Prajit

Fry one large whole onion in 2 tablespoonfuls of butter. Add 5 or 6 tablespoonfuls of well-washed rice and fry for 6 or 7 minutes. Sprinkle with a few sprigs of parsley finely chopped, stir and cover with one pint of beef stock or bouillon. Add salt to taste, stir well, cover and cook slowly. Add a little more beef stock from time to time, but do not stir any more. When the rice is cooked, remove the onion. Place tablespoonfuls of rice around boiled or roasted meats as a garnish.

RICE PILAF
Pilaf De Orez

extras from 4 to 6 chickens
salt
peppercorns
1 carrot
1 parsnip root

5 onions
3 tbs. butter
1 lb. uncooked rice
parsley

Cut into small pieces the extras of 4 to 6 chickens and boil in a quart of water to which have been added salt, a few peppercorns, one carrot, one parsley root, one parsnip root and one whole onion. While boiling, finely chop 4 onions and fry in 3 tablespoonfuls of butter until soft, but do not brown. Then add one pound of well-washed rice and fry for 6 or 7 minutes. Take out the extras, drain off liquid, then add them to the rice. Fry together for a few minutes, then pour over the rice slowly and a little at a time the strained soup in which the extras were boiled, but do not add the soup vegetables. Sprinkle with a little chopped green parsley, stir gently only once, cover the casserole and let cook very slowly until the rice is tender. Serve as a garnish with boiled or roasted lamb or veal, or as a dish by itself.

SQUASH WITH OIL
Dovlecei Cu Unt De Lemn

Brown one chopped onion in 5 tablespoonfuls of olive oil, add 5 or 6 very small squashes and brown with the onion. Add 2 to 3 tablespoonfuls of chopped parsley, a little thyme, salt and pepper and a very small quantity of water. Simmer until tender, cool and serve garnished with lemon.

BREADED SQUASH
Dovlecei In Pesmet

Take 4 squashes, cut each lengthwise into 4 parts, roll lightly in flour mixed with salt and pepper, dip in egg, then in bread crumbs. Fry in hot butter and serve immediately.

68 : VEGETABLE DISHES

SQUASH WITH CHEESE
Dovlecei Cu Brinza

Cut a few squashes lengthwise in halves. Boil in plenty of water and drain when done. Butter the bottom and sides of a baking dish and sprinkle with bread crumbs. Place the slices of squash in the casserole in layers, each one being covered with grated cheese, dotted with butter and sprinkled with chopped parsley and salt and pepper. Cover the last layer with crumbs and cheese. Bake in a moderate oven. Serve with heavy sweet cream.

STRING BEANS WITH MEAT
Fasole Verde Cu Carne

2 lbs. string beans	1 tbs. flour
1½ lbs. cubed veal	½ cup tomato sauce
2 tbs. bacon drippings	salt and pepper
1 onion	1 cup sour cream
parsley and fennel	

Slice lengthwise 2 pounds of green string beans, boil until nearly soft and let stand while you prepare the meat as follows. Cut into small cubes 1½ pounds of veal, brown in 2 tablespoonfuls of bacon drippings or lard, remove to another dish and let stand covered. Add one finely chopped onion to the frying pan, fry to a golden brown, add a little finely chopped parsley and fennel and simmer a little. Put in a tablespoonful of flour, heat with constant stirring until brown. Add ½ cup of tomato sauce and salt and pepper to taste. Cook a little longer, then add the meat and the beans, stir and cook until tender. Add one cup of sour cream and simmer for a few minutes. Serve very hot. Sprinkle with chopped parsley.

STRING BEANS PEASANT STYLE
Fasole Verde Stil Taranesc

Boil 2 pounds of yellow string beans until tender. Drain off the water, add finely chopped parsley, chives, fennel and a little dill if obtainable. Cover with one cup of heavy sour or

VEGETABLE DISHES : 69

sweet cream in which has been mixed a teaspoonful of flour.
Add ⅛ pound sweet butter and pepper and salt to taste. Cover
the pot and simmer very slowly. Serve hot or cold.

STRING BEANS IN OIL FOR LENT
Fasole Verde De Post Cu Unt De Lemn

Prepare the same as above, but instead of butter use olive oil
or cottonseed oil and instead of cream use tomato paste and
flour thinned with water. Add some chopped ripe olives and
cook slowly until tender. Serve cold.

GREEN STRING BEANS
Fasole Verde

Clean and wash 2 pounds of tender string beans and split
lengthwise in halves. Put 2 tablespoonfuls of lard or butter in a
casserole. When very hot, add the string beans. Stir while cooking. Add one tablespoonful of minced parsley and a little salt to
taste, cover and cook until the water is absorbed. Add 3 to 4
tablespoonfuls of beef stock or bouillon, a little at a time. Continue to add beef stock until the string beans have become tender.
When done, no liquid must be left, neither should the string
beans be dry. Serve with a topping of sour cream. Use to garnish
boiled or roast meats.

ROASTED TURNIPS
Gulii Prajite

Clean 10 to 12 tender turnips and cut into slices one inch
thick. Put 2 tablespoonfuls of butter in a casserole. When hot,
add the turnips. Stir while cooking. Add one tablespoonful of
powdered sugar, a few tablespoonfuls of beef stock and a little
salt. Cover the casserole tightly and cook slowly until tender.
Keep stirring to prevent burning and add a little liquid from
time to time as needed. When done, serve with a topping of
sour cream. Use to garnish boiled or roasted meats.

MUSHROOMS

Mushrooms are not so frequently used here as in Europe. Peasants pick them, growing wild in the woods, and make numerous delightful dishes out of them. The following recipes will add to your repertory and surely will bring you many compliments as payment for your efforts. Children just love them.

MUSHROOMS ROUMAINE
Ciuperci Gatite Romaneste

1 large or 2 small mushrooms for each serving	3 or 4 slices bacon
Roquefort cheese	1 tbs. chopped parsley
sweet butter	½ cup cognac or French brandy
shallots	¼ cup sweet vermouth
heavy sweet cream	4 or 5 tbs. light sweet cream
marjoram	

This dish is for epicures. I have made it many times and always I have been rewarded with ohs and ahs. Please try making it on a very special occasion.

Select very large mushrooms, one for each person served. If the mushrooms are smaller, buy two for each person. Gently trim away the white veil between the stem and the edge, being careful not to cut the edge. Wash each mushroom by holding

72 : MUSHROOMS

it upside down, the stem grasped by the fingers on the bottom, the cap being on top. Wash very gently the top of the mushroom with your fingers, and then wash the stem by tilting the mushroom slightly, first to one side, then to the other. The reason for this care is to prevent any water from getting into the area around the bottom of the stem. When washed, place the mushroom, turned on its side, on a board to permit any water to drain off.

When the mushrooms are dried, place them with the stem up and slice off a small piece from the stems, making a level cut. Make an incision in a lemon and squeeze enough juice into the circular trough of the mushroom caps to fill them. Let stand for 25 to 30 minutes.

Prepare in a small bowl a mixture of Roquefort cheese with a little sweet whipped cream butter and some finely chopped shallot. If you can obtain it, replace the Roquefort with Romanian brinza (sheep cheese). Stuff the caps of the mushrooms with this mixture and let stand for another 30 minutes. Now pour heavy sweet cream, using a small teaspoon, on the stems, letting the cream run all around the stem and covering well the cheese filling. Sprinkle with a little marjoram and let stand until you are ready to serve.

Have your guests already been served their soup or ciorba? Then you are ready to proceed. Fry in a large deep iron pan 3 or 4 slices of lean bacon cut up into small pieces, add one tablespoonful of finely chopped parsley and one tablespoonful of chopped shallot, cover and simmer slowly until cooked. Place the mushrooms in the pan leaving space between them, cover and simmer very slowly until the heat has penetrated through the mushrooms. Baste frequently with the liquid in the pan. Now pour over the mushrooms a small glass of cognac or good French brandy, ignite it immediately with a match and after the flame has burned itself out, cover for a few seconds. Remove cover, add ½ cup of sweet vermouth, cover again and simmer for 2 to 3 minutes. Try with a lighted match to see if any alcohol fumes are still present. Keep basting with the sauce. Add 4 or 5 tablespoonfuls of light sweet cream, cover and simmer for 2 to 3 minutes. Baste the mushrooms very well with the blended sauce, and serve on very hot medium-sized plates, one mushroom per

MUSHROOMS : 73

person, with the sauce equally divided. As is befitting an entree of such excellence, serve with it a glass of fine white wine.

GRILLED STUFFED MUSHROOMS
Ciuperci La Gratar — Umplute

mushrooms
salt and pepper
butter
sharp cheese
chives and parsley

lemon juice
flour
bacon drippings
¼ cup red wine

Select large mushrooms, clean and cut off the stems (the stems can be used in soup). Sprinkle with salt and pepper, add a little melted butter and fill the mushrooms with a mixture of sharp cheese, finely chopped chives, a little parsley and some lemon juice.

Grease a pan with bacon drippings and sprinkle over lightly with a little flour.

Place the stuffed mushrooms in the pan, pour in ¼ cup of red wine and grill under a flame. Serve the mushrooms on a hot plate topped with the sauce from the pan.

MUSHROOM STEW
Tocana De Ciuperci

1 lb. mushrooms
5 or 6 slices bacon
green scallions
1 tbs. chopped parsley

1 tbs. chopped fennel
salt and pepper
1 cup sour cream
1 tbs. flour

Wash one pound of mushrooms and dice with stems or cut into thick slices.

Place in a deep iron frying pan 5 or 6 slices of bacon cut into small pieces, a good portion of finely chopped green scallions (use the tender part of the greens), a heaping tablespoonful of chopped parsley and fennel and salt and pepper to taste. Cover and simmer a little, then add the sliced or diced mushrooms, mix and simmer for 10 minutes. Add slowly one cup of sour cream mixed with a level tablespoonful of flour, stirring con-

74 : MUSHROOMS

stantly. Cook slowly until done. Sprinkle over with chopped parsley. Serve with mamaliga (see MAMALIGA).

MUSHROOMS STUFFED WITH BRAINS
Ciuperci Umplute Cu Creeri

1 doz. mushrooms	1 egg
lemon juice	parsley, fennel, chives
butter	salt and pepper
brains	1 glass sherry

Select a dozen fat mushrooms, clean and cut off the stems. Sprinkle first with lemon juice, let stand for 15 to 20 minutes, cover with warm butter and let stand while you prepare the meat as follows. Mash brains with one egg, add a few finely chopped sprigs of parsley, fennel and chives and salt and pepper to taste, mix together well and stuff the mushrooms. Arrange in a buttered baking pan, pour over them ¼ cup of sherry, sprinkle with chopped parsley and bake in a hot oven. Baste the mushrooms now and then, add a little more butter if needed and bake until done. (Use the stems in soup or make a side dish of them with white sauce made with sour cream.)

MUSHROOMS WITH CHICKEN LIVERS
Ciuperci Cu Ficat De Pui

Prepare exactly as above, but replace the brains with tender chicken livers, broiled and then chopped.

MUSHROOMS WITH OMELET
Ciuperci Cu Omlete

1 lb. mushrooms	butter
lemon juice	6 eggs
brandy	bacon drippings
salt and pepper	sour cream
parsley and shallot	paprika

Select one pound fresh and firm mushrooms, rinse off and clean (but do not keep in water). Cut into slices, not too thick,

MUSHROOMS : 75

sprinkle over with lemon juice, a few drops of brandy, and add salt and pepper to taste, a few chopped sprigs of parsley and shallot. If you can't get shallot, use instead chopped chives or tender green scallions. Mix together and quickly sauté in a frying pan with butter. Let stand.

Beat 6 eggs and make an omelet, frying in bacon drippings. When your omelet is brown (take care not to burn), turn over on the other side. Immediately place the mushrooms on half of the omelet and, using a large spatula, lap the other half gently over the mushrooms, forming a sandwich. Brown both sides, taking care not to break during the turning, and serve quickly on a very hot plate. Top with a generous tablespoonful of sour cream and sprinkle with a little paprika.

MUSHROOMS IN WINE
Ciuperci Cu Vin

Select one pound of large firm mushrooms, clean and cut into thin slices. Sprinkle with a little lemon juice and let stand. Heat a frying pan containing pure olive oil. When the oil is quite hot, put in the sliced mushrooms. Add a cup of finely chopped onions and continue heating and stirring until the onions are brown. Now add 2 tablespoons of red wine, the juice of one lemon, salt and pepper to taste and very finely chopped parsley. Simmer for 5 minutes. Put in a bowl. Serve cold, garnished with water cress, radishes and black olives.

LENTEN MUSHROOMS IN WINE
Ciuperci De Post In Vin

Warm ¼ cup of pure olive oil in a deep frying pan and add one tablespoonful of chives, one tablespoonful of fennel and 2 tablespoonfuls of parsley, all finely chopped. Mix and sauté for 2 to 3 minutes. Now add one pound of thinly sliced mushrooms and sauté for 5 or 6 minutes. Sprinkle with the juice of a small lemon, add salt and pepper to taste, and sauté for 2 to 3 minutes longer. Pour in ½ cup of good white wine and cook slowly for

76 : MUSHROOMS

another 5 or 6 minutes. Let cool. Sprinkle with finely chopped parsley and serve.

MUSHROOMS WITH BUTTER SAUCE
Ciuperci Cu Sos De Unt

Wash and clean 24 to 30 mushrooms and cut into thin slices. Heat 2 tablespoonfuls of sweet butter in a casserole, put in the sliced mushrooms and add one tablespoonful of very finely chopped parsley and 3 tablespoonfuls of beef stock or bouillon. Keep tightly covered and let cook until tender. Make a butter sauce (see BUTTER SAUCE). When the sauce is done slowly add the juice of one lemon, mix, then add the mushroom mixture, mix again, and finally add a small glass of good white wine. Mix together gently and serve.

MUSHROOMS WITH BROWN SAUCE
Ciuperci Cu Sos De Rantasiu

24 to 30 mushrooms	4 tbs. sour cream
2 tbs. butter	2 tbs. flour
parsley	2 tbs. butter
beef stock or bouillon	chives
juice of 1 lemon	

Wash and clean 24 to 30 mushrooms and cut into thin slices. Put 2 tablespoonfuls of sweet butter into a casserole and when hot add the mushrooms. Stir gently, then add one tablespoonful of finely chopped parsley and 8 tablespoonfuls of beef stock or bouillon. Cover tightly and cook slowly until the mushrooms are tender.

While they are cooking prepare a sauce by browning 2 level tablespoonfuls of flour with 2 tablespoonfuls of sweet butter. When light brown add ½ teaspoonful each of finely minced chives and parsley. After it has been nicely browned add enough beef stock to make a sauce. Cook slowly for 10 minutes, then add the mushroom mixture and the juice of one lemon and stir. Add 4 tablespoonfuls of sour cream and serve.

MUSHROOMS : 77

JUST PLAIN MUSHROOMS
Ciuperci Simple

Clean as many mushrooms as you will need. Cut into pieces or use whole if the mushrooms are small. For the frying you may use butter, oil, bacon drippings or cut up into small pieces a few slices of bacon and render to obtain the bacon fat, using also the remaining pieces of bacon. Heat the fat in a frying pan, add a little onion cut into thin slices and fry to a golden brown. Add the mushrooms, salt and pepper to taste and cook until mushrooms are tender. Add one or two tablespoonfuls of sour or sweet heavy cream and serve hot. Eat with fresh bread and use it to absorb the juice.

MUSHROOM GARNISH
Ciuperci Garnitura

½ lb. mushrooms	1 tbs. chopped parsley
2 large onions	salt
lard	5 tbs. beef stock or bouillon
tabasco pepper	sour cream

Wash ½ pound of mushrooms. You may peel them or leave them unpeeled. Cut into thin slices. Fry 2 large onions very finely chopped in 2 tablespoonfuls of very hot lard in a small casserole to a golden brown. Add a little ground tabasco pepper, stir, then put in the sliced mushrooms and one tablespoonful of very finely chopped parsley. Cover the casserole and let cook until the liquid is absorbed. Now add a little salt and 5 tablespoonfuls of beef stock or bouillon. Stir and let cook for 10 to 15 minutes longer. Just before serving add 3 tablespoonfuls of sour cream and sprinkle over with a little chopped parsley. Serve with boiled beef, roast meat or chicken.

MUSHROOMS WITH LEMON
Ciuperci Cu Lamaie

Wash ½ to 1 pound of mushrooms. Do not peel. Leave the small ones whole and cut the large ones in half. Sprinkle with the juice of half a lemon. From here on prepare exactly as above.

Fish Dishes

EVEN THOUGH we are able here to get the fish cleaned, before starting to cook or to broil, give the fish a quick rinsing and let stand for a little while in the fresh air. Then start to cook. If it is only possible, the broiling should be done on an open fire. The fish is much more delicious then.

BROILED FISH
Peste La Gratar

Use only fat fish for best results with broiling and never stick a fork into the fish. Clean and cut deep crosswise incisions into the fish about ½ inch apart. Broil on an open fire, if possible. While broiling, sprinkle the fish with a little salt. The cuts will swell and make a very good crisp crust. Broil both sides, taking care to avoid burning. Serve either with small red or green sharp peppers, sprinkled over with sharp red paprika, or covered with white wine, to which a drop of olive oil has been added, and a few seeds of sharp peppers. Serve with white wine.

FISH AND TOMATOES
Peste Cu Paradie Rosii

2 to 3 lbs. fish	flour
4 or 5 tomatoes	parsley, leek, dill, garlic
4 or 5 onions	greens, lemon juice
3 tbs. butter or olive oil	salt and pepper

Cut 4 or 5 onions into slices, brown in 3 tablespoonfuls of butter or olive oil to a golden brown, add 4 or 5 sliced tomatoes

80 : FISH DISHES

and fry together with the onions 10 to 15 minutes. Butter well the bottom of a baking dish and sprinkle lightly with flour. Place into it the fried onions and tomatoes, add a little chopped parsley, leek, dill and if obtainable some garlic greens. Now add 2 to 3 pounds of any kind of fish cut into large pieces, then salt and pepper. Dot with butter.

Bake in a slow oven. Sprinkle the top while baking with finely chopped green parsley, basting now and then with the liquid in the dish and some added lemon juice. Keep in a cool, dry place. Serve cold with a sharp pepper and a mixed green salad. Very delicious.

FAT FISH STEW
Tocana De Peste

2 to 3 lbs. fat fish	1 tbs. grated carrots
2 onions	salt and pepper
2 tbs. olive oil	1 tsp. paprika
1 tbs. chopped tarragon or	red wine
dill	butter
parsley	heavy cream

Brown 2 chopped onions in 2 tablespoonfuls of olive oil. Combine with 2 to 3 pounds of large pieces of any fat fish (like carp, salmon or sturgeon), add one finely chopped tablespoonful of tarragon or dill, some chopped parsley, one tablespoonful of grated carrots, salt and pepper to taste and one teaspoonful of paprika. Cover with red wine or water. Dot with a little butter. Cook very slowly for 15 minutes, but do not stir. Add heavy cream to your taste and sprinkle with chopped parsley. Serve with well-seasoned green salad and sharp peppers.

CARP ALA OVIDIU
Crap Ala Ovidiu

2 to 2½ lbs. carp	1 tbs. sugar
8 to 10 onions	8 to 10 slices of lemon
¼ cup olive oil	2 tomatoes
salt and pepper	dill or parsley
1 laurel leaf	butter
1 tbs. vinegar	

FISH DISHES : 81

Fry 8 to 10 sliced onions in ¼ cup of olive oil until golden colored, add salt and pepper and one laurel leaf. Add 2 to 2½ pounds of carp cut into large pieces and fry together for a few minutes. In a small bowl mix 6 tablespoonfuls of water, one tablespoonful of vinegar (or more, if you wish) and one table-spoonful of sugar. Pour over the fish. Sprinkle with parsley and cover with 8 to 10 thin slices of peeled lemon. Dot with butter. Cook for 10 to 15 minutes, then add 2 sliced tomatoes and cook a little longer. Sprinkle the top with chopped dill or parsley. Serve cold.

MARINATED CARP
Crap Marinat

2 lbs. carp	salt and pepper
flour	1 clove and laurel leaf
6 tbs. olive oil	¼ cup dry wine (or 3 tbs.
1 large onion	vinegar)
celery, parsley, dill	

Cut 2 pounds of carp into pieces, roll in flour, let stand a while, then sear in ¼ cup of hot olive oil. Fry in 2 tablespoonfuls of pure olive oil in a saucepan one large sliced onion, a few slices of celery and a few sprigs of parsley and dill. When the ingredients are nicely browned, remove to an enameled dish and add the fish. Mix together. Add salt and pepper to taste, one clove, a very small piece of a laurel leaf and ¼ cup of dry wine (or 3 tablespoonfuls of vinegar diluted with water to make ¼ cup). Pour this over the fish, sprinkle with chopped parsley and cook slowly until tender. Cover, let cool, then place in a glass jar and put away in a cool place for a few days. Serve with salad or sour pickle.

MARINATED SALMON OR STURGEON
Stiuca Marinata

Make exactly as the MARINATED CARP above.

82 : FISH DISHES

STUFFED CARP
Crap Umplut

carp
1 cup ripe olives
2 tbs. fennel
1 clove garlic
parsley
lemon juice
6 tbs. olive oil

salt
onion slices
black pepper
2 tomatoes
1 small carrot
lemon slices

Get a nice, fresh carp, wash the inside well and let stand while you prepare the following dressing. Take one cup of ripe olives and chop fine, 2 tablespoonfuls of fennel, one clove of garlic crushed, a little parsley, lemon juice and one tablespoonful of pure olive oil. Mix together well, stuff the fish with it, then sew it up. Now with a sharp, pointed knife score the fish and sprinkle with salt.

Line a baking dish previously sprinkled with one tablespoonful of oil with thin slices of onion, sprinkle with black pepper, add 2 sliced tomatoes, a small shredded carrot and slices of lemon. Place the fish on top, pour on ¼ cup of boiling olive oil and bake until tender.

CARP WITH VEGETABLES
Crap Cu Zarzavaturi

3 to 4 lbs. carp
5 tbs. olive oil
4 onions
1 large carrot
1 small cabbage
2 tbs. chopped parsley

2 tbs. chopped fennel
2 or 3 slices of lemon
4 or 5 tomatoes
bouillon
butter

Slice 3 to 4 pounds of carp and fry slowly for a few minutes in 3 tablespoonfuls of olive oil until brown. Now fry in 2 table-spoonfuls of olive oil for 5 minutes 4 onions, one large diced carrot, one very small head of cabbage, 2 tablespoonfuls of chopped parsley, 2 tablespoonfuls of chopped fennel and 2 or 3 thin slices of lemon. Put vegetables into a baking pot, then

FISH DISHES : 83

arrange on top the fish slices, cover with 4 or 5 sliced tomatoes, pour over this sufficient bouillon, dot with butter and bake in a moderate oven until tender.

CARP ALA MACEDON
Crap Ala Macedon

Put into a baking dish the same vegetables and herbs exactly as in the making of ghivetch (see GHIVETCH). Place the fish on top and bake in a moderate oven until tender.

CARP IN BEER
Crap In Bere

1 carp	1 laurel leaf
¾ pt. beer	parsley and chives
garlic	peppercorns, cloves
butter	flour
1 onion	ground tabasco pepper
½ lemon	

Rub a stewing dish (glazed earthenware) generously with garlic, then add one tablespoonful of butter, one thin sliced onion, ½ lemon sliced, one laurel leaf broken into small pieces, one tablespoonful each of finely chopped chives and parsley and a few peppercorns. Cover and simmer slowly for 3 to 5 minutes. Now put in one medium-sized carp cut into large chunks and pour on ¾ pint of beer. Bring to a quick boil, cover and let simmer slowly for 25 to 30 minutes. When done, remove the fish to a hot serving plate. Quickly add to the sauce in the stewing dish a little more butter, a little flour, 2 cloves and a little ground tabasco pepper and cook for 5 minutes, stirring constantly. Strain over the fish and serve hot. It is also delicious if served cold.

COD WITH ONIONS
Peste Cod Cu Ciapa

2½ to 3 lbs. cod	paprika
olive oil	salt and pepper
parsley and fennel	2¼ tbs. flour
3 onions	3 or 4 tomatoes

84 : FISH DISHES

Cut 2½ to 3 pounds of the fish into slices of desired thickness and brown in hot, pure olive oil. Into a baking dish pour a little olive oil, sprinkle with chopped parsley and fennel, and place the browned fish on top.

Now fry in 3 tablespoonfuls of olive oil or butter 3 sliced onions, add paprika, salt and pepper, and 2¼ tablespoonfuls of flour. Mix well, add 3 or 4 sliced tomatoes and cook a little. Then add cold water, mix and cook for 5 minutes more. Pour this over the fish, stirring constantly, and bake until tender.

SALMON WITH ONIONS
Peste Salmon Cu Ciapa

Prepare the same as COD WITH ONIONS (see above).

STURGEON WITH ONIONS
Stiuca Cu Ciapa

Prepare the same as COD WITH ONIONS (see above).

SALMON WITH GARLIC
Peste Salmon Cu Usturoi

Cut 2 to 3 pounds of salmon into pieces of desired size, place in a pot, cover with water and boil. When tender add 5 or 6 crushed cloves of garlic in lemon juice. Add salt and a small red pepper. Cover and let stand one hour. Serve warm, sprinkled with chopped parsley and a little lemon juice.

STURGEON WITH HERBS
Stiuca Cu Mirositoare

3 tbs. olive oil	summer savory
4 onions	leek
½ cup hot water	4 or 5 small tomatoes
parsley	3 to 3½ lbs. sturgeon
fennel	butter

Fry in 3 tablespoonfuls of hot olive oil 4 sliced onions until yellow in color. Put into a baking dish, add ½ cup hot water, a few sprigs of parsley, a few sprigs of fennel, a little summer savory, a little leek and 4 or 5 small tomatoes cut in halves. Arrange 3 to 3½ pounds of sturgeon on top of the herbs, dot with a little butter and bake until tender and the juice has been absorbed. Serve cold.

FISH BAKED IN BROWN PAPER
Peste Fript In Hirtie

Use only fishes which are small (about 3 or 4 pounds), fresh and tender. Clean first and sprinkle with a little salt. Roll in brown paper and broil outdoors over an open fire or on top of charcoal. When all the paper has burned away, remove from the fire, and clean off the charred paper with wetted fingers. Serve immediately with cold potato salad or mixed sour salad. It is just simply out of this world.

# Chicken and Fowl

ROAST CHICKEN WITH ORANGES
Pui Prajit Cu Portocale

Clean and wash one roasting chicken and immerse in a pot of cold water for ½ hour. Drain, wipe, sprinkle with salt and dab generously with pieces of butter (or lard) both the inside and outside of the chicken. Arrange the chicken in a roasting pan and place in the oven. Start with low flame, then gradually increase it. When the chicken starts to roast, baste frequently with the juice of one large or two small navel oranges. After using up all the orange juice, baste with the liquid in the pan. Turn the chicken a few times to get done on all sides. If you like the skin to be crisp, place under the flame for a few minutes. When ready, cut into pieces, arrange on a hot plate and pour the sauce from the pan over the chicken. Garnish with fried potatoes, or small new potatoes baked whole in butter, and sprinkle with chopped parsley. Serve with vegetable salad.

ROAST CHICKEN IN CASSEROLE
Pui Prajit La Tava

1 large roasting chicken
3 tbs. butter
1 carrot and 1 onion
1 parsley root
1 or 2 turnips
3 or 4 cloves
peel of ½ lemon
stock

Cut one large roasting chicken into 8 parts and scald with boiling water. Place in a casserole on the fire with 3 tablespoon-

88 : CHICKEN AND FOWL

fuls of butter. Add one carrot, one parsley root and 1 or 2 young turnips, each sliced lengthwise, one whole onion with 3 or 4 cloves inserted in it and the grated peel of ½ lemon. Add a little stock or water. Shake from time to time to prevent burning, and add more stock or water as needed. Cover tight and cook until the meat is tender. When the chicken is done, remove to a dish. Make a sauce out of the liquid in the casserole with wine or sour cream and dill. Press it through a sieve into the casserole, put back the chicken and let cook for 5 to 6 minutes. Place on a serving plate, pour on the sauce and garnish all around with buttered cauliflower and buttered peas.

ROAST CHICKEN WITH RICE
Pui Prajit Cu Orez

ingredients for Roast Chicken in Casserole	2 eggs, plus yolks of 6 eggs
½ lb. rice	salt and pepper
beef stock	peel of ½ lemon
¼ lb. butter	mushrooms (optional)

Prepare as ROAST CHICKEN IN CASSEROLE. While the chicken is cooking with the vegetables, prepare the rice as follows. Scald ½-pound of rice in boiling water, drain, wash in cold water, drain well, then boil in beef stock or beef bouillon cubes dissolved in water. When done, strain and let stand.

Beat ¼-pound of butter to a foam, add the yolk of 6 eggs, beat both a little, then add 2 whole eggs and beat all together, well. Add the cooled rice, salt and pepper and the grated peel of ½ lemon. Mix well.

Butter a second casserole generously, put in half of the rice mixture, add the chicken pieces and cover them with the other half of the rice mixture. Cover the casserole, place it in a large pot of water and boil for one hour. Continue to cook the sauce in the first casserole to get a brown color, add a little stock or a solution of bouillon cubes and cook a little longer. Strain half of the sauce onto a heated serving plate and add the cooked chicken and rice. Add the other half of the sauce to butter fried mushrooms. Serve also with fried potatoes, noodles or fruit compote.

CHICKEN AND FOWL : 89

PIQUANT CHICKEN OR TURKEY LEFTOVERS
Mancara Piquanta Din Carnuri Ramase De Pui Or Curca

leftover chicken, turkey or	1 tbs. capers
capon	1 laurel leaf
1 dried roll	3 tbs. olive oil
tarragon vinegar	3 tbs. wine vinegar
5 hard-boiled eggs	parsley and chives

Use the leftover meat of chicken, turkey or capon. Cut into thin slices. Prepare in a mixing bowl the following. Chop very well together one dried roll soaked in tarragon vinegar, the yolks of 5 hard-boiled eggs, and mix well with one tablespoonful of capers and one laurel leaf. Add 3 tablespoonfuls of pure olive oil, mix, add 3 tablespoonfuls of wine vinegar and mix all together well. Press the sauce through a sieve onto a serving plate, place in it the slices of chicken or turkey and sprinkle over with finely chopped mixed green parsley and chives.

CHICKEN PEASANT STYLE
Pui Gatit Taraneste

2 or 3 small chickens	parsley
4 tbs. lard	salt
6 onions	½ cup sour cream
powdered tabasco pepper	

Clean and cut into small pieces 2 to 3 small chickens. Heat up 4 tablespoonfuls of lard in a casserole, add 6 finely chopped onions and fry to a nice golden color. Add a little powdered tabasco pepper and one tablespoonful of finely chopped parsley. Stir, add the chicken and salt to taste. Cover the casserole tightly and cook slowly, stirring from time to time to prevent burning, until the liquid is absorbed. Add ½-cup of heavy sour cream, mix gently and cook for 5 minutes. Cover the chicken with water and continue to boil slowly until the meat is tender. Remove to a hot serving plate and garnish all around with boiled farina or semolina balls covered with hot butter, or buttered dumplings sprinkled over with chopped parsley. Serve hot with fruit compote and vegetable salad.

90 : CHICKEN AND FOWL

CHICKEN WITH TOMATOES
Pui Cu Patlagele Rosii

Prepare exactly as above, but instead of water use the strained juice of home-cooked tomatoes or ready-made bottled tomato juice.

BREADED CHICKEN
Pui In Pesmet

Clean and cut into quarters 3 young broilers, salt a little and let stand for ½-hour. Dredge in flour, beat each piece between your palms, then dip in well-beaten eggs and dredge in bread crumbs. Place on a board and let stand awhile. Fry the chicken in deep and very hot fresh pork lard to a nice crisp brown. As the pieces are fried place them on a heated plate on absorbing paper. Serve hot with fried squash and sour cream or turnip and sour cream and green vegetable salad.

CHICKEN WITH WINE AND OLIVES
Pui Gatit Cu Vin Si Masline

1 roasting chicken	2 cups white wine
garlic	½ cup sour cream
olive oil	½ cup ripe olives
chives, fennel and parsley	salt and pepper

Clean, wash and cut into pieces one roasting chicken. Rub a deep frying pan with garlic, add some olive oil and sear in it the chicken pieces to a nice light brown. Remove from the pan, then prepare in it the following sauce. Add 2 tablespoonfuls of olive oil and one tablespoonful of flour, mix and fry a little. Now add one tablespoonful of chives, one tablespoonful of parsley and one tablespoonful of fennel, all of these finely chopped, mix and brown. Thin with 2 cups of white wine and cook for 5 minutes. Add ½-cup of sour cream slowly and mix, add ½-cup of ripe olives, then the chicken pieces and finally a little salt and pepper to taste. Cook slowly until tender.

CHICKEN AND FOWL : 91

CHICKEN WITH GARLIC AND BUTTER SAUCE
Pui Cu Usturoi In Sos De Unt

2 spring chickens	5 or 6 cloves garlic
5 tbs. butter	3 potatoes
scallions, dill	1 tbs. sour cream
1 tbs. flour	

Clean, wash and cut into pieces 2 spring chickens. Sear in 2 tablespoonfuls of butter, cover and let stand. Prepare the following butter sauce in a saucepan. Warm up 3 tablespoonfuls of butter, then add one small bunch of young scallions and a little dill, both finely chopped, and mix. Add one tablespoonful of flour, mix and fry a little, stirring constantly. Now add 5 or 6 large cloves of garlic well crushed and 3 boiled and peeled potatoes which have been broken into pieces with a spoon. Mix well, then thin with a little water and cook slowly for 5 to 10 minutes.

While the sauce is cooking, warm up the chicken in the casserole, then pour on the sauce slowly, mixing gently. Add a little more water, cover and cook slowly until tender. Just before it is done, add one tablespoonful of sour cream, mix, cover, then cook a little longer. Serve hot, sprinkled with finely chopped parsley. Garnish with flour dumplings or slices of mamaliga (see DUMPLINGS and MAMALIGA). Serve with a sour green salad on the side.

CHICKEN WITH ONIONS
Pui Cu Ceapa

This dish can be prepared very quickly. Clean, cut into small pieces 2 or 3 young small broilers and salt a little. Heat in a casserole 4 tablespoonfuls of bacon drippings. Chop finely a bunch of scallions or 2 onions, add to the fat and fry to a golden color, with stirring. Add the chicken pieces, one tablespoonful of parsley and salt and pepper to taste. Cover and cook until the liquid is absorbed. Then fry uncovered, with stirring, until crisp and brown. Add a tablespoonful of butter if needed and heat quickly on a hot flame. Serve hot with buttered rice or mushrooms.

92 : CHICKEN AND FOWL

CHICKEN WITH CREAM
Pui Cu Smantana

1 large chicken (or 2 small broilers)	1 pt. sour cream
¼ lb. butter	¼ lb. mushrooms
2 tbs. flour	salt and pepper
	parsley, fennel, chives

Clean and cut into pieces one large chicken or 2 small broilers. Brown in ¼-pound of hot butter in a frying pan and then remove to a casserole. Reheat the butter in the pan and add to it 2 tablespoonfuls of flour. Heat with stirring until light brown. Add slowly one pint of sour cream, mix well and simmer for a few minutes. Pour this over the chicken in the casserole, add ¼-pound of thinly sliced mushrooms, salt and pepper, a little finely chopped parsley, fennel and chives and a little water. Cover the casserole tightly and cook slowly until tender. Serve hot with fried potatoes or noodles and a vegetable salad.

CHICKEN WITH LEMON
Pui Cu Lamaie

Prepare exactly as above, but a few minutes before ready to serve add to the chicken a little lemon juice and very thin slices of peeled lemons. Simmer slowly a little while longer. Remove the chicken to a heated plate. Stir the sauce gently into 2 well-beaten egg yolks and pour over the chicken. Serve with MAMA-LIGA or steamed potatoes together with fruit compote.

CHICKEN STEW
Tocana De Pui

1 large chicken	2 onions
¼ lb. butter	½ pt. sour cream
2 tbs. chopped parsley	salt and pepper

Clean one large tender chicken, cut into small pieces and salt. Heat in a casserole ¼-pound of butter, bacon drippings or lard. When the fat is very hot fry 2 tablespoonfuls of finely chopped

CHICKEN AND FOWL : 93

parsley and 2 finely chopped onions until brown. Add the chicken, cover and simmer until the liquid is absorbed. Brown the chicken quickly, add ½-pint of sour cream and heat a little with constant stirring. Then add salt and pepper, cover with water and cook until tender in the covered casserole. Add farina balls (see FARINA BALLS) 10 minutes after the added water begins to boil. Serve hot, sprinkled with parsley.

ROAST GOOSE
Gasca Prajita

goose	6 to 8 mushrooms
salt and pepper	2 cups beef stock
garlic	2 glasses sherry
1 tbs. lard or butter	1 egg
1 large carrot	1 tbs. flour
1 parsley root	1 cup light cream
1 large onion	1 tbs. minced shallot
cloves, ground ginger	

Singe a young goose, clean and wash very well. Cut into 4 parts or it can be roasted whole. Salt and pepper and let stand for about one hour. Rub with garlic and place in a casserole with a tablespoonful of lard or butter. Add one large carrot and one parsley root, both sliced, one large onion larded with 5 or 6 cloves and sprinkled with a little ground ginger, and 6 to 8 thinly sliced mushrooms. Add slowly 2 cups of beef stock or a solution of bouillon cubes. Cover and roast slowly. When done add one glass of sherry, cover and simmer for 5 minutes.

Remove the goose to a heated plate and slice. Skim off all but about 3 tablespoonfuls of fat from the casserole and continue to cook the vegetables a little longer until light brown. Add a little more beef stock or bouillon and cook slowly a while longer. Prepare the following. Mix well one well-beaten egg and one tablespoonful of flour. Add one cup of light cream, one tablespoonful of minced shallot and one glass of sherry. Mix, bring to a boil and cook gently for 10 minutes more, with occasional stirring. Press through a sieve over the sliced meat. Serve with boiled noodles fried in butter and sprinkled with Parmesan cheese.

94 : CHICKEN AND FOWL

ROASTED DUCK WITH OLIVES AND BEER
Ratza Prajita Cu Bere Si Masline

duck
butter, flour
celery leaves
1 large onion
parsley, 1 laurel leaf

thyme
½ cup beer or ale
¼ lb. black olives
1 to 2 tbs. sour cream
¾ cup bouillon

Truss a young duck and sear. (If too fat, drain.) Butter well an oven pan, sprinkle a little with flour, then place the duck in it. Add some celery leaves, one large onion sliced crosswise, a few sprigs of parsley, one laurel leaf broken into 2 or 3 pieces and a little thyme. Baste with ½-cup of beer or ale and roast in a moderate oven. Shortly before it is done add ¼-pound of black olives, top with 1 to 2 tablespoonfuls of sour cream and sprinkle with about ¾-cup of bouillon. Bake slowly until done. Serve hot or cold with its sauce and garnished with any kind of dumpling or potatoes and a sour salad as a side dish.

DUCK ALA ROUMAINE
Ratza Ala Romania

duck
flour
butter
1 orange
¼ lb. bacon
shallot, fennel

thyme, marjoram
garlic, peppercorns
sage leaf
cabbage
sauerkraut juice
1 glass sherry

The most favored way to prepare duck in Romania is on sour cabbage and it is delicious. Singe and clean very well a young fat duck and keep it in the air to dry. Put on a rack over a dripping pan, place in a hot oven and heat until some of the fat will be melted. Remove from the oven, let cool a little, then dredge in flour and pat in well. Brown the duck in a little butter, in the meantime pouring over it slowly the juice of one orange. Prepare a brown sauce in the pan as follows. Fry ¼-pound of smoked bacon cut into small pieces. Add one tablespoonful each of finely chopped shallot and fennel and a little thyme and fry together for 2 or 3 minutes. Add a tablespoonful of flour, brown

CHICKEN AND FOWL : 95

well, stirring constantly, then thin with sauerkraut juice (not too sour) added slowly. Cook for about 10 minutes with continual stirring.

Cut the duck into pieces and place in a casserole, the bottom of which is rubbed with a clove of garlic. In the pan used for browning the duck add one sage leaf, then the head of one cabbage shredded (or use sauerkraut) and finally a little marjoram. Brown the cabbage and add it to the duck in the casserole. Pour on the brown sauce, cover the casserole and bake from 2 to 3 hours. Add a few peppercorns and let brown in the oven uncovered. Before removing the duck, add one glass of sherry.

YOUNG FAT GOOSE WITH SAUERKRAUT
Gasca La Tava Cu Varza Acra

Prepare exactly as DUCK ALA ROUMAINE, but be careful if the goose is too fat, to melt away most of it, so the meat will not be too greasy.

DUCK WITH GHERKINS
Ratza Cu Castraveti Mici

Prepare exactly as DUCK ALA ROUMAINE, but replace the sauerkraut with pickled gherkins.

DUCK WITH OLIVES
Ratza Cu Masline

Prepare exactly as DUCK ALA ROUMAINE, but make the brown sauce as follows. Fry one grated onion in 2 tablespoonfuls of butter or bacon drippings. Add one grated carrot and a tablespoonful of finely chopped parsley and simmer for 6 to 8 minutes. Add a heaping tablespoonful of flour. Brown with constant stirring. Dilute the sauce with water added little by little and cook for 5 minutes. Pour this over the duck and let simmer until tender. When done, remove the meat to a platter. Add to the sauce 1 to 2 tablespoonfuls of wine vinegar and one cup of ripe olives and simmer for 1 to 2 minutes. Replace the duck and finish cooking. Serve with lemon slices.

96 : CHICKEN AND FOWL

EXTRAS

GOOSE LIVER
Ficat De Gasca

Prepare exactly as the YOUNG LAMB EXTRAS, but instead of tarragon and dill use finely chopped chives.

GOOSE LIVER BREADED
Ficat De Gasca In Pesmet

Choose as many livers as needed. Cut into slices, not too thick, salt and pepper a little and let stand for ¼-hour. Dredge in flour, then in well-beaten eggs and finally in bread crumbs. Now fry the livers in very hot, deep lard until crisp and brown on both sides. Serve hot on top of buttered spinach, peas or potato purée.

GOOSE LIVERS STUFFED
Ficat De Gasca Umplut

Make a large and deep incision in 2 goose livers (from fat geese). Stuff the cuts with some sliced dry mushrooms which have first been soaked until tender in white wine to which has been added one clove and a pinch of cinnamon. Salt the livers and cover with fresh bacon slices.

Rub the bottom of a casserole with a little garlic, sprinkle with chopped shallot or chives, add the livers and pour over them a glass of white wine. Sprinkle over with finely chopped parsley, cover the casserole tightly and cook for one hour. Let cool, take out the livers and remove from them the bacon slices. Cut into thin slices, place in hot gelatin and cool. Serve with cold salads.

Meat Dishes

BROILED MEAT
Carne La Gratar

There are some things about broiled meats which all cooks should know, if they do not already. Meats which are to be grilled should be kept in the refrigerator for a number of days to tenderize them. Fillet of beef should be 2½ inches thick and flattened by pounding with the fist and the rib cuts, also of the same thickness, should be flattened with a wood mallet and cubed to tenderize them. Do not wash meat; wipe it with a damp cloth. The commercially available grill made of steel wire gives excellent results. Before using, wipe with a damp cloth and grease the grill with bacon fat. Avoid sticking a fork into the meat to prevent loss of the juices. The grill must be hot before putting the meat on it. Sear each side quickly on a hot flame, then reduce the degree of heat by either reducing the heat or moving the meat further away from the flame. Meats grilled on wood embers develop a characteristic deliciousness.

In Romania love of good food is a national trait, and it follows that good cooking must be found everywhere. These people know what a good dish is and will simply not eat anything that is not prepared well. Wherever you go in that colorful nation you will be captivated by its cooking.

98 : MEAT DISHES

In its exotic capital, Bucharest, called the Paris of the Balkans, there are an unusually large number of restaurants. As you pass them by, you can hear the exciting music of their gypsy bands, now gay, now plaintive and soon turning into a wild melody. Not only do you notice the music. Each restaurant is proud of its cooking and of its specialties. The kitchen is open and the wonderful aromas strike the nostrils and beg one to please enter, and few can resist, judging from the crowds eating.

There is a river in Bucharest called the Grivitza. On both sides of its muddy banks is the famous outdoor market. There are stalls where everything in creation is being sold; railings on which hang the colorful carpets of Romania, each different and each a work of art; and open-air aromatic bodegas with romantic terraces and little tables, where good cooking and broilings can be had at any time, day or night. Here can be seen peasants in their gay colored costumes, each one betraying in its design and coloring the district from which its wearer comes, mingling with tradespeople, ladies in silks, the famous gypsy girls, some selling flowers, others fresh bread, and visitors from foreign lands, speaking many strange tongues. Here a little crowd has collected. We see a man lying on the ground and a trained bear on a leash held by his gypsy master walking back and forth on the man's back. He is receiving a massage. It is very effective as the bear's paws are soft yet apply a great pressure due to its weight. It is a remedy for lumbago and for various aches and pains. In the evening barefooted urchins play on the wooden flute the national folk melodies full of haunting beauty and dance in the street, all in the hope of getting a few coins. Please believe me, once you have visited the banks of the Grivitza, it will remain with you forever.

In Romania where a girl must learn to cook at an early age, it is her duty to prepare the food whenever a young man comes to visit her. In order to have her daughter excel, the mother will begin to coach her days, even weeks before, in the making of a special ciorba or broiling. There is always much excitement, will she please her prince charming? And when he finally arrives, her face turns crimson. Will the broilings be the most flavorful he ever tasted, will she serve the meal with grace and charm? If she does, she may even be lucky enough to capture him, as she

MEAT DISHES : 99

believes fervently in the saying, "You can go to his heart through his stomach."

MITITEI

1 lb. rump beef	powdered cloves
1 lb. breast beef	thyme
3 or 4 cloves garlic	salt and pepper
bicarbonate of soda	½ cup beef stock
powdered allspice	

A favorite among the Romanians is *mititei,* homemade skinless sausages which are usually broiled outdoors on charcoal.

Buy one pound of beef from the rump and one pound of breast of beef, leaving some fat on the meat. Add 3 or 4 cloves of garlic and grind together. Place the meat in a bowl, add ¼ teaspoonful of bicarbonate of soda, about ½-teaspoonful of powdered allspice, ¼ teaspoonful of thyme, ¼ teaspoonful of powdered cloves, and salt and pepper to taste. Mix together with the hands, adding slowly ½ cup of rich or concentrated beef stock and continue mixing, adding a little beef fat if needed.

When thoroughly mixed, take some in your palms and roll the meat into sausages about 3½ inches long and one inch thick. See that your palms are kept wetted, so the sausages will remain smooth surfaced. Having formed all the meat into sausages, place them on a platter and keep them in a dry, cool place until the following day. This is necessary as time is required for the spices to penetrate deeply into the meat. You will get even better results if you will keep them in the refrigerator (not in the freezing compartment) for 2 or 3 days.

Before you start to grill the *mititei,* keep them in the air for 1 to 2 hours. Wipe the grill with a damp cloth and grease with bacon drippings. When the grill is very hot, put the *mititei* on and broil over a quick fire, turning and basting with beef stock on all sides and turning the sausages with flat tongs. Never use a fork or other sharp object, so as not to lose any of the juice.

Serve very hot with little sharp red or green peppers and sour pickles flavored with dill. And of course with a delicious grill like the *mititei* good wines are just begging to be drunk.

100 : MEAT DISHES

MIXED GRILL
Gratar Amestecat

The mixed grills occupy an important place among the Romanian broilings, second only to the *mititei*. When eaten at home or in a restaurant, the rule is to come in with an empty stomach. It is not unusual for people to keep eating it leisurely for 2 to 3 hours, and drinking wine at the same time.

The mixed grill is served on an enormous and very hot plate and consists of the following meats. *Mititei* is in the center of the plate, surrounded by grilled pig's kidney, pig's liver, pork chops, calf's udder, pork loin, fresh pork sausage, pig's brains and pork ribs. Serve very hot with french fried potatoes, sour cabbage or pickled cucumbers in liquid, and sharp red peppers.

GRILLED PORK CHOPS
Cotlete De Porc La Gratar

Choose pork chops one inch thick, trim off all the fat, sprinkle with salt and pepper and a little thyme. If you like, rub with garlic. Sear on a very hot grate to seal in the juice. Turn only once. Serve very hot with sour side dishes and sharp red peppers.

GRILLED KIDNEY
Rinichi La Gratar

Clean the kidney, remove the veins, wash in very cold water and let soak for a few minutes. Dry and sprinkle with salt and pepper. Sear quickly on both sides and grill. Serve very hot and sprinkle with garlic crushed in sour wine or if you prefer, serve the crushed garlic in a small saucer and dip the meat into the sauce as you eat.

FILLET OF PORK GRILLED
Muschiu De Porc La Gratar

Prepare the same as the Grilled Pork Chops and serve with apple sauce.

MEAT DISHES : 101

PORK LOIN GRILLED
Costita De Porc La Gratar

Prepare the same as the Grilled Pork Chops and serve with apple sauce.

GRILLED PORK BRAINS
Creeri De Porc La Gratar

Wash brains (whole or cut into halves) very well and immerse in wine for one hour before grilling. Let dry, add salt and pepper to taste, and dip into fine bread crumbs to which has been added a little thyme. Grill and serve with tabasco peppers.

PORK SAUSAGE GRILLED
Carnati De Porc La Gratar

Grill pure pork sausages or smoked sausages on racks. Serve very hot with mashed beans (see MASHED BEANS) or bean purée (see BEAN PURÉE) and sauerkraut. It is also delicious when cold.

PIGS LIVER GRILLED
Ficat De Purcel La Gratar

Remove the outside skin and veins of the liver, cut into thin slices of about ½ inch and broil, turning often. Add salt and pepper when ready to serve. Serve with nicely browned fried onions sliced crosswise and with sour side dishes.

PORK AND BEEF SAUSAGE
Carnati De Carne De Porc Si Vaca

Grind together 2 pounds of pork meat with the fat left on, 2 pounds of beef and 2 or 3 cloves of garlic. Add salt and pepper to taste, a pinch of marjoram and lovage and a little water. Mix well together. Fill into sausage casings, hang the sausages in a dry and cool place and let remain overnight. The following day grill on the grate.

102 : MEAT DISHES

PORK CHOPS IN SAUCE
Cotlete De Porc In Sos

3 pork chops	salt and pepper
2 tbs. fresh pork fat	paprika
1 small onion	1 tbs. flour
soup stock	

Sear quickly 3 or more pork chops in a large skillet and then fry to a dark brown. Add 2 tablespoonfuls of fresh pork fat. Make room by pushing the chops to one side and add one small finely chopped onion, salt and pepper to taste and a little paprika. When the onion is light brown, add a tablespoonful of flour and fry it to a nice light brown, stirring constantly. Add little by little, with stirring, enough cold water or soup stock to make a not too thick sauce. Move the chops into the sauce and let cook slowly, stirring now and then until the meat is done. When a bubble of fat rises to the surface, it is a sign that the meat and sauce are cooked. Serve very hot. Place the meat in the center of the plate, pour on the sauce and garnish all around the plate with peasant style potatoes (see POTATOES PEASANT STYLE) or potato purée. Fruit compote goes well with this dish.

PORK CHOPS WITH BEER
Cotlete De Porc Cu Bere

2 lbs. pork chops	1 tbs. butter
½ tbs. fresh melted pork fat	parsley
garlic	shallot or chives
2 onions	flour
2 large apples	2 cups beer
salt and pepper	cayenne pepper

Rub a deep oven casserole with garlic. Add 1½ tablespoonfuls of fresh melted pork fat (no other fat will give such a fine flavor). Slice 2 onions crosswise and spread on the bottom of the casserole. Peel and slice 2 large apples and place on top of the onion. Place on the fire until the heat has penetrated. Shut off the heat, cover and let stand. Trim well 2 pounds of tender pork chops, sear them quickly on both sides in a frying pan, then place the chops on top of the mixture in the casserole.

MEAT DISHES : 103

Sprinkle with salt and pepper, cover and heat over a very low flame.

Prepare a sauce in a frying pan with one tablespoonful of butter, a little finely chopped parsley and shallot (or chives). Add a little flour, mix, then brown lightly. Thin with 2 cups of beer and add a pinch of cayenne pepper, stirring constantly. Pour this sauce over the meat. Place in a hot oven and bake with a moderate heat until done.

ROASTED SUCKLING PIG
Purcel Mic La Gratar

1 small suckling pig	whole cloves
salt and pepper	2 glasses wine
butter	cinnamon bark
4 or 5 red apples	parsley

Get a small suckling pig from your butcher. Have him clean the outside as well as the inside, but also see that you get all the meat extras, the heart, the lungs, kidney, etc. Wipe the meat with a damp napkin and prepare as follows. Salt the inside and outside of the little pig well and let stand for one hour. Make a few long gashes through the skin on each side of the backbone. Brush the entire outside and inside with butter and sprinkle with pepper. Place inside the pig 4 or 5 small red apples into which you have stuck 2 or 3 whole cloves. Put the little pig on a rack over a dripping pan, having first tied the front and back feet with wood sticks, so that the pig is in a kneeling position. Brush once more the outside of the pig with butter (or lard), put one apple in the mouth and pour around the pig so that it will run into the pan ¼ cup of hot water together with 2 glasses of hot wine in which you have put a little cinnamon bark. (If you can afford it, or perhaps you feel like making it a festive occasion, then replace the wine with champagne.) Now butter a large white sheet of paper, cover the pig with it, and place the pan with the pig into a hot oven. Use a slow fire at first, then increase the heat to moderate. Baste with the liquid from the pan every 15 minutes. If needed, add more wine to the pan.

When the back of the little pig is half roasted, turn it over, roast with basting until the meat is cooked. Now turn the pig

104 : MEAT DISHES

over again, to its original kneeling position on the wood sticks. Again baste very well. Increase the heat and roast to a dark brown and crisp surface. Put the roasted pig on a hot serving plate, decorated with flowers in its ears. Garnish all around it with fried potatoes over which pour the sauce. Sprinkle with green parsley. Serve with fried sauerkraut or wine sauce or freshly grated horseradish root and apple mixed together.

PORK ALA ANISOARA
Porc Ala Anisoara

Cut 2 pounds of pork tenderloin into very small cubes, sear very quickly in a deep frying pan, then add 2 tablespoonfuls of pork fat or bacon drippings and 3 finely chopped onions and fry with the meat until nice and brown. Now peel 2 large tomatoes, cut into very thin slices, add to the pan. Add pepper and salt to taste and cook together until done. Sprinkle with a little finely chopped parsley and a little thyme. Serve very hot on a hot plate with boiled or mashed potatoes and sour side dishes.

GRILLED BEEF STEAK
Biftec La Gratar

Before using the steak keep for at least 2 to 3 days in the refrigerator, but not in the freezing compartment. About 4 or 5 hours before broiling take out the steak and let it warm up in the kitchen. Rub both sides with garlic, place on the hot grill and broil to taste, raw, medium or well-done. Serve immediately on a hot plate. In Romania grilled meats are served on wooden plates, garnished with potatoes, tomatoes sprinkled with chopped parsley and sour dill pickles.

GRILLED FLANKEN STEAK
Fleica La Gratar

Prepare like the Grilled Beef Steak. Before the grilling is finished, pour over the steak garlic crushed in lemon juice or

MEAT DISHES : 105

wine vinegar. Serve hot sprinkled with chopped parsley. Cut into individual portions according to taste. Serve with sour side dishes.

GRILLED BEEF RIB STEAK
Biftec De Coaste La Gratar

Select nice pieces of steak, do not remove the bones, add salt and pepper to taste and sprinkle well with garlic crushed in lemon juice. Let stand for a while before placing it on a very hot greased grate. Serve very hot with cauliflower and sour pickles.

GRILLED BEEF CHOPS
Antrecote De Vaca La Gratar

Keep chops 2 days in refrigerator, warm in kitchen a few hours before using, flatten with the fist, dip in hot butter and broil on a hot grate. Add salt and pepper, arrange the chops on a long very hot serving plate, pour over them a little hot butter and garnish with fried potatoes and sour cabbage.

GRILLED BEEF FILLETS
Frigarui De Vaca La Gratar

Beef fillets may be broiled in the usual way or they can be made by frying in very hot butter in a frying pan, quickly and with a full flame. Serve with French mustard and sour dill pickles.

BEEF CUTLETS WITH ONIONS
Cotlete De Vaca Cu Ciapa

4 to 6 beef cutlets	pepper seeds
salt	soup stock
2 tbs. lard	1 pt. cream
4 large onions	parsley, chives

Clean 4 to 6 cutlets of the film, fat and bones, flatten a little, add salt and let stand. Heat a pan, put in 2 tablespoonfuls of

106 : MEAT DISHES

lard. When very hot, add 4 large onions chopped very fine and a few pepper seeds and fry the onions to a nice golden color. Now add the cutlets, fry together for a few minutes, then add just enough soup stock or water to cover. Cover tightly and fry until the meat is tender. When the liquid is absorbed and the cutlets are a nice pink, drain off the fat, pour over the meat one pint of cream, a tablespoonful of finely chopped parsley and a little chives and cook for a short while longer. Place the cutlets on a very hot long serving plate, pour the sauce on and garnish with potatoes, butter dumplings, noodles or macaroni.

CUTLET IN CREAM
Cotlete Cu Smantana

4 to 6 cutlets	1 pt. cream
2 tbs. lard	yolk of 3 or 4 eggs
salt	parsley and chives
beef stock	juice of one lemon

Ask the butcher to trim and flatten 4 to 6 cutlets. Put 2 tablespoonfuls of lard in a pot and when the lard is very hot, put in the cutlets which have been slightly salted and fry quickly on both sides to a ruddy color. Now add beef stock slowly until the cutlets are covered. Cover the pot tightly and fry slowly until the cutlets are tender, adding from time to time a little more beef stock if needed. When the meat is tender, drain off the fat and pour over the cutlets one pint of cream mixed with the yolks of 3 or 4 eggs, finely chopped parsley and chives and the juice of one lemon. Heat very slowly, but be sure it does not boil. Arrange the cutlets on a previously heated large serving plate, pour over them the cream sauce, and garnish with fried carrots, baked macaroni or pot cheese dumplings.

ROAST BEEF
Carne De Vaca Prajita

roast of beef	3 tbs. butter
fresh bacon	1 large onion
salt	12 peppercorns
garlic and parsley	beef stock

MEAT DISHES : 107

Buy a nice piece of roast beef, sprinkle with salt and cover with a few slices of fresh bacon. Rub the bottom of a frying pan lightly with garlic. Add 3 tablespoonfuls of butter, one large onion sliced, 12 peppercorns, one tablespoonful of finely chopped parsley and a few tablespoonfuls of beef stock. Put the beef into the pan and place in a hot baking oven. Bake with a high heat, basting with the sauce from time to time and adding more beef stock if needed. Bake the meat to a nice color, or until tender.

Cut crosswise into thin slices, arrange the slices one next to each other on a hot serving plate, then pour on the sauce. Garnish with mixed side dishes, such as red cabbage, mushrooms or any garnish you wish.

STUFFED ROAST BEEF
Carne De Vaca Umpluta

roast of beef	1 egg
1 onion	garlic
chopped lean ham	fresh bacon
1 tbs. ea. chopped chives,	beef stock
parsley and fennel	6 or 8 tbs. cream
salt and pepper	lemon juice
½ small roll	

Get a well-trimmed piece of beef for roasting and wipe with a damp cloth. Cut lengthwise in half through the center and scoop out with a sharp knife as much as you can, leaving 2 shells with cavities which are to be stuffed.

Chop the cut out meat, place in a bowl and add to it one finely chopped onion, a little lean ham chopped, a tablespoonful of finely chopped chives, parsley, fennel and salt and pepper to taste, then ½ small roll well soaked and the excess water pressed out, and one egg, all mixed together well. Fill this stuffing into the meat shells, join both halves and sew together, so that the original shape is again formed.

Rub the bottom of a frying pan with a little garlic, put in a few pieces of fresh bacon, add a few tablespoonfuls of beef stock and 3 or 4 tablespoonfuls of cream. Place the stuffed roast beef in the pan and place in a hot oven. Baste frequently with the sauce. When the meat is ruddy and tender, add 3 or 4 more

108 : MEAT DISHES

tablespoonfuls of cream and 1 or 2 tablespoonfuls of beef stock. Continue heat for 5 minutes. Skim the fat from the sauce. Pour lemon juice over the meat. Cut the stuffed roast beef into slices, place on a hot serving plate, pour on the sauce and garnish all around with cauliflower, carrots, peas and boiled cabbage and sprinkle with hot butter and parsley.

ROAST BEEF ALA BUCURESTI
Vaca Prajita Ala Bucuresti

roast beef
fresh bacon
salt and pepper
beef stock

cream
lemon juice
parsley and chives

Buy a large piece of roast beef, trimmed of fat and bone, and have the butcher flatten it. Season with pepper and salt and interlard with fresh strips of bacon. Let stand for 2 hours. Place the meat on a grate with a pan underneath to catch the drippings and juice. Add a little beef stock and 3 tablespoonfuls of cream to the pan. Baste frequently with this sauce until the meat is tender. When the meat is done, remove to a board and continue to cook the sauce until it is a nice reddish brown. Add 3 tablespoonfuls of cream and the juice of one lemon and if needed, a little salt. Continue to cook a little longer. While the sauce is cooking, cut the roast on the board into thin slices and arrange on a large heated plate. Squeeze the juice of a lemon over the slices, pour on the sauce from the pan and sprinkle with finely chopped parsley and chives. Garnish with red beets, fried potatoes and mustard.

BEEFSTEAK ALA SINAIA
Biftec Ala Sinaia

Ask your butcher to cut and trim a very tender piece of beefsteak. Cut crosswise into slices 1½ inches thick and flatten a little. Dip each slice in hot butter, pile one on top of the other and let stand for one hour. While you are warming up a pan con-

MEAT DISHES : 109

taining 3 tablespoonfuls of butter (or lard), drench the slices of meat in flour and fry quickly both sides over a high flame to a red brown color. Add a little beef stock and some salt to taste, cover very tightly and heat for about 5 to 6 minutes. When done, serve on a very hot serving plate. Place the meat in the center, pour on the sauce and garnish all around with fried red cabbage, mushrooms, green beans, red beets, fried brains and peas. On top of the meat place some eggs sunny side up. Prepare the garnishing before you finish the meat.

A quickly prepared and tasty meat can be prepared by frying the steak in plenty of very hot butter (or lard) for 4 to 5 minutes. Salt to taste, garnish and serve immediately.

RAW BEEFSTEAK
Biftec De Carne Cruda

Get 2 to 2½ pounds of well-trimmed beefsteak, wipe and clean off all small fibers, chop very fine and place the chopped meat in the center of a glass plate in the form of a mound. Flatten the top and form in the center of the mound a little nest, in which put the yolk of one egg. Garnish all around the mound with 2 tablespoonfuls each of black caviar, finely chopped capers, chopped onions and french mustard, blended with olive oil and vinegar. Arrange artistically and decorate with green parsley.

RASOL PIQUANT

beef for soup	salt and pepper
⅓ lb. bacon	1 cup tomato juice
¼ lb. ham	1 cup beef stock
1 onion	1 laurel leaf
large glass white wine	

Prepare a piece of beef as above. While the soup is boiling prepare the following sauce. Cut ⅓ pound of fresh bacon into small pieces and fry in a pot. Add a finely chopped onion and ¼ pound of finely chopped raw ham and fry well together. Add a large glass of white wine and salt and pepper to taste. Cover

110 : MEAT DISHES

the pot tightly and cook slowly for ½ hour. Now add one cup of tomato juice, one cup of beef soup and one laurel leaf. Cook a little longer, then add the sliced boiled meat and boil together for 15 minutes.

Arrange the meat on a hot serving plate and garnish around the meat with fried, boiled or steamed rice, or with small whole new potatoes fried in butter. Sprinkle with finely chopped chives and parsley.

BOILED BEEF
Rasol Ardeal

Boil 4 to 5 pounds of beef for soup with the regular vegetables. When done, remove the meat, clean off all the bones, cut into suitable pieces and arrange on a plate. Pour a few tablespoonfuls of the beef soup over the meat, sprinkle with finely chopped parsley and serve with a sauce of your choice. Garnish all around the beef with rice, carrots and mushrooms, all cooked or sautéed separately.

ROASTED BOILED BEEF
Carne Fiarta Prajita

boiled beef	2 tbs. cooked rice
2 tbs. lard	⅓ lb. boiled ham
6 large potatoes	1 pt. cream
4 eggs	parsley and chives

Remove bones from the boiled beef, prepared as above. Heat 2 tablespoonfuls of lard in a pot. When very hot, add in this order 6 large boiled potatoes cut into slices, 4 sliced hard-boiled eggs, 2 heaping tablespoonfuls of boiled rice obtained from the beef soup, and ⅓ pound of boiled tender ham well-chopped. Now add the boiled beef in one piece and over the beef pour one pint of cream, and sprinkle over with finely chopped parsley and chives. Place in a moderately hot oven and bake for 15 minutes.

MEAT DISHES : 111

Place the beef on a board and slice according to taste. Arrange the slices all around a hot serving plate and in the center put all the ingredients remaining in the pot. Serve immediately with a sauce to your liking.

LEFTOVER BEEF
Carnuri Ramasita

Use any kind of leftover meat, boiled, roasted, fried or baked. Cut into small pieces. Salt and pepper to taste, sprinkle over with lemon juice and let stand for 30 minutes. Dredge in flour, then in eggs and finally in bread crumbs. Fry in deep and very hot lard. Serve immediately on top of peas, green beans or any kind of salad.

BEEF BRAINS
Creeri De Vaca

Wash the brains, remove the skin and soak in cold water for one hour. Drain and let dry. Fry 3 medium-sized onions thinly sliced in one tablespoonful of butter or lard to a golden color, but do not brown. Add the brains and salt and pepper to taste. Break the brains into pieces with a wooden spoon from time to time. Add a small glass of brandy, stir and fry quickly. Serve hot as garnishing with steak or roasted beef.

BEEF TONGUE
Limba De Vaca

Wash well one fresh beef tongue. Boil until tender in salt water containing 10 to 12 peppercorns, one onion, a few sprigs of parsley and a few sprigs of fennel. Cool the tongue and peel off the skin. Cut into thin slices on a board and arrange on a plate garnished with potato salad and red radishes. Serve with horse-radish or sorrel sauce.

112 : MEAT DISHES

SMOKED TONGUE
Limba Afumata

Wash a smoked tongue in a few changes of hot water and put in a casserole with water to which have been added 2 cloves, a piece of a laurel leaf, a few peppercorns, one onion and ½ cup of vinegar. Boil slowly for 2 hours or until cooked. Peel, cut into slices, arrange on a heated plate and garnish with hard boiled eggs sliced into quarters, olives and horseradish sauce. If you wish, you may boil the smoked tongue in plain water and serve with a well seasoned sauce.

SMOKED BOILED TONGUE WITH TOMATOES AND OLIVES
Limba Afumata Fiarta Cu Patlagele Rosii Si Masline

Prepare exactly as above. When making the sauce which goes with this dish use tomato juice instead of stock and add a cup of ripe olives and a bunch of mixed herbs tied together, which will be removed from the sauce when ready. Serve hot or cold.

FRESH PORK TONGUE
Limba De Porc Proaspata

pork tongues	1 tbs. pulverized sugar
2 tbs. lard	1 pt. wine
2 tbs. flour	seedless raisins
chives, thyme	almonds, cloves

Wash a few fresh pork tongues and boil exactly as the beef tongue. While they are boiling, prepare a brown sauce as follows. Heat in a deep iron pan 2 tablespoonfuls of lard or bacon drippings. When very hot add 2 heaping tablespoonfuls of flour, stirring constantly. When light brown add a little finely chopped chives and a little thyme, stir, then add one tablespoonful of pulverized sugar with stirring. When browned, thin slowly with one pint of good wine and enough liquid in which the tongues have been cooked to make a sauce, neither too thick nor too thin. Taste and if needed add more salt and sugar. Add a handful of rinsed seedless raisins, a handful of almonds which have

MEAT DISHES : 113

been first scalded, peeled and then finely sliced, and a few cloves. Stir together and add the sliced tongue. Cook slowly for ½ hour, then serve with lemon sauce.

COLD FRESH TONGUE WITH SAUCE
Limba Rece Proaspata Cu Sos

Prepare exactly as above, but when the tongue is boiled, peel the skin, then replace in the pot and let cool in its own liquid. Serve cold with olive oil sauce or horseradish sauce and cold salads.

ROAST VEAL
Carne De Vitel Prajita

leg of veal	2 tbs. butter
fresh bacon	1 pt. cream
beef stock	juice of 2 lemons

When you buy a leg of veal have the butcher remove the bone and flatten the meat. Salt well and interlard with fresh bacon. Place the leg in a pan over a grill. Put into the pan a little beef stock, 2 tablespoonfuls of butter, one pint of cream and the juice of 2 lemons (without seeds) and mix them well. Put in the hot oven and roast for 2 hours, basting frequently with the sauce. When the meat is tender and of a nice color cut the leg of veal into slices and arrange them on a very hot plate. Pour on a little of the sauce from the pan. Garnish with cauliflower and the meat of a lobster boiled in salt water. Serve in a serving dish the remaining sauce, sprinkled over with finely chopped parsley.

LEG OF VEAL ALA CLUJ
Carne De Vitel Ala Cluj

leg of veal	parsley, chives and thyme
fresh bacon	2 tbs. flour
salt	beef stock
1 tbs. capers	6 to 8 tbs. cream
1 onion, 1 clove of garlic	dried tabasco pepper
2 tbs. butter	1 lemon

114 : MEAT DISHES

Buy a leg of veal with the bone removed and then flattened. Salt well, interlard with fresh bacon and let stand one hour. Make a mixture of a few slices of bacon cut into small pieces, the grated peel of ½ lemon, a tablespoonful of capers, one chopped onion, one clove of garlic and one tablespoonful of chives. Let stand while you prepare a brown sauce as follows: heat in a pan 2 tablespoonfuls of butter. Fry in it one tablespoonful of chopped chives, one tablespoonful of chopped parsley and a little thyme. Stir constantly until tender. Add 2 tablespoonfuls of flour with constant stirring. When dark brown add slowly little by little beef soup or broth until you get the desired consistency (do not make it too thick). Add to the sauce 6 to 8 tablespoonfuls of cream, a very little crushed dried tabasco pepper (what you can pick up on the tip of a knife) and the juice of one lemon. Cook 5 minutes longer. Now add the above mixture, simmer for another 5 minutes, cover the pan tightly and let stand. Now roast the leg of veal in a pan in a hot oven, basting frequently with the above sauce until tender.

When the leg is done, cut into thin slices, place on a hot serving plate and pour over the slices the hot sauce from the pan. Garnish with fried rice, fried mushrooms or any garnishing you may choose.

VEAL ALA ANISOARA
Carne De Vitel Ala Anisoara

leg of veal	cloves
salt	2 laurel leaves
fresh bacon	beef soup or broth
garlic	chives and parsley
1 large carrot	1 tbs. flour
1 large parsley root	4 or 5 tbs. cream
1 large parsnip root	1 lemon
2 small onions	

Ask your butcher to cut a few slices of veal cutlets one finger thick and to flatten them as thin as possible, without breaking through the meat. Salt and let stand for 30 minutes. Remove all the rest of the meat from the leg of veal, leaving the bone clean of meat, and put through the grinder. Arrange the cutlets on a board next to each other. On each place a

MEAT DISHES : 115

square of the chopped veal about ½-inch thick, roll as tightly as you can and tie with a strong thin string.

Now rub with a little garlic the bottom of a stew pan, put in a few slices of fresh bacon, one large carrot sliced, one parsley root sliced and one parsnip root sliced. Place on top 2 small onions in each of which you will insert 3 or 4 cloves. Cover with the grated peel of ½ lemon. Add 2 laurel leaves, sprinkle over with a little beef soup or broth and lay on top the rolled veal. Sprinkle over with finely chopped chives and green parsley. Cover tightly and cook slowly until the meat is tender and a nice red, adding from time to time beef soup or broth, as the liquid evaporates.

When the meat is done, remove the liquid to another pan, leaving the vegetables in the same pan to roast longer with the veal rolls.

Sprinkle the vegetables with one tablespoonful of flour. When nicely browned, thin with a little beef broth and add with mixing 4 or 5 tablespoonfuls of cream, the liquid previously removed from the pan and the juice of one lemon. Simmer 5 minutes longer. Remove the veal rolls to a hot plate and cut into ½-inch slices. Place all the contents of the pan in a sieve held over the plate of the veal rolls. Crush the vegetables with a spoon until all of them have been strained through. Garnish with stuffed eggs (see EGGS) and serve with a fruit compote.

VEAL PEASANT STYLE
Carne De Vitel Stil Taranesc

3½ lb. shoulder veal	parsley
4 tbs. lard	beef broth
7 or 8 large onions	6 to 8 tbs. cream
crushed tabasco pepper	1 tsp. flour
salt	1 onion

Cut into small pieces 3½ pounds of veal from the shoulder. Heat 4 tablespoonfuls of lard in a deep frying pan. When hot add 7 or 8 large onions finely chopped, fry to a nice gold color, add a pinch of crushed tabasco pepper, then the meat. Sprinkle with salt to taste and fry. When the juice from the meat has been absorbed and the veal is nicely browned, sprinkle with 3 tablespoonfuls of finely chopped parsley. Fry a little longer,

116 : MEAT DISHES

then add just enough beef broth (or water) to cover the meat. Cover the pan tightly and cook slowly about one hour.

While the meat is cooking, beat in a bowl 6 to 8 tablespoonfuls of cream with a teaspoonful of flour, add the juice of one lemon and pour this over the meat when ready to serve. Bring to the boiling point and serve as usual on a hot plate, garnished with fried potatoes or dumplings.

FRIED VEAL CHOPS
Cotlete De Vitel Fripte

Choose 4 to 5 pounds of thick veal chops, trimmed and well flattened. Salt each chop, dredge in flour, then in eggs and finally in bread crumbs and fry quickly in deep and very hot butter or lard on both sides till it turns brown and crisp. While the chops are frying, place the serving plate on the stove to get hot. When done, arrange the chops on the plate and garnish with lemon slices and green scallions. Serve any kind of sour salad you want.

VEAL CHOPS NATURAL
Cotlete De Vitel Nature

Take some veal chops, ¾-inch thick, flatten, salt and dredge in flour. Shake off the excess flour and fry very quickly on both sides in a deep pan in very hot and deep butter or lard. When the chops have turned crisp and brown, place on a serving plate and keep on the stove to remain hot. Skim off the fat, add a little beef soup or broth to the remaining sauce in the pan, bring to a boil and pour it over the chops. Serve with peas in butter and sliced red beets.

VEAL WITH GARLIC
Carne De Vitel Cu Usturoi

3 lbs. veal	salt and pepper
5 or 6 cloves garlic	1 cup broth
4 tbs. butter	1 glass wine
parsley and chives	3 tbs. sour cream

Cut 3 pounds of veal into small cubes. Cut 5 or 6 cloves of garlic into very small pieces and sear for a few minutes in 4 tablespoonfuls of butter or lard. Add the meat and fry, with constant stirring until brown. Add chopped parsley and a little chives. Sauté for a few minutes. Add salt and pepper to taste and one cup of broth or water. Cook slowly until meat is tender, adding from time to time more broth. When done, add one glass of wine and 3 tablespoonfuls of sour cream and cook for 5 minutes longer. Serve with mamaliga or purée of potatoes with a sour salad.

VEAL WITH MUSHROOMS
Carne De Vitel Cu Ciuperci

Pound with the back of a knife a few large-sized, thick veal cutlets. Sprinkle with salt and pepper to taste and sear quickly on both sides in 4 to 5 tablespoonfuls of butter or lard. Slow the fire, cover the top of the chops thickly with cream and sprinkle with finely chopped chives and parsley. Add one cup of thinly sliced mushrooms. Simmer for 5 minutes, then turn the cutlets over and simmer for 5 minutes longer. Add a little more cream and a glass of sherry. Heat to a point just short of boiling. Serve hot. Garnish with cauliflower and asparagus tips in butter and sour salad.

STUFFED VEAL LIVER
Ficat De Vitel Umplut

veal liver	1 tbs. bread crumbs
bacon	flour
¼ lb. butter	garlic
onions	1 laurel leaf
parsley and chives	lemon slices
salt and pepper	beef soup
1 egg	white wine

Wash veal liver in cold water, wipe with a clean cloth and remove skin and veins. Make a deep horizontal cut in one side of the liver and fill with the following stuffing. Beat together ¼ pound of butter with ⅛ pound of shredded bacon until foamy.

118 : MEAT DISHES

Add a finely chopped small onion, one tablespoonful of finely chopped parsley, a little salt and pepper, one egg and one tablespoonful of bread crumbs. Mix well together.

Stuff this mixture into the liver and sew the opening together. Dredge in flour, place in a pot previously rubbed with a little garlic, add a few slices of bacon, one sliced onion, one laurel leaf, a few slices of lemon, a few tablespoonfuls of beef soup and the same amount of white wine. Sprinkle with a little finely chopped chives and parsley. Cover the pot tightly and cook slowly for 45 minutes. When done, remove from the pot, place on a hot serving plate, take out the thread and cut into slices. Press the sauce through a sieve over the liver. Garnish with stuffed squash or kohlrabi.

VEAL LIVER FLORA
Ficat De Vitel Flora

1 veal liver	1 large carrot
fresh bacon	1 parsnip
salt and pepper	1 laurel leaf
parsley, chives and fennel	1 glass wine
garlic	beef soup
3 onions	4 tbs. cream

Wash a nice veal liver in cold water, wipe with a clean cloth and remove skin and veins with a very sharp knife. Interlard with fresh bacon, add salt and pepper, then sprinkle with one tablespoonful of finely chopped parsley aand one of chives. Let stand while you prepare the pot. Rub the bottom with a little garlic and cover with fresh bacon. On top of the bacon put 3 sliced onions, one large sliced carrot, one sliced parsnip, one laurel leaf broken into small pieces and spread evenly over the surface and sprinkle with one tablespoonful each of chopped fennel and parsley. Now put in the liver and pour over it one glass of good wine. Cover the pot tightly and cook slowly for 2 hours.

Remove the liver to a board. Skim off the fat from the pot and add to the remaining sauce a little beef soup (broth), 4 tablespoonfuls of cream and a little chopped parsley. Bring to a boil, remove the pot from the fire, cover and let stand. Cut the liver

MEAT DISHES : 119

into long thin slices and arrange around the outside of a hot serving plate, leaving the center empty. When the liver is on the plate, again apply heat to the pot, bring to a boil and press the sauce through a sieve onto the center of the plate. Garnish with fried sliced tomatoes, carrots and mushrooms.

FRIED VEAL BRAINS
Creeri De Vitel Fripti

Immerse in very cold water two or more veal brains for one hour and remove. Heat salted water in a pot. When it is boiling rapidly, pour it over the brains, let drain off and stand for 10 minutes. Then rinse in cold water. Place on a board, remove the skin and cut into slices about an inch thick. Dip in egg, salt and pepper to taste and dredge in roll crumbs. Fry in hot lard to a nice brown. Serve on top of spinach, peas, kohlrabi or carrots cooked in butter, or by itself with wine sauce.

BRAINS WITH CREAM OR WINE SAUCE
Creeri Cu Sos De Smantana Sau Vin

Prepare exactly as above, except that the brains are cut into small sections. Place in either cream or wine sauce (see SAUCES), and simmer slowly until heated through. Garnish with green beans, fried cabbage or potatoes, sprinkled over with parsley.

VEAL EXTRAS
Maruntaie De Vitel

veal liver, heart, lungs	1 tomato
1 large onion	3 tbs. lard
parsley and fennel	2 tbs. flour
1 or 2 laurel leaves	2 onions
15 to 20 black peppercorns	4 tbs. cream
celery	1 lemon

This is a very delicious and inexpensive dish, rich in calories, vitamins and flavor. Boil in salted water one large onion, a bunch of green parsley and fennel, 1 or 2 laurel leaves, 15 to 20 black peppercorns, a few bunches of celery and one tomato. Add to the

120 : MEAT DISHES

pot the liver, heart and lungs of one calf, and boil together until tender.

While the extras are boiling prepare a brown sauce as follows. Put into a large saucepan 3 tablespoonfuls of lard and add 2 tablespoonfuls of flour. Heat with constant stirring until light brown in color. Add 2 finely chopped onions and fry to a dark brown. Strain the liquid from the pot in which the extras were boiling and add slowly enough liquid to the saucepan to make a sauce. Add the grated peel of one lemon and let simmer slowly. Cut the meat extras into strips (like noodles), add to the sauce and let simmer slowly for 10 minutes. Then add 4 tablespoonfuls of cream, continue to simmer for 5 minutes longer, stirring slowly. Then add the juice of one lemon (or more if you like it more sour). Serve on a large hot plate, garnished with dumplings made with butter or elbow macaroni, and a sour green salad.

VEAL LIVER
Ficat De Vitel

Prepare exactly as YOUNG LAMB OR SUCKLING PIG EXTRAS, but instead of tarragon and dill use finely chopped chives.

YOUNG SPRING LAMB
Carne De Miel

1 quarter spring lamb	2 tbs. olive oil
salt	1 glass white wine
garlic	leek and parsley

Clean and wipe well one quarter of a spring lamb, which has been cracked in 2 or 3 places by the butcher. Salt and let stand for 45 minutes. Fry in a pan previously lightly rubbed with garlic with 2 tablespoonfuls of lard or olive oil. Add one glass of white wine and sprinkle over with one tablespoonful each of finely chopped green leek and parsley. Cook for one hour in a moderate oven or until nicely browned, basting and turning the meat from time to time.

When done, cut into large pieces and place them back into the original shape of the quarter of the spring lamb. Add a few

MEAT DISHES : 121

tablespoonfuls of wine or water to the sauce in the pan, let boil a few minutes, then pour it over the lamb. Sprinkle with finely chopped parsley. Garnish with potato salad, baked peppers or tomatoes, and serve with a green vegetable salad.

SPRING LAMB EXTRAS
Maruntaie De Miel

lamb extras (heart, liver, lungs)	10 or 12 black peppercorns
6 onions	1 tbs. capers
1 large carrot	lard or olive oil
1 parsley root	parsley, fennel, scallions
1 laurel leaf	5 eggs
	salt and pepper

Boil the young spring lamb extras (heart, liver and lung) in salted water with one large onion, one large carrot cut lengthwise in half, one parsley root, one laurel leaf, 10 or 12 black peppercorns and one tablespoonful of capers from tarragon vinegar or one tablespoonful of chopped tarragon leaves. Boil until tender. Remove the extras from the pot to a board and cut into very small pieces. Fry 5 very finely chopped onions in a pan with 2 tablespoonfuls of lard or olive oil, add the cut extras and fry a little longer. Now add finely chopped fennel, scallions and parsley, 3 chopped hard-boiled eggs and 2 whole raw eggs, mix very well, add salt and pepper, mix again and let stand.

Wash the stomach lining of the lamb well in cold water and stretch out carefully on a board. Place the mixture prepared above on the lining, spread evenly, roll and tuck in the sides. Add 2 tablespoonfuls of lard or olive oil to a frying pan. When very hot, add the meat roll and cook slowly until done. Cut into slices about ¾-inch thick. Serve with cauliflower, mushrooms and a sour red cabbage salad.

YOUNG LAMB OR SUCKLING PIG EXTRAS
Maruntaie De Miel Or Purcel

Cut into very small cubes the extras from a young (5 to 6 weeks) lamb or suckling pig. Cut 6 onions into very thin slices

122 : MEAT DISHES

and fry in 2 tablespoonfuls of very hot bacon drippings or lard until nicely browned. Add a little ground tabasco pepper and 1 or 2 sprigs of tarragon or thyme. Then add the extras and salt to taste, mix, cover and cook slowly, stirring from time to time, to prevent burning. When nicely fried add 5 tablespoonfuls of beef stock or bouillon and let cook 10 minutes longer. When done, sprinkle over with chopped dill (if obtainable) or one tablespoonful of finely chopped parsley. Serve as garnishing for roasted meats or as a dish by itself.

SPRING LAMB SCHNITZEL
Snitel De Miel

Cut steaks from the leg of lamb, palm size and ¾-inch thick, flatten well, add salt and pepper and fry quickly in hot butter. Place the steaks on a large heated serving plate. Skim off the fat from the pan, add to the remaining liquid a glass of wine, let come to a boil, then pour it over the meat. Sprinkle with finely chopped parsley. Garnish with rice pilaf, peas and tomatoes and serve with a sour vegetable salad.

SPRING LAMB CHOPS
Cotlete De Miel

lamb chops	1 tbs. each chopped parsley
salt	and celery
butter	juice of one lemon
garlic	beef soup
1 onion	

Wipe and trim a few chops one-inch thick. Flatten and salt. Fry in butter slowly just for a few minutes until the meat becomes white on both sides. When the chops are cooled, dip in hot butter and place one on top of the other and let stand.

In the meantime in a pot lightly rubbed with garlic add one tablespoonful of butter and fry in it one chopped onion, one tablespoonful each of chopped parsley and chopped celery. Now complete the frying of the chops in very hot butter and place

MEAT DISHES : 123

on top of the fried onions and the greens. Pour the juice of one lemon and a little beef soup over the meat, cover the pot tightly and cook slowly until the liquid is absorbed. Arrange the chops when ready on a heated plate and pour over them the hot sauce from the pan. Garnish one side with sour red cabbage, the other with stuffed eggs. Serve with a sour vegetable salad.

SPRING LAMB CHOPS YOU LOVE
Cotlete De Miel La Tava

Remove the bones from a few thick spring lamb chops, flatten a little to give a nice form, then with a sharp knife score the surface. Salt and then fry each in butter slowly just for a few minutes until the meat becomes white on both sides. Remove to a plate. After they are cooled dip them in a sharp sauce (or you may experiment with other sauces to suit your desire), place on a plate and put in the refrigerator. When cooled, dip the chops in well-beaten eggs, dredge in roll crumbs and fry quickly in deep and very hot lard. Arrange on a heated plate and garnish with potato dumplings, kohlrabi fried in butter and mushroom or dill sauce.

MUTTON WITH GARLIC
Carne De Oaie Cu Usturoi

leg of mutton	1 large onion
salt	12 to 14 peppercorns
fresh bacon	1 glass wine vinegar
lard	parsley and thyme
garlic	beef stock

Clean, trim well and flatten a nice leg of mutton. Salt, interlard with garlic and fresh bacon, then sear a little on both sides in lard or bacon fat. Add one sliced large onion, fry a little with the mutton, then add 12 to 14 black peppercorns, one glass of wine vinegar and a little water. Sprinkle with a little chopped parsley and thyme. Cover the casserole tightly and cook for 3 hours, adding from time to time a little beef stock or water, to prevent the sauce from drying out. When the meat is tender,

124 : MEAT DISHES

remove the cover, place the casserole in the oven under the flame and brown nicely, basting the mutton now and then with the sauce in the casserole.

Put the leg of mutton on a board, cut into slices and arrange on a hot platter. Garnish with fried mushrooms, stuffed green peppers or tomatoes. Serve with garlic, cucumber, sour or mustard sauce. It can also be served cold with red beets, capers, red cabbage or freshly shredded horseradish.

MUTTON LEG ALA FLORA
Carne De Oaie Ala Flora

leg of mutton	2 red peppers
fresh bacon	butter
salt	parsley, thyme and chives
garlic	½ glass red wine
2 each	wine vinegar
onions, parsley roots	5 to 6 tbs. cream
carrots, parsnip roots	soup stock
14 to 16 peppercorns	1 lemon
2 tbs. fennel	

Clean a leg of mutton and trim well. Salt and let stand. Rub the bottom of a casserole with garlic and cover with cut pieces of fresh bacon. Slice 2 onions, 2 carrots, 2 parsley roots and 2 parsnip roots. Place the onion slices on top of the bacon and add the other sliced vegetables in the order given. Now spread over the surface 14 to 16 peppercorns, 2 tablespoonfuls of fennel, 2 red meaty peppers sliced crosswise (and with the seeds left in) and finally add 3 ounces of butter spread all over in small dots.

Now rub well into the leg of mutton some chopped onion, parsley and thyme, and place the leg on top of the vegetables in the casserole. Pour ½ glass of red wine over the meat and let stand for about 10 minutes. Then pour on a little water and a little wine vinegar. Sprinkle with finely chopped chives and parsley, cover tightly and cook for 2 hours very slowly until tender. Remove the mutton leg, slice and arrange on a heated serving plate. To the sauce remaining in the casserole add 5 to 6 tablespoonfuls of cream and a little soup stock or cold water.

MEAT DISHES : 125

Let boil a little, add the juice of one lemon, and again bring to
a boil. Press the sauce through a sieve over the sliced meat.
Garnish with red or green stuffed tomatoes or stuffed eggs. Serve
with a sour vegetable salad. It is simply delicious.

MEAT PUDDINGS

THE MEAT PUDDINGS are not popular here and are not served
in many homes. Yet they are easy to make, very nutritious and
really a joy to eat. Children as a rule do not relish liver and I
myself felt the same way, until I actually experienced the
delectable liver pudding for myself. I remember, as if it happened yesterday; my first trip to Bucharest. It was after the first
World War, when my province of Transylvania was reunited
with its mother country of Romania after 1,000 years of sub-
jugation. I was very young and unworldly. I came from a land
of deep forests, mountains, valleys, happy running brooks and
patriarchal farms, and landed smack in the center of sophistica-
tion. To the Bucharestians I was nothing but a hick and anyone
seeing my amazed face when I got off the station would have
agreed. The store windows were richly stocked with food, and
after years of war and privation you may well imagine what the
effect was on me. On the sidewalks meats were being broiled
and there was something new that I hadn't seen in my native
Transylvania, the piping hot *pudinga cu carne* or meat puddings, cut into generous squares and inside different meats,
liver, etc. Here in New York, in the large market neighborhoods, delicious old world dishes are similarly prepared and sold
right in the streets, like pizza, knishes, etc.

My uncle and aunt who were my escort forgot their ideas
about propriety and dignity and asked me if I wanted some
meat pudding. I shocked them by not only accepting, but eating quite a few. Of course, when I arrived at our destination,
this did not prevent me from eating a really big luncheon. You
see, all my life I have been rather on the plump side, and enjoyed the eating of good food.

Why not surprise your family some day by making these
puddings and watch the faces of your children. It will give you
an idea how I looked when I first met the Romanian *budinca.*

126 : MEAT DISHES

LIVER PUDDING
Budinca De Ficat

1½ lbs. liver	salt and pepper
1 onion	8 egg yolks
4 tbs. butter	5 to 6 tbs. bread crumbs
marjoram, ginger	flour

Scrape on a meat scraper (or mince) 1½ pounds of liver. Fry one finely chopped onion in a tablespoonful of butter, add this to the liver and combine with one tablespoonful of finely chopped parsley, a little marjoram, pepper to taste and a little ginger. Press through a sieve. Beat 3 tablespoonfuls of butter with a fork to a foam, add the yolks of 8 eggs, and beat well. Add a teaspoonful of salt and combine with the liver. Add 5 to 6 tablespoonfuls of bread or roll crumbs. Mix all well together. Butter a dish, sprinkle over with flour and shake from side to side so the flour lightly covers the butter. Put in the liver mixture and cook in a double boiler. When done, turn over on a serving plate and serve with any sauce of your choice. This dish can also be made from veal, pork, minced chicken or goose.

MEAT PUDDING
Budinca De Carne

1½ lbs. fried veal or	1 roll soaked in milk
leftovers	pepper
1 tbs. sweet butter	flour
10 eggs	

Chop well 1½ pounds of fried veal or leftovers. Beat to a foam one tablespoonful of sweet butter, add the yolks of 10 eggs, mix and combine with one roll soaked in milk and squeezed out, and a little pepper. Add the meat and mix well together. Now beat the whites of 8 eggs and add gently to the mixture. Rub a pudding form with butter, sprinkle with flour and turn into it the meat mixture. Place in a double boiler and cook for 45 minutes. When done, turn out on a large serving plate. Serve with mushroom or butter sauce poured over the pudding.

MEAT DISHES : 127

PUDDING WITH RICE AND TONGUE
Budinca De Orez Cu Limba

Wash well one pound of long kernel rice, then boil in milk
until it swells and becomes tender. Put into a casserole and
while still hot add to it 2 tablespoonfuls of sweet butter and
mix well. When cooled add 5 eggs and a little salt and mix.
Butter very well a pudding form and sprinkle with flour. Line
the dish with very thinly sliced boiled tongue, add the rice
mixture, place in a double boiler and cook for 45 minutes.
When done, turn over on a serving plate and pour on a sauce
to your liking.

PUDDING WITH POTATOES AND HAM
Budinca De Cartofi Cu Sunca

Boil 6 or 7 large potatoes, let cool, then scrape. Beat 2 tablespoonfuls of sweet butter until it foams, then add 6 egg yolks
one by one, mixing in each well before adding the next. Combine with the potatoes, add some salt and mix. Add ½ pound
of lean boiled ham cut into small pieces and mix all well together. Now add the stiff beaten whites of 6 eggs and mix
gently. Place the mixture in a buttered dish and cook for one
hour in a double boiler. Turn over on a plate, sprinkle with
Parmesan cheese and over the cheese pour very hot fresh
butter.

CHOPPED MEAT DISHES AND FILLINGS

CHOPPED MEAT ROLL
Placinta Cu Carne Tocata

Make a strudel dough (see STRUDEL DOUGH) from one pound
of pastry flour. Use chopped meat for a filling (see CHOPPED
MEATS FOR FILLING). Bake in oven to a crisp brown. Cut into
squares and serve plain or with a sauce.

128 : MEAT DISHES

PATTIES WITH CHOPPED MEAT
Pasteu Mic Cu Carne Tocata

Make a dough of butter (see BUTTER DOUGH), stretch to
½-inch thickness and cut with a form medium-sized pieces.
Place on a piece of dough a tablespoonful of chopped meat filling, cover with another piece of dough and press edges of both
together. Avoid breaking the edges. Smear all over with a well-
beaten egg, place them in a baking pan and bake quickly in a
hot oven. Serve hot.

MINCED BEEF FOR FILLINGS
Carne Macinata Pentru Umplaturi

1 lb. beef	parsley, fennel and thyme
½ lb. fresh bacon	2 eggs
1 roll soaked in milk	salt and paper
1 onion	

Mince one pound (or more) of tender beef and mix with
¼-pound of fresh bacon separately chopped. Add to a mixing
bowl one roll soaked in sweet milk and pressed of excess liquid,
one finely chopped small onion, one tablespoonful each of
chopped green parsley and fennel, a little thyme, 2 eggs and salt
and pepper. Mix all together gently but very well with a wooden
spoon. Fry in a deep pan ¼-pound of fresh bacon cut into small
pieces, add the above mixture and when hot, add the meat. Mix
together and simmer for 5 minutes. Use for fillings.

MIXED MINCED MEAT FOR FILLINGS
Carne Macinata Amestecata Pentru Umplaturi

½ lb. beef	salt and pepper
½ lb. pork	½ cup uncooked rice
¼ lb. fresh bacon	1 egg
1 onion	thyme and dill
parsley, fennel, scallions	

Mince ½-pound of beef, ½-pound of pork and ¼-pound of
fresh pork bacon. Fry the bacon, then add one finely chopped

MEAT DISHES : 129

onion, one tablespoonful each of finely chopped parsley, fennel and green scallions and salt and pepper to taste, and fry for 6 to 8 minutes. Add ½ cup of rice well rinsed in cold water, mix and fry a little longer. Now add the meat, sear quickly, remove from the fire and let cool. Add one egg, salt and pepper, a little thyme crushed in your palms and a little powdered dill. Mix well. Use this mixture for stuffing green peppers, pickled cabbage leaves, kohlrabi and green vine leaves.

MINCED VEAL FILLINGS
Carne De Vitel Macinata Pentru Umplaturi

1 lb. cooked veal	salt and pepper
2 tbs. butter	1 roll soaked in milk
2 onions	2 eggs
parsley, fennel and thyme	2 tbs. cream

Mince one pound of cold fried or roasted veal. Fry in 2 table-spoonfuls of butter 2 finely chopped onions. Add one table-spoonful of chopped parsley and fennel, a little thyme and salt and pepper to taste. When all are fried together, place in a mixing bowl. Add one roll soaked in milk and pressed out and 2 eggs. Combine with the meat, add 2 tablespoonfuls of cream and mix together. Use for fillings or shape into small sausages or balls. Roll the balls in beaten eggs, then in crumbs and fry in hot butter quickly. This meat mix can be used in puddings and in soups.

MINCED COLD MEATS
Carnuri Amestecate Raci

Mince ½-pound of any kind of cold meat and ½-pound of boiled ham. Mix with a tablespoonful each of finely chopped parsley and fennel and a little thyme. Beat to a foam one table-spoonful of butter in a bowl, add 3 eggs slightly beaten, then combine with the meat. Add salt and pepper and 3 tablespoon-fuls of cream and mix very well. Use for filling potatoes, squashes, puddings and patties.

130 : MEAT DISHES

MINCED LAMB MEAT
Carne Macinatà De Oaie

1 lb. lamb meat	1 egg
2 large onions	bread soaked in milk
2 tbs. bacon drippings	salt and pepper
parsley and marjoram	3 tbs. cream
2 tbs. uncooked rice	

Mince one pound of young lamb meat. Fry 2 large, finely chopped onions in 2 tablespoonfuls of bacon drippings or lard. Add one tablespoonful each of finely chopped parsley and marjoram and fry a little longer. Add 2 tablespoonfuls of washed rice, mix and simmer for 5 minutes. Put the minced meat in a mixing bowl, add one egg and a little bread soaked in milk and pressed free of excess liquid. Add the rice mixture, salt and pepper to taste and 3 tablespoonfuls of cream. Mix all well together. Use for filling turnips, vine leaves, tomatoes and green peppers.

MINCED LAMB EXTRAS FILLING
Maruntaie De Oaie Macinate Pentru Umplatura

lamb extras	1 or 2 cloves
carrot	salt and pepper
parsley root, parsnip root	2 tbs. bacon drippings
laurel leaf	parsley and marjoram
12 peppercorns	1 tbs. bread crumbs
6 to 8 onions	2 tbs. sour cream

Boil the extras of a young lamb with one carrot, one parsley root, one parsnip root, one laurel leaf, 12 peppercorns, 2 or 3 onions, 1 or 2 cloves and salt to taste. When the extras are done, remove to a board, let cool, then mince. Fry in a casserole in 2 tablespoonfuls of bacon drippings or lard, 4 or 5 finely chopped onions to a nice brown. Add the minced meat and mix well. Now add one tablespoonful of finely chopped parsley, a little marjoram, a little salt and pepper and one tablespoonful of bread crumbs and mix well. Then add 2 tablespoonfuls of heavy sour cream and mix. Use as a filling for strudel (see STRUDEL), also for soups.

MEAT DISHES : 131

MINCED MEAT FILLING FOR PATTIES
Carne Macinata Pentru Pasteuri

Mince 1¼-pounds of tender beef and 1¼-pounds of pork meat. Rub a casserole with garlic and fry in it one pound of chopped onions with ¼-pound of fresh bacon or lard. Add one tablespoonful of chopped parsley, a little ginger and lovage, 2 tablespoonfuls of cream and salt and pepper. Mix and simmer a few minutes. Add the meat and mix well. Cook until the liquid is absorbed, stirring from time to time to prevent burning. When the meat starts to brown, remove from the fire and let cool. Use for the filling of patties.

MINCED FILLING FOR CHICKEN
Pui Macinata Pentru Umplaturi

Mince 4 chicken livers. Fry one finely chopped onion in 2 tablespoonfuls of butter. While frying add a little finely chopped green parsley and fennel and salt and pepper to taste. Soak 2 small rolls in milk, press out the excess liquid and put into a bowl with 3 eggs. Add the onion mixture, mix, then add the liver and again mix all gently together. Use to fill the chicken.

FILLING FOR BREAST OF VEAL OR YOUNG LAMB
Umplaturi Pentru Piept De Vitel or Miel

Beat with a fork in a casserole one tablespoonful of butter to a foam. Add 4 eggs and beat well together. Now add one tablespoonful of finely chopped chives, ½ tablespoonful of green parsley, salt and pepper to taste and one cup of biscuit crumbs soaked in milk. Mix together to make a soft dough and use to fill veal or lamb breast.

FILLING OF HAM
Umplatura De Sunca

Fry 10 sprigs of finely chopped chives in ¼-pound of butter or lard. Add some finely chopped green parsley and simmer for

132 : MEAT DISHES

6 to 8 minutes. Cool, then add one roll soaked in beef broth and squeezed of excess liquid, salt and pepper to taste and 2 eggs, then mix. Chop ¾-pound of boiled lean ham and add to the above mixture. Mix again well. Use for filling breast of veal, chicken or squash.

FILLING FOR FISH
Umplatura Pentru Peste

Fry in a pan 5 large, finely chopped onions in a large tablespoonful of bacon drippings or lard. When the onions are fried, remove from the fire, add 4 tablespoonfuls of washed and half-boiled rice, salt and pepper to taste and a few sprigs of green parsley finely chopped. Mix all together well. If you wish you can add small black raisins. Use to fill a fish.

NUT FILLING FOR FISH
Umplatura De Nuca Pentru Peste

Fry 6 finely chopped onions in 2 large tablespoonfuls of lard or butter. When the onions are fried, remove from the fire. Add one slice of bread soaked in water and squeezed out, salt and pepper to taste, one cup of chopped walnuts and the grated peel of 1½ lemons. Mix all these ingredients together well. Use to fill a fish.

MUSHROOM FILLING
Umplatura De Ciuperci

Fry in a tightly covered casserole with 2 tablespoonfuls of butter, 15 to 20 mushrooms, together with a few finely chopped sprigs of chives and parsley. When fried, remove from the fire and let cool. Soak one roll in milk, press out excess liquid, add one whole egg and the yolks of 2 eggs, one chopped liver of a goose or capon and salt and pepper to taste. Now mix gently and very well all the ingredients. Use for filling breast of veal or lamb or chicken.

MEAT DISHES : 133

MIXED MEAT BALLS
Perisoare De Carne Amestecata

½ lb. lean pork   salt and pepper
½ lb. veal   eggs
parsley and fennel   crumbs
1 roll   lard
1 onion

Please try this excellent hot appetizer. Put through the meat chopper ½-pound of lean pork meat, ½-pound of veal and a few sprigs of parsley and fennel. Place in a bowl and add one dry roll which is first soaked in water or milk and then squeezed of excess liquid, one finely chopped onion and salt and pepper to taste. Mix together well.

Dip your hands in cold water, take small portions of the chopped meat and form into small balls. Roll them in eggs, then in crumbs. Place on a board, let stand, then fry them in a large frying pan in a generous quantity of very hot deep lard. Drain off the excess fat of the meat balls on brown paper. Serve quickly very hot in a heated serving dish with toothpicks stuck in the meat balls. Serve with little sour pickles. The meat may be kept in the refrigerator. When needed, just fry for a few minutes and serve. They are a fine after theatre snack.

BEEF MEAT BALLS
Perisoare De Carne De Vaca

Prepare exactly as above, but make the meat balls bigger and flatter and fry very quickly in deep fat on both sides. Serve hot with a sauce of your choice.

LIVER BALLS
Perisoare De Ficat

Prepare as the mixed meat balls, except that you will chop the liver by hand, fry in butter and add also some finely chopped scallions to the liver.

134 : MEAT DISHES

BRAINS BALLS
Perisoare De Creeri

Prepare as the meat balls, except that you will first boil the brains till tender and then chop by hand. Add only to the brains a little flour when mixing and form the balls flat and as large as the beef balls. Serve with mushrooms in any style.

MEAT BALLS IN WINE SAUCE
Perisoare in Sos De Vin

1 lb. beef	2 laurel leaves
onion, parsley and fennel	6 to 8 peppercorns
salt and pepper	hot paprika
1 egg	½ cup stock
flour	peel of ½ lemon
bacon drippings	sour cream
wine	Brown Sauce

Chop one pound of inexpensive beef, place in a mixing bowl one finely chopped large onion and one tablespoonful each of chopped parsley and fennel. Mix well. Add salt and pepper to taste and one egg, mix together and shape into flat balls. Dredge in flour and fry in very hot and deep bacon drippings or lard to a nice brown on both sides. Remove to a plate and cover to keep hot, while you make a brown sauce. Prepare the sauce with some of the fat in which the meat balls were fried (see BROWN SAUCE). Thin the sauce with wine, add 2 laurel leaves, 6 to 8 black peppercorns, salt and pepper, a little hot paprika and ½ cup of stock or bouillon cubes dissolved in water. Bring to a boil, then add to it the meat balls and sprinkle with the grated peel of ½ lemon. Simmer slowly for 10 to 15 minutes. Serve hot topped with one tablespoonful of sour cream, garnished with dumplings or potatoes and sour vegetable salad.

MEAT BALLS WITH RAISINS
Perisoare De Carne Cu Stafide

Prepare exactly as above, but in the sauce omit the wine and use instead wine vinegar and one cup of raisins first soaked in sugared water and then drained of liquid.

MEAT DISHES : 135

CHOPPED MIXED MEAT FOR FILLINGS
Carne Tocata Pentru Umplaturi

¾ lb. pork
¾ lb. beef
¼ lb. bacon
bacon drippings
1 small onion

4 tbs. uncooked rice
parsley, scallions, thyme
salt and pepper
1 or 2 eggs

Chop together ¾-pound of pork and ¾-pound of beef (tender cut) and mix with ¼-pound of chopped bacon. Fry one small finely chopped onion in one tablespoonful of very hot bacon drippings. When golden brown add 4 tablespoonfuls of well-washed rice and stir. Fry until the rice is dry and remove from the fire.

Add a little bacon drippings to another pan and when very hot add the chopped meat and one tablespoonful each of finely chopped parsley and green scallions. Sear for a few minutes, stirring constantly, then reduce the heat, add salt and pepper, mix and when the heat has penetrated through the meat, remove from the fire.

Place in a bowl the ingredients of both frying pans. Add ¼-pound of chopped bacon and 1 or 2 eggs. Mix well together. Taste and if needed add more salt and pepper. Add a little thyme and mix again.

Use for stuffing sauerkraut leaves and fresh cabbage (see STUFFED SAUERKRAUT LEAVES and STUFFED FRESH CABBAGE).

OLD FASHIONED CHOPPED MEAT FOR FILLINGS OR MEAT BALLS
Carne Tocata Pentru Umplaturi or Perisoare Moda Veche

Chop together ½-pound of pork and ½-pound of beef. Fry in an iron pan ¼-pound of bacon and ¼-pound of smoked raw ham, each diced very small. Add ½ cup of well-washed rice, stir and continue heating until the rice is dry. Add the meat, salt and pepper to taste and ½ teaspoonful each of powdered thyme and dill. Mix well and fry until the heat has penetrated through the meat. Let cool, remove the meat to a bowl, add 2

136 : MEAT DISHES

eggs and mix well. Use for filling sour or pickled cabbage leaves, green peppers, kohlrabi and squash.

CHOPPED VEAL AND PORK FOR FILLINGS OR MEAT BALLS
Carne Tocata De Vitel Si Porc Pentru Umplaturi or Perisoare

Prepare exactly the same as above, except that you replace the rice with stale bread or roll, moistened in milk or water, and instead of bacon or pork use butter.

CHOPPED LAMB FOR FILLINGS OR MEAT BALLS
Carne De Oaie Tocata Pentru Umplaturi or Perisoare

Prepare as above either with rice or with roll or bread crumbs. Instead of fats or butter, use pure olive oil.

CHOPPED LAMB MEAT SURPRISE
Surpriza De Carne De Oaie Tocata

Grind 1½-pounds of rather lean lamb meat, well trimmed of fat. Chop finely 3 onions, 2 large meaty green peppers and enough peeled tomatoes to make 2 cups. Add 2 tablespoonfuls of finely chopped parsley, one tablespoonful of finely chopped fennel, a little marjoram and salt and pepper to taste. Mix all together well.

Prepare a biscuit dough and roll into any shape you like or cut in forms. Cover dough with the meat mixture and bake for 40 to 45 minutes. Serve hot with sour cream or lemon sauce.

BROILED MIXED CHOPPED MEAT SURPRISE
Surpriza De Carne Amestecata Tocata Le Gratar

Have your butcher grind 1½-pounds of leg of lamb and ½-pound of round steak. Place in a large mixing bowl. Add 2

MEAT DISHES : 137

tablespoonfuls of chopped scallions, 2 tablespoonfuls of chopped parsley, one tablespoonful of fennel, a little thyme, salt and pepper to taste, a pinch of dried crushed tabasco peppers and the yolks of 2 eggs. Mix well with the hands and shape into pork sausage forms. Put them on a pan broiler and broil to a nice brown, turning constantly to broil evenly. When done, serve quickly on a heated plate with potatoes and French mustard, and a mixed vegetable bowl.

CHOPPED MEAT LOAF
Carne Tocata La Tava

1½ lbs. top round steak	2 tbs. bacon drippings
½ lb. shoulder of pork	parsley, fennel, green garlic
6 slices bacon	salt and pepper
5 slices bread	5 eggs
1 large onion	½ cup stock

Grind together 1½-pounds of top round steak and ½-pound of pork shoulder. Take the crust off 5 slices of white bread and soak in water. Put the bread into a large mixing bowl and add the meat. Fry one large onion finely chopped to a nice golden color in 2 tablespoonfuls of bacon drippings. Add one tablespoonful each of finely chopped parsley, fennel and green garlic (if obtainable), and salt and pepper to taste and fry a little longer. Let cool, then add the fried mixture to the meat and bread in the bowl and add one egg, and the yolk of one egg (the white will be used for smearing the meat loaf). Then add slowly ½ cup of stock of broth and mix gently. Now add 3 chopped hard-boiled eggs and mix together.

Grease a baking dish, put 3 slices of bacon on the bottom, form your meat loaf and place it gently on the bacon. Beat the white of the egg and with a feather or a brush smear the whole of the meat loaf, including the bottom. Place 2 or 3 slices of bacon on top and bake in a moderate oven. Baste frequently with hot stock or boiling water, later with the liquid from the dish. Bake for 1 to 1½ hours. Serve hot or cold with cheese sauce.

138 : MEAT DISHES

GRAPEVINE LEAVES STUFFED WITH LAMB
Sarmale Cu Foi De Vita Cu Carne De Oaie

1 lb. lamb
2 slices bacon
olive oil
1 onion
parsley, fennel and chives
thyme or dill

4 tbs. uncooked rice
salt and pepper
grape vine leaves
sauerkraut juice
cream

Sear one pound of not too finely chopped lamb meat in 2 tablespoonfuls of olive oil or small pieces of bacon together with one finely chopped onion, one tablespoonful each of finely chopped parsley and fennel and a little thyme or dill. When done, cover and let cool. Smooth out enough grape vine leaves to hold the chopped meat. Scald with salted water. If you use grape vine leaves preserved in salt, then keep in cold water overnight, rinse, then smooth out the leaves. Mix the cooled meat with 4 tablespoonfuls of rinsed rice and salt and pepper to taste. Now place a full teaspoonful of mixed meat on a leaf, turn in both sides, then roll loosely and tuck in the ends of the roll.

Butter an earthenware casserole and place on the bottom a few chopped leaves and a few sprigs of parsley and chives. Now put in the rolls, placed next to each other. On top place chopped leaves (or not too sour sauerkraut), 2 slices of bacon and a little thyme or dill. Continue to alternate these layers, until you finish with the rolls. Cover the top with chopped leaves or sauerkraut and pour on ½ cup of hot bacon drippings or pure olive oil (or any good fat). Then add salt and pepper.

Cover with sauerkraut juice (if too sour, dilute with water). If not available, then use lemon juice diluted with water. Let stand, tightly covered, for 1 to 2 hours. Then place on the fire and simmer slowly until cooked, shaking the casserole from time to time, to prevent burning. Serve on a heated plate topped with a generous portion of heavy sweet or sour cream. Sprinkle with chopped fresh dill or parsley.

STEWS

There is hardly a people on this earth which does not prepare stews in one form or another. Not only has this delectable dish a changing personality from country to country, but in each nation there are variations in different regions and even from household to household. No two dishes can ever be made exactly alike. This is because no two people are alike. A pinch of a fragrant herb will vary with different size of fingers and this immediately will cause a difference in the result. Remember that the fingers are still a measuring tool in many parts of the world. Also the tongue and the nose are of the greatest importance in creating a new dish or duplicating something you have eaten. Have you ever partaken of something really tasty, perhaps a well-known dish with a trace of something new? I have many times, but very often I do not ask the hostess for her recipe. I try to recreate it in my kitchen. Sometimes I get just the right flavor, and sometimes even an improvement.

Even to this day I keep trying to get exactly the same delicious flavor that I remember my beloved *bunica* (grandmother) got in her cooking. One day I was attempting to create a stew, but somehow it was not like grandmother's. Something was missing.

140 : STEWS

Then I thought of a certain herb, but the name escaped me. Perhaps my friend who lives nearby could help me. She was none other than Romany Marie. Who has not heard of her charming little Bohemian restaurant in the heart of Greenwich Village, New York? For 40 years, together with Dr. Damon Marchand, her husband and partner in life, they have been hosts to artists, writers, royalty and people who accomplished much and those who as yet had only dreams of doing great things. They both loved people, that was the secret of their success. People came to confide in them, to talk over their problems and worries, and always came away with renewed confidence in their own capacities and in what life had as yet to unfold to them. They were both patrons of the artists, and when necessary (and that happened often) fed them in their early struggling days. Who will ever forget, after a visit to Marie's, the delicious Romanian stews and ciorbas, with fresh green dill floating lavishly on the surface! Or the colorful stories and piquant incidents that they related with so much gusto.

Luckily, Marie was in. I wanted the name of a certain herb and started to describe it. "It is used to flavor stews, soups and in preparing wild game. In Romania some of it is tied around a baby's wrist as the babies love to suck on it." You see, they are both Romanians, having come to America 50 years ago.

"I know what it is," she replied. "It is sas—sas—yes, sassafras."

Do you know that right here in New York you can eat nearly 50 different nationality stews? Of course you will have to get off the beaten path, visit strange neighborhoods, go into little hidden streets, climb stairs or go into cellar taverns. But for your trouble you will be rewarded. You will get the feel of the "old country" there, and truly native dishes which have not been changed in any way. You will hear strange tongues, and in your imagination you will be traveling to the far corners of the earth. You will love it. There will be plenty to tell your family and friends and there will be memories that will remain with you always.

All the stews given here can be made from the inexpensive cuts of meat. Despite this, they are truly delicious. Not much work is required in making them. They can be kept for 2 or 3 days and all you have to do when reheating is to use a double boiler and serve with a little wine or brandy added to the stew.

STEWS : 141

STEW OF CHICKEN LIVER
Tocana De Carne De Pui

1 lb. chicken livers	1 glass brandy
salt	1 glass sherry
chives, parsley, fennel	¼ cup sour cream
3 tbs. butter	

This is excellent for Sunday brunch. Get one pound of fresh chicken livers, rinse them in cold water, salt, place in a dish, cover and put into the refrigerator for use the following day. Before starting to prepare this dish, have your table set and place the serving plates on the stove to heat up, as it must be eaten immediately when finished to have the livers at the peak of their flavor.

Remove the livers from the refrigerator, rinse off the salt with cold water and let stand, while you chop finely enough chives, parsley and fennel to make one tablespoonful each. Place 3 or more tablespoonfuls of butter in a large frying pan, heat, put in the chopped greens, stir well, cover the pan and cook slowly for 8 to 10 minutes. Now increase the flame to a high heat, put in the whole livers (or you may cut them into halves), sear for 2 or 3 minutes, stirring constantly, and add quickly one glass of brandy. Ignite with a lighted match, cover the pan for a second, add one glass of sherry, mix, then add ¼ cup of sour cream and stir constantly until it is well blended. While it is slowly cooking, add a little finely chopped parsley. Bring nearly to the boiling point, but do not boil. Remove from the flame and serve immediately on very hot plates. Eat with fresh rye or French bread and use the bread to dunk up all of the sauce. Do not waste any of it. Leave your plate dry. Serve hot coffee with it.

CHICKEN LIVER WITH ONIONS
Ficat De Pui Cu Ciapa

Prepare ¼ pound of chicken livers as above. Heat in an iron frying pan 1 to 2 tablespoonfuls of bacon drippings and when very hot add 2 chopped onions and fry to a golden brown. Add one tablespoonful of chopped parsley, simmer for 1 to 2 minutes, raise the heat and add the chicken livers (whole or cut into

142 : STEWS

halves). Sear for a few minutes, stirring constantly. Now lower the heat, add one glass of white wine and continue to heat for 5 or 6 minutes more, with stirring. Serve quickly on a hot plate.

GOOSE LIVER STEW PEASANT STYLE
Tocana De Ficat De Gasca Stil Taranesc

1½ lbs. goose liver	½ pt. sour cream
2 tbs. bacon drippings	¼ cup beef soup
1 onion	salt and pepper
parsley and sweet marjoram	

In a casserole to which has been added 2 tablespoonfuls of bacon drippings fry one sliced onion to a golden brown. Add one tablespoonful of finely chopped parsley and a little finely chopped sweet marjoram, stir and add 1½ pounds of goose liver cut into pieces. Sear for a few minutes on a quick flame, then lower the heat and add ½ pint of sour cream. Simmer a little, then add ¼ cup of beef soup or bouillon and cook until tender. Add salt and pepper and sprinkle with finely chopped parsley. Serve hot with rice, asparagus or fried potatoes and a vegetable salad.

SPRING CHICKEN STEW PEASANT STYLE
Tocana De Pui Stil Taranesc

2 or 3 spring chickens	salt
5 or 6 onions, chopped	4 or 5 tbs. sour cream
3 tbs. lard	beef soup or water
dried tabasco peppers	fennel, parsley and dill

Clean 2 or 3 spring chicken and cut into pieces. Fry 5 or 6 onions, chopped into small pieces, to a golden brown in a casserole with 3 tablespoonfuls of lard. Add the cut up chicken to the casserole. Add a pinch of crushed dried tabasco peppers, salt, cover the casserole and cook until the liquid is absorbed, stirring from time to time. When no liquid remains, add 4 or 5 tablespoonfuls of sour cream, simmer for 5 minutes, then add enough beef soup or water to just cover the chicken, one table-

STEWS : 143

spoonful of finely chopped fennel, one tablespoonful of finely chopped parsley and a little dill. Cover and cook for ½ hour, then serve hot with butter dumplings, noodles or potatoes fried in butter.

CHICKEN STEW WITH TOMATOES
Tocana De Pui Cu Tomate

Prepare exactly as above, but instead of soup or water use strained tomato juice. Serve the stew topped with a tablespoonful of sour cream.

CHICKEN STEW WITH TARRAGON
Tocana De Pui Cu Tarcon

2 chickens	1 tbs. flour
garlic	wine
4 tbs. lard or butter	salt and pepper
scallions, parsley, tarragon	

Clean, wash and cut into pieces 2 spring chickens. Rub the bottom of a casserole with a little garlic, add 3 tablespoonfuls of lard or butter and when very hot sear the chicken quickly. Cover and let stand. Prepare a sauce in a saucepan as follows. Place one tablespoonful of lard or 1½ tablespoonfuls of butter in a saucepan and when very hot put in one tablespoonful of chopped green scallion and one tablespoonful of chopped parsley. Fry for 2 to 3 minutes. Add one tablespoonful of flour, mix and brown. Now thin with enough wine which has been diluted with a little water to make a good sauce, not too thick. Add salt and pepper to taste, mix, then put in 2 tablespoonfuls of finely chopped tarragon, mix again and cook for 2 to 3 minutes.

Heat up the chicken in the casserole and when hot pour the sauce over it slowly. Stir well, cover tightly, then cook slowly until tender. Stir from time to time, also shake the casserole. Serve topped with sour cream and sprinkled with finely chopped parsley. Garnish with dumplings or slices of mamaliga.

144 : STEWS

SPRING CHICKEN STEW IN CREAM
Tocana De Pui Cu Smantana

1 broiling chicken	2 eggs
5 tbs. butter	farina
parsley, green scallions	salt and pepper
1 pt. cream	

Cut a broiling chicken into small pieces. In a deep frying dish holding 4 tablespoonfuls of butter fry one tablespoonful of chopped parsley and a goodly portion of finely chopped green scallions until nice and tender. Add the cut chicken pieces and fry with constant stirring until they get a little color. Add slowly one pint of cream and simmer for 10 minutes with stirring. Now add enough water to cover the chicken, stir, add salt and a little pepper, cover the dish and simmer while you prepare quickly the farina balls as follows. Beat one tablespoonful of butter, chicken fat or lard in a bowl to a foam. Add 2 eggs, beat well together and add the farina, letting it trickle slowly through your fingers, while stirring constantly in one direction. When the mixture is rather soft and very light, pick up with a teaspoon, which has first been wetted in the frying dish, about ½ teaspoonful of farina mixture and drop into the dish holding the chicken. Move the chicken to one side, so it will be easier to reach the liquid while dipping the teaspoon into it. When finished dropping the farina mixture into the liquid, cover and cook until the farina balls are done. Serve hot with a vegetable salad of your choice.

VEAL STEW
Tocana De Vitel

2 lbs. shoulder of veal	dried tabasco peppers
garlic	salt
3 tbs. lard	fennel
7 or 8 large onions	sour cream

Cut 2 pounds of veal shoulder into pieces. Rub the bottom of a casserole with a little garlic, add 3 tablespoonfuls of lard and fry in it 7 or 8 large onions cut into thin slices to a golden brown. Add a pinch of crushed dried tabasco peppers, stir, then

STEWS : 145

add the meat. Salt to taste, add a tablespoonful of finely chopped fennel, cover the casserole tightly and cook slowly until the juice is all absorbed. Stir from time to time to prevent burning. Add 2 tablespoonfuls of sour cream and simmer for 5 to 8 minutes. Add enough water to cover the meat, cover the casserole tightly and cook slowly for one hour. Serve hot with rice fried in butter, farina balls or dumplings. Sprinkle with finely chopped parsley.

VEAL STEW IN WINE
Tocana De Vitel In Vin

breast of veal	1 glass white wine
flour	sour cream
4 tbs. lard	2 cups broth
1 small onion	1 egg
fennel, parsley, thyme	1 lemon
2 tomatoes	salt and pepper

Buy a nice piece of breast of veal, have the bones cracked by the butcher, wipe and dredge in flour. Heat in a deep iron pan 3 tablespoonfuls of lard or even better, bacon drippings, and when hot fry a finely chopped small onion to a nice brown. Add one tablespoonful each of chopped parsley and fennel and simmer slowly. Heat in a separate pan one tablespoonful of lard and when very hot sear the meat quickly to crispness and a brown color on both sides. Add the veal to the simmering greens and on top of the meat place 2 sliced tomatoes and sprinkle with a little thyme. Into the pan where you seared the meat add a glass of white wine, bring it to a boil and pour this over the tomatoes. Boil slowly for one hour, then add 2 or 3 tablespoonfuls of sour cream and one cup of hot broth, and continue cooking until tender.

Make a sauce as follows. Mix one well-beaten egg with the juice of one lemon and add to it slowly one cup of broth. Heat over a slow fire, stirring constantly, until the sauce is thick, but be careful not to boil. Add salt and pepper. When ready to serve, pour the sauce over the meat and sprinkle with a little finely chopped parsley. A very delicious dish, becoming even more tasty the following day. When reheating use a double boiler.

146 : STEWS

VEAL STEW FROM THE NECK
Tocana De Vitel Grumazi

Prepare exactly as above, replacing the cup of broth with a cup of clear tomato juice. Instead of the egg and lemon sauce use sour cream and sprinkle with dill instead of parsley.

VEAL STEW FROM THE SHOULDER
Tocana De Vitel Dela Umeri

Prepare exactly as VEAL STEW IN WINE, replacing the egg and lemon sauce with sour cream. Serve with butter dumplings.

VEAL STEW WITH VEGETABLES
Tocana De Vitel Cu Zarzavaturi

3 lbs. veal shank	1 branch celery
1 bunch scallions	1 small onion
3 tbs. lard or bacon drip-	3 tomatoes
pings	1½ lemons
1 tbs. parsley	2 cups broth
1 large carrot	salt and pepper
1 parsley root	½ cup cream

Cut 3 pounds of veal shank into pieces. Fry a bunch of finely chopped scallions in 3 tablespoonfuls of lard or bacon drippings, add one tablespoonful of finely chopped parsley and simmer until tender. Add the meat and sear quickly on a high flame, with constant stirring, until brown. Lower the heat. Add one large carrot, one parsley root, one branch of celery, one small onion and 3 tomatoes, all these being sliced crosswise, the grated peel of ½ lemon, one cup of hot broth and salt and pepper to taste. Cover tightly and cook slowly for one hour, shaking the dish from time to time. Now add slowly ½ cup of cream well beaten with the juice of one lemon. Pour over one cup of broth, cover and continue cooking until tender. Serve hot with potato dumplings.

STEWS : 147

VEAL STEW WITH MUSHROOMS
Tocana de Vitel Cu Ciuperci

2 lbs. veal	¼ lb. mushrooms
5 tbs. sweet butter	2 tbs. sour cream
garlic	salt and pepper
1 large onion	1 cup soup stock
parsley and thyme	

Cut 2 pounds of veal into pieces and sear quickly in 2 tablespoonfuls of sweet butter in a deep frying pan rubbed very well with garlic. When nicely browned, reduce the heat and add 3 more tablespoonfuls of butter, one large chopped onion and one tablespoonful of finely chopped parsley. Stir together and fry until brown. Now add ¼ pound of sliced mushrooms, 2 tablespoonfuls of sour cream, a pinch of thyme, salt and pepper to taste and one cup of soup stock. Cover tightly and cook slowly until the meat is tender. Serve hot, garnished with dumplings or potatoes, with sharp peppers on the side.

PORK STEW
Tocana De Porc

2 lbs. pork meat	2 glasses white wine
garlic	beef stock
3 tbs. lard	2 tomatoes
12 large onions	thyme
dried tabasco peppers	1 small glass brandy
pepper and salt	sour cream

Wipe clean 2 pounds of pork meat, trim off fat, flatten with a wood hammer and cut into large cubes. Rub the bottom of a casserole with a little garlic, put in 3 tablespoonfuls of lard (or an equivalent amount of the fat you have trimmed off) and when hot, add 12 large onions sliced very thin and fry to a golden color with the casserole uncovered. Add a pinch of crushed dried tabasco peppers, stir, then add the meat. Cover tightly and cook, stirring from time to time to avoid burning. When the liquid is absorbed, sprinkle with pepper and salt to taste and add a glass of white wine. Cover and continue to cook slowly. Stir frequently. Add some beef stock, 2 tomatoes sliced cross-

148 : STEWS

wise and a good pinch of thyme. Stir and add slowly some more beef stock and cook on a low flame until meat is tender. Shortly before meat is done, add one more glass of wine and cook a little while longer. When meat is tender, see that you have enough sauce to supply each serving. Pour on a small glass of brandy and top with 4 tablespoonfuls of sour cream. Serve very hot on heated plates, garnished with fried or boiled potatoes and sour pickles in dill or sour vegetables.

PORK STEW WITH POTATOES
Tocana De Porc Cu Cartofi

Prepare the same as above, execpt that you omit the brandy and replace the wine with tomato juice. About 15 minutes before the meat is tender, add 4 large potatoes cut into cubes, ½ cup of sour cream and one large red or green pepper, sliced crosswise. Cover tightly and cook until done. Add more stock if needed. Serve hot with red cabbage and mamaliga.

PORK STEW PEASANT STYLE
Tocana De Porc Stil Taranesc

3 lbs. pork shoulder	parsley, caraway seeds
8 onions	salt and pepper
1 tbs. lard	stock or water
garlic	1 tbs. sweet paprika
2 lbs. sauer kraut	1 cup sour cream
thyme, dill, fennel, leek	

Trim some of the fat from 3 pounds of pork shoulder. Fry the fat in a large iron pan. Meanwhile slice 8 onions. Remove the pork shoulder fat from the pan and skim off all except about 5 tablespoonfuls of the fat. Add the onions and fry to a golden color. Cut the meat into large pieces (as pork reduces in size quicker than other meats), place in another frying pan with a tablespoonful of lard and sear quickly, with constant stirring. Cover and let stand.

Rub the bottom of a casserole very well with garlic and place the fried onions in it. When the casserole has been heated up

STEWS : 149

add 2 pounds of sauerkraut squeezed of all juice. Heat on a high flame for 5 to 6 minutes with constant stirring, then sprinkle with one tablespoonful of thyme and one tablespoonful of chopped dill (if dry, crush between your palms over the mixture). Mix together and add one tablespoonful of chopped fennel, one of leek and a little parsley and simmer for a few minutes. Now add the meat, sprinkle with a little caraway seeds, stir, add salt and pepper to taste and slowly add stock or water until the meat is just covered. Cook slowly for one hour or until the meat is tender. About 15 minutes before ready to serve add one tablespoonful of red sweet paprika and one cup of sour cream and simmer slowly until ready. Serve on a hot plate. Delicious with mamaliga or fresh pumpernickel or rye bread. It will keep for a whole week. For reheating use a double boiler. Serve with a topping of one tablespoonful of sour cream, but it is equally good without it.

BEEF STEW
Tocana De Carne De Vaca

Prepare the same as the PORK STEW, but cook longer. Cook slowly covered for 2 hours or until tender. Serve with dumplings or mamaliga.

BEEF STEW IN ALE
Tocana De Vaca Cu Bere

2 lbs. beef stew	parsley, fennel, thyme
garlic	½ tsp. red paprika
5 tbs. bacon drippings	1 tbs. butter
4 onions	1 tbs. flour
1 bottle ale	stock
salt and pepper	sour cream

Get 2 pounds of good beef for stewing, wipe and cut into cubes. Rub the bottom of a frying pan with a little garlic, add 2 tablespoonfuls of bacon drippings, and when very hot sear the meat for a few minutes, stirring constantly. Let stand while you fry 4 thinly sliced onions in 3 tablespoonfuls of lard or

150 : STEWS

bacon drippings to a golden brown. Add the meat from the pan, stir and let simmer slowly.

Add one bottle of ale to the pan in which the meat was sautéed and heat. Uncover the casserole which contains the meat, bring to a boil, and, stirring constantly, add enough of the ale to just cover the meat. Cook 10 minutes uncovered, add salt and pepper to taste, one tablespoonful of chopped fennel, one crushed clove of garlic, one tablespoonful of finely chopped parsley, a little thyme and ½ teaspoonful of red paprika, and let simmer while you prepare the following sauce. Blend one tablespoonful of butter with one tablespoonful of flour and thin with a little stock or water. Pour the sauce over the meat, add one cup of sour cream, stir together and continue to cook until the meat is tender. Serve with slices of mamaliga or dumplings and a sour salad.

BEEF STEW WITH POTATOES
Tocana De Carne De Vaca Cu Cartofi

Prepare the same as the PORK STEW WITH POTATOES, but cook longer, about 2 hours, or until tender.

MIXED MEAT STEW
Tocana De Carnuri Amestecate

1 lb. chuck beef	3 or 4 large tomatoes
1 lb. neck veal	1 carrot
2 lbs. spareribs	parsley, tarragon, thyme
garlic	3 tbs. sour cream
3 tbs. bacon drippings	beef stock
4 onions	

Cut into pieces one pound of chuck beef, one pound of veal from the neck and 2 pounds of spareribs (ask the butcher to crack the ribs in two). Rub an iron casserole with garlic, add 3 tablespoonfuls of bacon drippings or lard and when very hot, add the meat and sear quickly to a nice color, stirring constantly to prevent burning. Add 4 onions (finely chopped in advance), stir together, cover the casserole, reduce the heat and fry slowly until the onions are golden colored. Stir from time to time to

STEWS : 151

avoid burning. Add 3 or 4 large sized peeled tomatoes or a pound can of whole tomatoes (retain the juice to be added later). Stir together. Add one tablespoonful each of chopped parsley and tarragon or dill, one carrot thinly sliced and a little thyme. Mix well and cook slowly for ½ hour. Add 3 tablespoonfuls of sour cream, cook for 5 minutes longer, then add the tomato juice from the can. If necessary add beef stock or water slowly, enough to cover the meat. A solution of bouillon cubes can be used instead. Simmer together until the meat is tender. This dish can keep for 2 or 3 days. Serve with dumplings, noodles or macaroni.

LAMB STEW
Tocana De Carne De Oaie

Prepare exactly as the VEAL STEW, except that you will trim the fat from the lamb, sprinkle with salt and pepper, rub with garlic and let stand for ½ hour.

LAMB STEW WITH GREEN HERBS
Tocana De Carne De Oaie Cu Zarzavaturi

3 lbs. stewing lamb	3 tbs. bacon fat
garlic	2 onions
salt	2 tbs. flour
green parsley, fennel, scal-	paprika
lions, shallots	2 tomatoes
1 stalk celery	stock
2 tbs. olive oil	1 glass brandy

Trim very well the fat from 3 pounds of lamb meat for stewing, rub well with crushed garlic, then salt and let stand. Take one bunch of green parsley, fennel, scallions and shallot and one stalk of celery, quickly dip in boiling water, place on a board and chop finely. Place in a pan with 2 tablespoonfuls of olive oil and sear the chopped greens, stirring constantly. Cover and let stand while you cut the meat into pieces.

Put 3 tablespoonfuls of bacon drippings or lard into a casserole and when very hot, add the meat and sear very quickly, but do not burn. Add 2 finely chopped onions, stir well and simmer

152 : STEWS

a little. Sprinkle the meat with 2 tablespoonfuls of flour and brown together at a moderate heat, stirring constantly. Add a little paprika and 2 sliced tomatoes, heat a little, then pour on slowly sufficient stock, a solution of bouillon cubes or water. Simmer slowly for 30 minutes, add the fried greens and more stock, bouillon or water as needed. Cook slowly until the meat is tender, and see that enough liquid remains to be sufficient for each serving. Before serving pour one glass of brandy over the meat. Serve with slices of mamaliga, potatoes or dumplings and sour salads.

LAMB STEW WITH OKRA
Tocana De Oaie Cu Bame

2 lbs. lamb	parsley, chives, celery
salt	1 glass wine
garlic	3 tbs. sour cream
3 tbs. bacon drippings or oil	2 cups tomato juice
2 onions	thyme
½ lb. okra	

Wash 2 pounds of lamb, sprinkle with salt and let stand. Rub the bottom of a casserole with garlic, add 3 tablespoonfuls of bacon drippings or oil and when hot fry in it 2 sliced onions to a golden brown. Add the meat after cutting into pieces, simmer a little, then add ½ pound of okra and a tablespoonful each of finely chopped parsley, celery and chives. Pour on a glass of wine, simmer for 5 minutes, then add 3 tablespoonfuls of sour cream and cook for ½ hour. Add 2 cups of fresh tomato juice, sprinkle over with a little thyme and cook until the meat is tender. Serve hot with sliced mamaliga or potatoes.

LAMB STEW WITH GREEN PEPPERS AND CARROTS
Tocana De Oaie Cu Ardei Verde Si Morcovi

Prepare exactly as above but replace the okra with meaty green peppers (use red ones if green peppers are not available) sliced crosswise and with the seeds remaining in them, and one large carrot sliced crosswise.

OMELETS

I WILL remember as long as I live a little sad yet comical incident whenever I hear the word *Omelete*. It was during the first World War in my native Romania. Food was scarce and things went from bad to worse. It was a cold spring day. We children began to talk about a subject always in our thoughts. When the stomach is empty, the least desired food looks appetizing and even shines before our eyes surrounded with a halo.

My sister Florica said, "Oh, how I hate eggs, but just now I think I could enjoy even that." Right at that moment our trouble started. We decided to collect a dozen eggs, from barns, attics or any dark corner where hens were setting. We planned to borrow them only and to return them one at a time. To our young minds it didn't seem to be a crime. Well, we succeeded all right. We were already thinking about that large beautiful *omelete* fried in sunflower seed oil, without jam or cheese, it's true, but with commonplace onions, and we were all excited. But how does the saying go—"We propose, but God disposes." We sneaked into the kitchen and tried to talk our beloved Aunt Nastasia into letting us prepare the *omelete*. At once she demanded to know, "Where in the good God's name did you get these eggs?" We became suddenly speechless, but seeing our guilty faces she knew what had happened. Tanty Nastasia came close, towering over us like a giant, but yet controlling herself marvelously, not to frighten us and perhaps make us drop the eggs, which I was carrying in my lifted up skirt. Then we got it, I mean the rod. But the greatest humiliation came when

154 : OMELETS

we had to return the eggs to their rightful owners, tell them the true story and beg for forgiveness. It was comical, but painful also, as our disappointment over the lost *omelete* was very great. Since that day I have loved eggs in any form, but especially *omeletes*.

The variey of omelets in Romania is very great. We children were taught to become not only eaters of eggs, but to excel in perfecting an *omelete par excellente* of our own. We prided ourselves on our ability to create a good *omelete*. Here are a few eggs dishes, very delicious yet quick to make.

OMELET WITH STRAWBERRIES
Omlete Cu Fragi

10 to 12 eggs	¼ lb. sweet butter
¼ lb. powdered sugar	strawberries
vanilla	bread crumbs
¼ cup warm milk	

Break into a bowl 10 to 12 eggs, separating the whites from the yolks. Mix the yolks in the bowl with ¼ pound of powdered sugar, add vanilla to taste, then stir for 15 to 20 minutes but in one direction only. Now add ¼ cup of lukewarm milk and ¼ pound of melted sweet whipped butter. Again mix well, but only in one direction. Beat very well the egg whites and add to the yolk mixture. Clean, wash and dry well a handful of whole strawberries and add to the egg mixture. Butter well the bottom and sides of an omelet form, sprinkle with fine bread crumbs and tilt and pat gently the form to spread the crumbs evenly. Now pour in the mixture, put into a hot oven and bake till a nice light brown. Serve quickly on a hot plate.

OMELET WITH CHERRIES
Omlete Cu Cirese

Prepare exactly as above, but instead of strawberries use a handful of whole cherries, cleaned, pitted and well dried.

OMELETS : 155

OMELET WITH STRAWBERRY JAM
Omlete Cu Dulceata De Fragi

3 eggs	1 tbs. flour
1 tbs. powdered sugar	1 tbs. butter
salt	2 or 3 tbs. strawberry jam
1 tbs. sweet cream	

Put into a bowl 3 egg yolks and one tablespoonful of powdered sugar. Stir in one direction only until it foams. Then add a little salt, one tablespoonful of heavy sweet cream and slowly one tablespoonful of flour a little at a time, mixing all the time in one direction. Add the egg whites first beaten to stiffness and mix together very gently. Heat one level tablespoonful of sweet butter in a large iron pan, add the egg mixture and place in a preheated oven. When the omelet becomes light brown, remove the pan from the oven and add quickly 2 or 3 tablespoonfuls of strawberry jam and spread it evenly on only half of the surface of the omelet. Now flap over the other half of the omelet onto the jam, so that you really have a semicircular sandwich. Put back in the oven under the flame until you get a light brown color, then serve quickly on a hot plate, sprinkled over with sugar. It is simply delicious.

OMELET WITH POT CHEESE
Omlete Cu Brinza De Vaca

4 eggs	3 tbs. pot cheese
salt and pepper	1 tbs. parsley
½ tbs. lard or butter	

Beat well 3 eggs and add a little salt and pepper. Heat a large frying pan with ½ tablespoonful of lard or butter. When the fat is hot pour into the pan the eggs and fry slowly. Move the omelet around in the pan to prevent burning. Mix together 3 heaping tablespoonfuls of pot cheese, a little salt and pepper, one tablespoonful of finely chopped parsley and the yolk of one egg. When the omelet is done on the bottom, turn over with a spatula, adding at the same time a little more lard to the pan. Add the pot cheese mixture and spread it evenly on only half of the surface of the omelet. Now flap over the other half of the

156 : OMELETS

omelet onto the cheese mixture, so that you obtain a sort of semicircular sandwich. Fry quickly to a nice light brown and serve immediately. If you wish, you can put some sour cream on top.

OMELETS WITH VARIOUS WHOLE FRUIT JAMS
Omlete Cu Dulceata De Fructe

Any whole fruit jam may be used to prepare an omelet. Make it according to the above recipe. You can choose as many eggs as you wish, but vary the other ingredients accordingly. This is a very successful surprise dish when unexpected guests arrive, and has never failed to bring to the hostess not only appreciation, but compliments and even gifts of perfumes. And if you want a new hat and want to receive it graciously, try asking your husband that important question some Sunday morning, after he has finished one of these jam omelets.

OMELET WITH SOUR CREAM
Omlete Cu Smantana Acra

It is very easy to make and is a meal by itself. Beat slightly 3 whole eggs, add 3 full tablespoonfuls of sour cream, mix together a little, then add 2 tablespoonfuls of flour a little at a time, and mix well. Add a level tablespoonful of lard or butter to a pan and when hot, pour in the egg mixture and fry uncovered on a slow fire, moving the omelet around in the pan to prevent burning. When a nice light brown, turn the omelet over with a spatula, adding at the same time a little more lard under the omelet. Fry to a nice light brown and serve quickly on a hot plate.

SCRAMBLED EGGS
Jumari De Oua

Put one tablespoonful of lard or butter in a large iron frying pan and when it is very hot pour in 6 to 8 eggs, to which you have first added a little salt and pepper and then beat well

OMELETS : 157

in a bowl with a fork. Stir a few times and remove from the
fire when it is neither too soft nor too hard. Serve on a heated
plate with fried potatoes and sliced tomatoes, or simply with hot
rolls and coffee.

SCRAMBLED EGGS WITH ONIONS
Jumari De Oua Cu Ciapa

Prepare exactly as above, but when the lard is very hot first
add 4 onions very finely chopped and fry to a light golden color.
Then add the beaten eggs.

SCRAMBLED EGGS WITH MILK
Jumari De Oua Cu Lapte

Beat well in a bowl 6 to 8 eggs with 6 tablespoonfuls of boiled
milk. Add salt and pepper to taste, mix, then pour into a large
iron pan in which you have one tablespoonful of very hot butter.
Cover the pan, lower the flame and cook slowly. Do not turn, but
with the end of a knife lift one side slightly to see if it is a nice
light brown. When it is, turn out on a large plate, but be careful
not to break it. Spread the top with grated Cascaval cheese, and
serve quickly on a very hot plate.

SCRAMBLED EGGS WITH PARMESAN
Jumari De Oua Parmesan

Prepare like the SCRAMBLED EGGS WITH ONIONS, but replace
the onions with Parmesan cheese or if you wish, with Cascaval
cheese.

SCRAMBLED EGGS WITH HAM
Jumari De Oua Cu Sunca

Prepare exactly as above, but replace the cheese with ham.

158 : OMELETS

THE ROMANIAN EYES
Ochiuri Romanesti

Half fill a large dish with water, add salt and heat. When the water is boiling break 6 (or more) eggs, one at a time, gently on top of the water. Be careful not to break them and also see that each egg is broken on the surface of the water and not touching any other egg. Cover the dish tightly, remove from the fire, and let it stand in a warm place on the stove for 15 minutes. Then remove each egg carefully with a large slotted spoon so as not to mar it in any way. Arrange them on a large and very hot serving plate. While you are removing the eggs, heat strictly fresh sweet butter and when very hot pour it over the eggs. Sprinkle with finely chopped parsley and serve quickly.

EGG OMELET WITH CASCAVAL
Jumari De Oua Cu Cascaval

Beat very well 8 large fresh eggs in a bowl with a fork (always use a fork for beating eggs). Add 4 tablespoonfuls of sweet milk and ½ pound of grated Cascaval (the cheese made from sheep's milk) and mix well together. Heat 2 tablespoonfuls of butter in a large pan. When very hot, add the egg mixture and cover tightly. Let cook slowly over a very low flame. Do not stir, but move the pan from side to side to brown evenly and nicely. When done, skim off a little of the fat, then turn over on a large hot serving plate. Cover the top with grated Cascaval cheese. Then cut crosswise into slices 2 inches in width. Serve on a heated plate.

Mamaliga Dishes

MAMALIGA or maize bread is the staple national food of the Romanian people. To the Romanian peasants, who comprise 85 percent of the population, mamaliga is revered as a gift from God. In the early morning they start with the cold corn bread, and they eat it in various other forms throughout the day. They call it *mamaliga de aur* or the bread of gold. It is the staff of life, and as long as the peasant or mountaineer has his mamaliga, he feels safe. Even though the mountains of Transylvania are so rich in metallic gold, the poor tsarani (countrymen) would trudge down its slopes to the valleys below with their woodenware, fashioned primitively by hand but each a beautiful work of folk art, to barter them for a sack of golden corn to sustain their families.

And yet this healthful food which is used extensively in all parts of the Balkans and whose praises have been sung by poets in beautiful rhymes, is an importation from America. It is the American Indians whom we must thank for maize. It was they who cultivated it here for thousands of years. From America it was brought to Europe, even to faraway Romania.

I myself learned to appreciate mamaliga during the first World War, when we didn't even have this staple to eat. It was hunger that forced nearly all the city people to try the food of

160 : MAMALIGA DISHES

the peasants and they soon came to love it. Because this food is prepared in many forms, all of them delicious, I hope you will try the following recipes.

MAMALIGA—TRADITIONAL METHOD

This is the way the country people prepare mamaliga. Put on the fire a deep and heavy soup pot with 2 quarts of salted water. When it is boiling fast pour in at once enough yellow corn meal to form the shape of a pyramid. After the corn meal has been boiling for about 30 to 40 minutes make a hole in the pyramid from the top through the center with a wooden mash stick (a sort of a thin rolling pin). In Romania it is called *facalet* and is made by the menfolk especially for preparing mamaliga. The top is artistically carved with an individual design and the name of the owner. It is a handy instrument to have around as a protection against burglars and excitable wives have been known to use it on straying husbands. If a youngster gets a little out of hand, all a mother has to do is to look in the direction of the *facalet* and he will suddenly become very obedient.

While the mamaliga is boiling, prepare the cheese, stew (*tocana*) or any other dish you wish to serve on the side. See that you always have enough water in the pot. After it has been cooking for 3 hours, pour out one large or 2 small cups of the liquid, wrap the pot with plenty of towels, place it between your knees and begin to stir slowly with the *facalet*. Continue stirring until the mush is thick and smooth. The longer you stir, the smoother the mamaliga will be. Return slowly the liquid you took out while you are stirring. If you want to use the mamaliga as bread, stir until it is very thick, cover, put back on the fire and let heat for 5 or 6 minutes. Remove from the fire, let stand for 10 minutes, then turn out on a board. Leave it in the shape of the pot or form into any desired shape. To make it easy to turn out the mamaliga, use a large flat knife dipped in cold water to loosen the sides of the pot. I have given the traditional country method of preparation, but there is an easier way. It follows.

MAMALIGA DISHES : 161

MAMALIGA—MODERN METHOD
Mamaliga Metoda Moderna

1 qt. water
1 tbs. salt

1 box yellow corn meal

Put on the fire a deep and heavy soup pot with one quart of water and a level tablespoonful of salt. Bring to a fast boil. Empty a box of yellow corn meal into a soup plate. Take a handful and let it sift slowly through your fingers into the boiling water, stirring constantly with a large heavy wooden spoon. Continue adding corn meal until you get the desired thickness. Be careful when adding the corn meal to lower the flame when it begins to boil again, as there is a tendency to boil up suddenly and you may burn yourself. Continue to heat and to stir until the mush is very smooth. Then cover the pot and let cook slowly for 10 to 12 minutes longer. Wet a long flat knife in cold water and cut around the sides of the pot, loosening and pushing away the mush from the sides. Then turn out on a wooden board. Form into a nice shape, as a torte, with a spoon dipped in cold water, and cut slices with a white thread. Serve instead of bread with meat stews, soups, milk, etc.

MAMALIGA LAYER WITH CHEESE
Mamaliga Cu Brinza

mamaliga
¼ lb. bacon

grated cascaval cheese
1 tbs. bacon fat

Prepare the mamaliga as above, but leave the corn meal mush rather soft. Before you make the mamaliga, cut ¼ pound of bacon into small pieces, fry and let stand to remain warm. Have ready grated Cascaval cheese (or you may use grated Parmesan or Swiss or even pot cheese). Also have ready a deep frying pan or oven proof glass or porcelain dish. Now into this dish put a tablespoonful of bacon fat to cover the bottom and some of the bacon pieces. With the same spoon take some of the mamaliga and spread on a layer (not too thin nor too thick). Now sprinkle with the cheese (please do not be stingy). Continue forming these layers, bacon pieces and fat, mamaliga and

162 : MAMALIGA DISHES

cheese, and end up with a layer of cheese on top. Be generous with the fat and the cheese. Keep uncovered in the oven for a few minutes or until the heat has penetrated through. Serve very hot on heated plates with very cold sauerkraut juice, sauerkraut or sour salads.

MAMALIGA WITH BUTTER
Mamaliga Cu Brinza

Prepare exactly as above but replace the bacon fat and bacon pieces with butter, which you should use generously.

MAMALIGA DUMPLINGS WITH CHEESE
Mamaliga Galuste Cu Brinza

Prepare mamaliga and when the mush is cool enough mix in a generous amount of butter and cheese with the mamaliga by working with the hands. Form into dumplings or large balls, then fry in hot butter to a nice light brown. Serve hot with any sour salad.

STUFFED MAMALIGA
Mamaliga Umpluta

Form mamaliga dumplings or balls as above. Make a hole in the middle and fill with cubed ham, bacon cut into small pieces, mushrooms or eggs. Close the opening in the top with a little mamaliga, place in a pan and bake. Serve with a topping of sour cream, or as a side dish with cooked vegetables.

FRIED MAMALIGA SLICES
Mamaliga Felii Prajita

Cut long slices of cold mamaliga, dip in well-beaten eggs, then dredge both sides with grated cheese and pat in well. If possible always use sheep cheese. Fry to a nice light brown. Serve hot covered with yoghurt (fermented, concentrated milk), or sour cream. It also goes well with sour salads.

MAMALIGA DISHES : 163

COLD MAMALIGA PEASANT STYLE
Mamaliga Rece Stil Taranesc

Cut cold mamaliga into thin slices with a cotton thread. Rub a glazed earthenware casserole with a clove of garlic, butter well the bottom of the dish (or use lard or slices of bacon), then put in a layer of mamaliga slices and cover with cheese. Continue forming these layers, butter, mamaliga slices and cheese, ending with the cheese on top. Be generous with cheese and butter. Cover and cook slowly on top of the stove until well heated throughout, or bake in the oven. Serve cold.

MAMALIGA WITH CREAM
Mamaliga Cu Smantana

Serve hot or cold slices of mamaliga with heavy sweet or sour cream. This dish is nourishing, yet light and delicious. Wonderful for Lent and summer.

MAMALIGA WITH MILK
Mamaliga Cu Lapte

Put some mamaliga, enough for one portion (either slices or bulk), into a soup plate. If the mamaliga is hot add to it cold milk mixed with sweet cream. If it is cold, then pour over it boiling hot milk. Serve as a first course in a dairy meal or for breakfast.

MAMALIGA WITH SAUERKRAUT
Mamaliga Cu Varza Acra

Serve cold or hot slices of mamaliga with plain or stuffed sauerkraut. It is more delicious even than bread. Won't you please try it?

DUMPLINGS

FARINA DUMPLINGS
Gogoase De Gris

1 tbs. cold lard	farina
2 whole eggs	soup stock or water
salt	

Beat in a mixing bowl one tablespoonful of very cold, solid lard or 1½ tablespoonfuls of sweet butter to a foam with a fork. Break into it 2 whole eggs, beat, then add a little salt to taste.

Before you add the farina, see that some of the soup strained from the chicken or meat (or water if you prefer to cook the dumplings in water) is boiling gently, not fast. Now take a handful of farina in one hand and let it sift through your fingers into the egg mixture, while with a fork held in your other hand you stir constantly in one direction. Add enough farina to form a rather soft mixture. Test a small ball of the mixture by dropping it into the boiling soup. If it holds together, the mixture is all right, but if it crumbles add a little more farina to it and mix in well.

With a spoon dipped in the boiling soup pick up some of the mixture, form into an oval shape and drop into the soup. Repeat

166 : DUMPLINGS

this until all the dumplings have been put into the boiling liquid. Work quickly so that the farina mixture will not have time to become hard. Now cover the pot tightly and boil gently until done. Do not overboil the dumplings, nor cook in water which is boiling fast, as this will harden them. When ready, transfer gently into a soup casserole and add slowly the soup in which you boiled the chicken or meat and which has been kept hot all the time.

It is necessary to repeat that the dumplings must be cooked only in gently boiling liquid and that stirring of the mixture must be in one direction only. If you want a nice color, add a little saffron. Use for garnishing also meats and soups, with or without cheese.

BUTTER DUMPLINGS
Galuste De Unt

Prepare some butter dough (see BUTTER DOUGH). Roll out to a sheet ½ inch thick. Choose two tin cutting forms of the same shape, one a little smaller than the other. Cut the dough into an equal number of small and large pieces. Place the larger pieces of dough into a baking pan wetted with water. Smear over with beaten egg and let stand. Cover with the smaller pieces of dough and smear these also with beaten egg. Bake to a nice brown at a high heat. Serve with soup, sauces or garnishing for meats together with sauces, either by itself or topped with sour cream.

FLOUR DUMPLINGS
Galuste De Faina

Beat 1½ tablespoonfuls of very cold sweet butter to a foam with a fork. Add 3 eggs and beat together with the butter very well. Add one tablespoonful of cold water, then let flour sift slowly through the fingers of your left hand while with the right you keep stirring constantly until you get a soft dough. With a tablespoon drop pieces of the dough into boiling salted water. Let boil, covered, for about 20 minutes or until done (test by tasting one). Drain, then sprinkle with hot butter and chopped

DUMPLINGS : 167

green parsley. Serve with sauce as a garnishing for stews, meat or chicken, or as a dish by itself with hot butter and plenty of cheese.

DUMPLINGS WITH OLIVE OIL
Galuste Cu Unt De Lemn

1 egg	salt
1 tbs. olive oil	flour

Beat one whole egg in a deep bowl with 2 tablespoonfuls of very cold water. Add one tablespoonful of pure olive oil and beat together again very well. Add salt to taste. Let enough flour sift slowly through your left hand while stirring constantly with the right hand to form a soft dough. No lumps please. Then knead very well with a spoon.

Put a pot of salted water to boil. With a small spoon wetted in the boiling water, pick up some of the dough and drop it into the pot. Repeat until all the dough has been put into the water. Cover and boil gently until done. Test by tasting to know when they are cooked. Drain off all water, but do not wash or rinse. Now add to the chicken stew (or any other stew). Let it remain in same long enough to absorb the flavor. It can be used as a garnishing with any sauce and served with grated or melted cheese or with sour cream, sprinkled with parsley.

CHEESE DUMPLINGS
Gogoase Cu Brinza

1 lb. cottage or pot cheese	1 tbs. sugar
2 eggs	flour
salt	

Mix well one pound of cottage or pot cheese (without added cream), 2 egg yolks, a little salt and one tablespoonful of sugar. Now mix in the 2 egg whites first beaten to stiffness, and a little flour added slowly, enough to make a rather soft dough. Test the dough by shaping a little of the mixture into a small ball with your wet hands and put into boiling water. If the ball holds

168 : DUMPLINGS

together, the mixture is all right, but if it crumbles, then add just a little more flour, but use the flour sparingly, as too much will make the dumplings too heavy. If necessary, make another test ball until it comes out just right. Then wet your hands and shape into balls, spherical, oval or any shape you like. Make them the size of a small apple and prepare 1 or 2 per person.

Boil them in salted water gently on a very slow fire until done. Take one out, cut in two. If it is sticky, it still needs more cooking. When done, drain and put directly on a serving plate. Top with hot butter or sour cream and sprinkle with finely chopped parsley. They can be used as a garnish or even as a dessert if you pour over them some fruit sauce.

POT CHEESE DUMPLINGS
Galuste In Pesmet Cu Brinza

Prepare exactly as the CHEESE DUMPLINGS. While they are boiling, get a large frying pan, put in 2 tablespoonfuls of butter, warm up, then add 1 to 2 cups of bread crumbs. Roast slowly to a nice brown. When the dumplings are done, roll them in the crumbs and continue to heat uncovered on a very low flame until well heated throughout. Serve as a side dish, plain or sprinkled with sugar, or as a garnishing topped with sour cream. All dumplings made without meat are delicious vegetarian dishes.

LIVER DUMPLINGS
Galuste De Ficat

½ lb. liver	parsley, chives, thyme
1 tbs. lard	salt and pepper
3 eggs	bread crumbs

Scrape ½ pound of liver (beef, veal or chicken) which has first been cleaned of skin and veins. Use only the liver that comes through the scraper. Beat in a mixing bowl one tablespoonful of lard or 1½ tablespoonfuls of butter to a foam with a fork. Break into it 3 whole eggs, beat again very well, add a few drops of water then add the liver and mix. Add a few sprigs of parsley and chives, very finely minced, salt and a little pepper to taste and a pinch of thyme. Mix well. Now add enough very fine bread crumbs to make a dough, neither too soft nor too hard.

With a spoon dipped in the boiling soup pick up some of the mixture, form into the desired shape and drop into the soup. After all the dumplings are in the pot, cover and boil gently until done. Take out a dumpling and cut in two. If sticky it means they are not yet done. Use for soup garnishing by itself or with a sauce of your choice.

Sauces

WHEN WE are preparing sauces, be they hot or cold, it is well to remember a few directions. If we adhere to them the sauce will have the superb flavor every cook strives to get. First, it is well to have all the ingredients at hand and in condition to be quickly used, that is already chopped, grated, beaten, etc. When browning flour, if we use lard or bacon drippings, these fats must be very hot to sear the flour immediately at the start, then reducing the heat and stirring all the time. But if you use butter, it must be just melted, not hot, and the heating must be done slowly, otherwise the taste and flavor will suffer.

The sauce should be prepared only a little while before using, not more than ½ hour, as standing will detract from its color and taste. However, if you need to keep the sauce for 1 to 2 days, remove it after being made to an earthenware or porcelain dish. When ready to use it, reheat in a double boiler. The sauce must not be too thick, nor too thin.

When pouring soup stock or water over sauces which will be used in soups, add the liquid very slowly on a not too high flame, and stir constantly to avoid lumps.

172 : SAUCES

HOT SAUCES

WINE SAUCE
Sos De Vin

2 tbs. lard or bacon drippings	1 tbs. powdered sugar
	8 to 10 cloves
2 tbs. flour	1 piece cinnamon bark
shallot	small black raisins
white wine	20 to 25 almonds
salt and pepper	

Warm a deep iron pan, put in 2 tablespoonfuls of lard or bacon drippings (the bacon drippings give a fine flavor, especially in brown sauces). When the fat is hot, add 2 tablespoonfuls of flour, with constant stirring, and one tablespoonful of minced shallot. Stir and brown to a nice color. When you get the color you want, thin with a very good white wine, adding just a little water after the wine, and stir constantly to prevent lumps. Use a wooden spoon for the stirring. Salt and pepper to taste and add one tablespoonful of powdered sugar, 8 to 10 cloves, one piece of cinnamon bark, a handful of small black raisins and 20 to 25 almonds, peeled and sliced as thin as possible. Stir together gently and very well and boil slowly for 20 minutes. When done, remove the cloves and the cinnamon bark. Serve this sauce with boiled tongues or with any kind of boiled or even roasted meats and game meats.

LEMON SAUCE
Sos De Lemaie

6 egg yolks	sugar
1½ tbs. flour	1½ tbs. butter
4 lemons	4 to 6 tbs. white wine

In a mixing casserole beat 6 egg yolks a little, add 1½ tablespoonfuls of flour and mix. Add one full large cup of water, the juice of 4 lemons, enough sugar to be sweet to your taste, the grated peel of one lemon, 1½ tablespoonfuls of sweet butter and 4 to 6 tablespoonfuls of very good white wine. As you put in each

SAUCES : 173

of the above ingredients mix in a little, then when the last one is added, mix all together well but gently. Now place the casserole on the flame and with constant stirring bring to a boil, but do not let it boil. Remove from the fire and press through a sieve. Serve immediately with any kind of roast or boiled meats.

CREAM SAUCE
Sos De Smantana

1½ tbs. lard or bacon drippings	6 to 8 tbs. beef broth
1¾ tbs. flour	1 cup sour cream
chives and parsley	salt
	lemon juice

Add 1½ tablespoonfuls of lard or bacon drippings to a deep iron pan and when hot add 1¾ tablespoonfuls of flour and with stirring heat until light brown. Add one tablespoonful of finely minced chives, a few finely chopped sprigs of parsley, and mix after each addition. Now add slowly 6 to 8 tablespoonfuls of beef broth or bouillon to thin, then add slowly and with constant stirring one full cup of sour cream and a little salt. Bring to the point of incipient boiling, that is when you see 2 or 3 bubbles coming to the surface, but definitely do not boil. Then add enough lemon juice to be sour to your own taste and serve immediately with any kind of roasted or boiled meats.

BROWN SAUCE
Rantas

3 tbs. bacon drippings	scallion and parsley
1½ tbs. flour	broth or bouillon

To obtain a really piquant flavor in the brown sauce the secret is to use fresh or smoked pork fat, lard, bacon drippings or even bacon cut into small pieces and rendered in the pan. If you wish you may add the bacon pieces to the melted fat in making the sauce. If butter, olive or vegetable oil is used, a fine sauce will result, but with quite a different flavor. This sauce is excellent for soups, ciorbas, boiled vegetables, stuffed green peppers, etc.

Heat a deep iron pan and put into it 3 tablespoonfuls of bacon

174 : SAUCES

drippings. When hot, add 1½ tablespoonfuls of flour, stirring constantly until the color becomes light brown. Now add one tablespoonful of finely chopped green scallion (or leak, chives or even a very finely sliced small onion). Stir, then add a sprig of parsley finely chopped, and continue to stir until you get a nice dark brown color. Now add slowly, with constant stirring, enough cold or hot water, broth or bouillon to make a thick sauce. When it is the desired thickness, cook on a slow flame for 10 minutes. Pour this sauce, strained or unstrained, into the boiling soup, stir well and continue to cook on a slow fire until the soup or whatever else you use it on is done. The amount of sauce in this recipe is enough for 2 quarts of soup or ciorba.

An intriguing variation is to replace the water or broth with tomato juice. Blend in a good portion of sour cream. This makes a delicious sauce for potatoes and hamburgers.

WHITE SAUCE
Sos Alb

Beat one large tablespoonful of butter to a foam in a sauce bowl. Add one large tablespoonful of flour and mix. Now pour on very slowly, stirring constantly, one cup of water, soup stock or bouillon cubes dissolved in water to make a thin sauce without lumps. Even milk or wine can be used as the thinning agent, but soup stock or strong broth give best results. Add any kind of herb flavoring you wish. You may also blend in sweet or sour cream.

Use this sauce in soups, ciorbas, stews, vegetable or meat dishes. A little while before the soup or other dish is done, add the white sauce slowly and with constant stirring. Continue to cook until done.

BUTTER SAUCE
Sos De Unt

Place a porcelain bowl in a double boiler with boiling water. When the dish has become warmed put in ⅓ pound of sweet butter. Now add 6 egg yolks one at a time, mixing in each yolk well by stirring always in one direction before adding the next.

SAUCES : 175

Heat until the mixture comes to an incipient boil, but please do not boil. Add salt and pepper to taste and the juice of 2 lemons, or more if you like it more sour. Serve with asparagus or cauliflower or as an addition to other sauces.

GARLIC SAUCE
Sos De Usturoi

2 tbs. flour	soup stock
2 tbs. bacon drippings	salt
1 cluster of garlic	wine vinegar
parsley and thyme	

Brown 2 tablespoonfuls of flour in 2 tablespoonfuls of very hot bacon drippings or lard with constant stirring. Add a cluster of garlic cloves which have been peeled and very finely chopped, but do not brown. Add a little finely chopped parsley and thyme and mix well. Thin with soup stock and add salt and wine vinegar to taste. Let cook slowly for 10 to 15 minutes. Thin if needed with diluted wine vinegar. Top with 2 tablespoonfuls of sour cream before serving. Serve with lamb or other meats.

ONION SAUCE
Sos De Ciapa

2 tbs. flour	salt and pepper
2 tbs. bacon drippings	wine vinegar
3 onions	tabasco pepper
soup stock	3 tbs. sour cream

Make a brown sauce by adding 2 tablespoonfuls of flour to 2 tablespoonfuls of very hot bacon drippings or lard. When light brown add 3 finely minced onions and brown with the flour. Thin with soup stock, adding it slowly and with constant stirring to prevent lumps. When as thin as desired add salt and pepper to taste and let cook slowly for 15 minutes. Add wine vinegar to your taste, a pinch of ground tabasco pepper and 3 tablespoonfuls of sour cream, mix well and press through a sieve onto a sauce dish. Serve with boiled beef or roasts.

176 : SAUCES

SAUCE FOR ROAST MEATS
Sos De Friptura

1 large glass white wine	3 tbs. butter
1 cup bouillon	ground tabasco peppers
parsley, chives, thyme	1 onion
1 laurel leaf	salt and pepper

To the sauce in the dish where the meat was roasted add one large glass of good old white wine, one cup of bouillon, one tablespoonful of chopped green parsley, one tablespoonful of minced chives, one laurel leaf, 3 tablespoonfuls of butter, a pinch of ground tabasco peppers, one sliced onion and a little thyme. Stir all the ingredients together, cover the dish and let cook slowly for 2 hours. When done, skim off the fat and press the sauce through a sieve with a wooden spoon, taking care that all the juice has been squeezed out. Now add salt and pepper to taste, and serve with roast meats.

SAUCE FOR GAME MEATS
Sos De Vanat

3¾ tbs. lard or bacon drippings	coriander, laurel leaf
	salt
2 tbs. flour	2 carrots
2 onions	1 parsley root
1 tbs. pulverized sugar	1 parsnip root
beef stock	1 white turnip
12 peppercorns	lemon juice or wine vinegar

Prepare this brown sauce as follows. Heat in a deep iron pan 2¼ tablespoonfuls of lard or bacon drippings and brown in it 2 tablespoonfuls of flour. When the flour turns to a light brown, add one minced onion and fry until soft. Add one tablespoonful of pulverized sugar, brown a little, then thin slowly with beef soup, stock or water to the consistency you want. Add 12 peppercorns, a pinch of coriander, salt to taste and one laurel leaf. Mix well and let simmer a little longer.

Into another pan put 1½ tablespoonfuls of lard, heat, then add 2 carrots, one parsley root, one parsnip root and one young small white turnip, all of these being grated, and one sliced onion.

SAUCES : 177

Stir and fry. When fried, add it to the above brown sauce and cook for 15 to 20 minutes. Press through a sieve, then add the juice of a lemon or wine vinegar. Make this sauce as sour as you like it. Serve for all game meats.

LAMB AND MUTTON SAUCE
Sos De Oaie

2 or 3 large red onions	1 cup Butter Sauce
2 tbs. butter	nutmeg
½ lb. boiled ham	salt and pepper
thyme, parsley	horse-radish
1 large glass wine	3 egg yolks

Chop finely 2 or 3 large red onions and fry in 2 tablespoonfuls of butter. Now add ½ pound of boiled lean ham, a little thyme, a few whole sprigs of parsley, one large glass of boiling wine, one cup of butter sauce (see BUTTER SAUCE), a little grated nutmeg, salt and pepper to taste and a little grated horse-radish. Mix together and let boil for 10 to 12 minutes, then press through a sieve. Beat 3 egg yolks in a sauce dish, then add slowly the above mixture little by little, while stirring constantly. Serve with lamb or mutton.

FISH SAUCE
Sos De Peste

2 tbs. flour	4 egg yolks
2 tbs. butter	grated nutmeg
fish ciorba	juice of 1 lemon

Brown well 2 level tablespoonfuls of flour in 2 tablespoonfuls of hot sweet butter. Pour over this enough fish ciorba (see CIORBAS) to make a sauce. Let cook slowly for 15 minutes, then strain. Beat 4 egg yolks in a dish, pour the sauce over this slowly, stirring constantly. Add a little grated nutmeg and the juice of one lemon and beat with an egg beater until it begins to thicken. Then serve immediately by pouring it over the boiled fish. If it cannot be served right away, keep the dish containing the sauce hot by immersing it in another dish of hot water. Sprinkle with chopped parsley.

178 : SAUCES

ANISE SAUCE FOR FISH
Sos De Anis Pentru Peste

Make a butter sauce (see BUTTER SAUCE). Add a teaspoonful of minced anise, bring to an incipient boil, but do not boil. Then serve with the fish.

SAUCE FOR CHICKEN OR VEAL
Sos Pentru Pui or Vitel

Mix in a small casserole 6 egg yolks with 2 level tablespoonfuls of flour, add a little finely minced shallot or chives, one large tablespoonful of sweet butter, a glass of good wine and the juice of one lemon. Mix well together, place over the fire, stirring gently while it is getting hot, and heat until it begins to thicken, but do not boil. Serve immediately. If your guests are late, do not despair. Keep the casserole in hot water until ready to serve. And if you think the sauce is too thick, thin with a little more wine.

ALMOND SAUCE WITH HORSE-RADISH
Sos De Migdale Cu Hrean

Mix well a teaspoonful of flour with a full cup of sour cream, then thin by adding slowly some beef stock a little at a time to prevent lumps. Shell a handful of almonds and mince fine. Add the almonds and a little sugar to the mixture and let boil for 5 minutes. Just before serving, add a little grated horse-radish. Serve with boiled meats and roasts.

HORSE-RADISH WITH CREAM SAUCE
Sos De Hrean Cu Smantana

Put one tablespoonful of lard in an iron pan, add a little chopped chives and a tablespoonful of flour and brown lightly while stirring. Add one grated horse-radish root, a few tablespoonfuls of beef stock, a large full cup of sour cream, a little

SAUCES : 179

salt and sugar enough to give the desired sweetness. Let boil about 5 minutes. Serve immediately with any boiled meat.

CURRANT SAUCE FOR GAME
Sos De Coacaza Pentru Vanat

Heat 2 tablespoonfuls of fine crumbs in a large tablespoonful of butter. When only half roasted, add 6 to 8 tablespoonfuls of good white wine, one pound of cleaned currants and a little salt and sugar to taste. Let boil together for 10 to 15 minutes. Serve with game.

CURRANT SAUCE
Sos De Coacaza

Combine 1½ pounds of cleaned currants, one large cup of beef stock, one tablespoonful of pulverized sugar and a little salt. Let boil. While this is boiling, prepare a brown sauce with one tablespoonful of flour and a little finely minced chives in one tablespoonful of lard. When nicely browned, add the currant mixture, mixing well to prevent lumps, and let boil for 10 to 12 minutes longer. Press through a sieve and serve with boiled birds.

SOUR WILD CHERRY SAUCE
Sos De Visine

Prepare exactly as above, but replace the currants with one pound of sour wild cherries from which the pits have been extracted. Before serving press through a sieve.

CHERRY SAUCE
Sos De Cirese

Prepare exactly as the above, replacing the wild cherries with sweet cherries. Before serving press through a sieve.

180 : SAUCES

BRIAR SAUCE
Sos De Maces

Take two pounds of ripe briars, cut into halves, take out the pits, peel and wash in cold water. Boil until they become soft, then press through a sieve. Now replace the currants with the briars and prepare exactly as the Current Sauce (see above). Serve with game or roasts.

GOOSEBERRY SAUCE
Sos De Agrise

Clean one pound of gooseberries of stems and tails, add 2 cups of soup stock, one tablespoonful of finely chopped parsley and one tablespoonful of sugar and let boil until done. Beat very well 3 egg yolks with 4 tablespoonfuls of sour cream, then add it to the gooseberries with constant stirring. Heat until boiling is about to begin (when you see a bubble form), then serve immediately with boiled chicken, capon or meats.

APPLE SAUCE
Sos De Mere

Prepare exactly as the gooseberry sauce but replace the gooseberries with 6 or 7 apples, sliced thin. Serve with boiled chicken, capon or beef.

GAME APPLE SAUCE
Sos De Mere Pentru Vanat

6 to 8 apples	1 large glass white wine
2 tbs. butter	cinnamon, sugar
3 tbs. beef stock	4 or 5 cloves
2 tbs. fine bread or roll crumbs	1 tbs. raisins

Choose very acid apples (Winesap, Northern Spy or Roman Beauty). Peel 6 to 8 of them, cut into thin slices and brown in one tablespoonful of butter. Then add 3 tablespoonfuls of beef

SAUCES : 181

stock, cover and cook until tender. In another pan roast lightly 2 tablespoonfuls of fine bread or roll crumbs in one tablespoonful of butter, then add to it the apple mixture and stir. Now add one large glass of old white wine, stir, and add a little cinnamon, 4 or 5 powdered cloves, sugar to taste and one tablespoonful of small black raisins, cleaned and washed. Stir and let boil slowly for 15 to 20 minutes. If the sauce is too thick, thin with more wine. Serve with game of all kinds.

SOUR GRAPE SAUCE
Sos De Agurida

Clean and wash ½ pound of sour unripe grapes. Add one large cup of beef stock and boil. When done press through a sieve. Make a brown sauce without onions, then put into it the sour grape sauce and add a little finely chopped parsley and thyme, a little salt and sugar to taste and let cook for 10 to 12 minutes. Serve with boiled or roasted meats.

ORANGE SAUCE
Sos De Portocale

Heat a large tablespoonful of butter and brown in it one tablespoonful of pulverized sugar. Grate the peel of 3 oranges, then squeeze out the juice, strain and add to the browned sugar. Now add the grated orange peel, 10 to 12 tablespoonfuls of good white wine and a small dry roll grated. Mix well together, cook for about 10 to 14 minutes on a slow fire, strain through a sieve and serve immediately.

CAPER SAUCE
Sos De Capere

Make a brown sauce using 2 tablespoonfuls of lard or bacon drippings. When very hot, add 2 level tablespoonfuls of flour, stirring constantly. When it turns light brown add one tablespoonful of chopped chives and a little thyme and stir. When

182 : SAUCES

fully browned, thin slowly with soup stock to avoid lumps. Add
2 tablespoonfuls of washed and chopped capers and a few sprigs
of green parsley. Let cook slowly. Add 4 to 5 tablespoonfuls of
sour cream and serve.

CELERY KNOB SAUCE
Sos De Telina

Cut 3 celery knobs into small cubes and boil in water. When
only half boiled, drain off the water and combine the cut celery
knobs with butter sauce (see BUTTER SAUCE). Add to this the
juice of one lemon. Beat 2 egg yolks in a sauce dish, then add
the above mixture little by little. Mix well and serve immediately.

GREEN SORREL SAUCE
Sos De Macris

1¾ tbs. flour	soup stock
2 tbs. bacon drippings	salt
chives and parsley	3 tbs. sour cream
3 tbs. green sorrel	

Make a brown sauce by adding 1¾ tablespoonfuls of flour to
2 tablespoonfuls of very hot bacon drippings or lard with constant stirring. When light brown add one tablespoonful of
finely chopped chives, fry a little, then add one tablespoonful of
finely chopped parsley, stir, then add 3 tablespoonfuls of finely
chopped green sorrel, which was first well cleaned and washed.
When fully browned thin with soup broth (make a rather thin
sauce). Add salt and let cook slowly for 15 minutes. Then add
3 tablespoonfuls of sour cream and mix well. Serve with boiled
or roasted meats.

TARRAGON SAUCE
Sos De Tarcon

Prepare exactly like the GREEN SORREL SAUCE, but replace the
sorrel with 2 tablespoonfuls of finely chopped tarragon and a
little sugar.

SAUCES : 183

GREEN DILL SAUCE
Sos De Marar

Prepare exactly like the GREEN SORREL SAUCE, but use 3 table-spoonfuls of finely chopped dill.

GREEN PARSLEY SAUCE
Sos De Patrunjel

Prepare exactly like the GREEN SORREL SAUCE, but use 3 table-spoonfuls of finely chopped green parsley.

CUCUMBER SAUCE
Sos De Castraveti

Prepare exactly like the GREEN SORREL SAUCE, but replace the sorrel with 3 or 4 sour pickles, thinly sliced.

PURE TOMATO SAUCE
Sos De Patlagele Rosii

9 or 10 tomatoes	1 large parsley root
parsley, celery leaves	1 parsnip root
onion, chives	butter

Very delicious for all kinds of cold or hot dishes is the fresh tomato sauce. It can be prepared from canned tomatoes or canned tomato juice, but it will not be the same, nor have the same appealing flavor unless you use fresh ripe tomatoes. Do not be afraid to get acquainted with and buy the very, very ripe and soft tomatoes. They are extremely cheap, yet give gratifying results. Won't you please try them? They make the sauce so very tasty. The Romanians break the tomatoes into smaller pieces with their hands, as they believe the natural fruit and vegetable juices are good for the skin and for one's health and beauty.

Wash 9 or 10 ripe tomatoes, break into small pieces and put them in a pot. Add some parsley and celery leaves, one onion finely sliced and enough cold water to just cover. Place the pot on the fire and boil slowly until cooked. Now remove from the

184 : SAUCES

fire and let stand for 30 to 40 minutes. Strain and press through a sieve until all the juice is extracted. Add one large or 2 smaller fresh whole roots of parsley, one root of parsnip and a few sprigs of chives. Boil slowly till you get the thickness desired. Before using the sauce, remove the vegetables. Add some butter. Serve with 1 or 2 tablespoonfuls of sour cream. Use for potatoes, hamburgers or any kind of boiled or fried meats.

TOMATO SAUCE
Sos De Patlagele Rosii Cu Rantas

12 large tomatoes	2 tbs. lard
1 onion	1 tbs. flour
celery, parsley, fennel	

Wash 12 very ripe large red tomatoes, break up into pieces and put into a casserole with one sliced onion, a few branches of celery, a few sprigs of parsley and one sprig of fennel. Cover with water and boil for ½ hour, then strain and press out all the juice through a sieve. Make a light brown sauce from 2 tablespoonfuls of lard or bacon drippings with one tablespoonful of flour. When the sauce starts to get brown, slowly add the tomato sauce with constant stirring to prevent lumps. Add a little salt and pepper and sugar to taste. Let cook slowly, with occasional stirring, for 10 to 12 minutes. Before serving add 2 or 3 tablespoonfuls of sour cream. Serve with boiled meats, roasts and meat balls.

MUSHROOM SAUCES

The mushrooms should be well washed and cleaned of sand. If you wish you can peel the mushrooms and use the peelings, although I myself do not peel them. The stems can be cut or broken off, but when the mushrooms are sliced, then slice the stems too. If you peel the mushrooms, then place immediately in cold water to prevent them getting black. If you want the mushroom meat to remain white, rinse a few times in cold water, then cook slowly for 8 minutes in a little salt water with one tablespoonful of sweet butter and some lemon juice. When cooked, strain, cover and heat until done, then add to the sauce that will follow. Use the strained liquid in which the mushrooms

SAUCES : 185

were cooked for basting roasts or to thin sauces. If saved, keep it in a porcelain dish.

After the peelings and stems of the mushrooms are washed, put them to boil in a little soup stock, strain and use them for other sauces.

MUSHROOM SAUCE WITH WINE
Sos De Ciuperci Cu Vin

12 to 24 mushrooms	salt and pepper
4 onions, finely chopped	6 to 8 tbs. beef soup
2 tbs. warm butter	nutmeg
1 tbs. parsley, finely	1 lemon
chopped	3 egg yolks
1 glass white wine	

Wash and clean 12 to 24 mushrooms, then cut into thin slices. While slicing the mushrooms fry 4 very finely chopped onions in 2 tablespoonfuls of warm butter. When lightly browned add the mushrooms, stir together and add one table-spoonful of very finely chopped parsley. Cover the casserole tightly and cook slowly until all the liquid is absorbed. Then add one glass of good white wine, salt and pepper to taste and 6 to 8 tablespoonfuls of beef soup or bouillon. Cook until the mushrooms are soft, and then add a little nutmeg, the grated peel of one lemon and finally the juice of this lemon and mix well. Just before serving beat well 3 egg yolks in a sauce serving dish, then add slowly little by little the mushroom mixture to the egg yolks with constant stirring. Serve with chicken, veal or anything you have made. No one will refuse it; rather they will praise you and kiss you for it.

COLD SAUCES

APPLE SAUCE WITH HORSE-RADISH
Sos De Mere Cu Hrean

Peel 6 to 8 apples, grate and mix with one tablespoonful of grated horse-radish, 2 tablespoonfuls of pulverized sugar and 2

186 : SAUCES

tablespoonfuls of wine vinegar. Mix the ingredients well together and serve with boiled chicken or boiled beef.

HORSE-RADISH SAUCE
Sos De Hrean

Clean and grate one root of horse-radish and scald with a little boiling beef stock or bouillon (free from any fat or grease). Add a little salt, enough wine vinegar to your taste and 3 tablespoonfuls of sour cream or yoghurt. Mix all together very well in a sauce dish and serve with all kinds of boiled or roasted meats.

OLIVE OIL SAUCE
Sos De Unt De Lemn

Mix together well 5 tablespoonfuls of pure olive oil, 1 to 2 tablespoonfuls of wine vinegar and one tablespoonful each of parsley, onion and chives, all of these being minced. Now add the yolks of 6 hard-boiled eggs, which you have pressed through a sieve. Mix all very well, add a little salt and pepper to taste, then again mix. Put in a sauce dish and serve.

HARD-BOILED EGGS SAUCE
Sos De Oua Fierte

Make 8 hard-boiled eggs, cool, then mince very finely all the eggs except 3 yolks, which you will press through a sieve. Beat a dab of sweet butter in a casserole to a foam, add the eggs and 1 to 2 tablespoonfuls of wine vinegar (use enough to suit your taste). Mix and then add one tablespoonful of minced chives, salt and pepper. Mix again and turn into a sauce dish and serve.

SALADS

When green vegetables have to be cooked, they should be cooked in salted water, but first they must be well cleaned and rinsed. When done, they must be cooled, then prepared according to the recipe. Green vegetables that will be served raw must be carefully cleaned of small bugs, etc., and well rinsed.

GREEN LETTUCE SALAD
Salata Verde

Choose 2 (or as many as you need) heads of lettuce, remove the outside wilted leaves, clean and rinse, then cut lengthwise into 2 or 4 pieces and place them in a deep salad bowl. Mix together a cupful of wine or apple vinegar, a little salt and pepper and pure olive oil to taste, and pour this over the lettuce slowly. Gently mix the lettuce and the oil-vinegar mixture with a wooden fork and spoon, being careful as you turn the lettuce that you do not break it. When ready, place each quarter of lettuce on an individual plate and pour over it enough of the oil-vinegar mixture so that each quarter will have an equal amount. Sprinkle with finely chopped parsley. Prepare salad only when ready to serve.

GREEN LETTUCE SALAD WITH EGGS
Salata Verde Cu Oua

Prepare as above, but garnish with hard-boiled eggs cut lengthwise. Sprinkle the eggs with a little salt and pepper and some finely chopped parsley. Surround with a few ripe olives, if you wish.

188 : SALADS

GREEN LETTUCE SALAD WITH SUGAR
Salata Verde Cu Zahar

Prepare exactly as the GREEN LETTUCE SALAD, but instead of the olive oil add 2 level tablespoonfuls of sugar. Do not use eggs in this salad.

GREEN LEAF LETTUCE SALAD
Salata De Laptuci

Prepare the same as the GREEN LETTUCE SALAD, but instead of cutting the lettuce into quarters, pull individual leaves from the head, and use the sugar-wine vinegar mixture.

MIXED LETTUCE AND SCALLION SALAD
Salata Amestecata Cu Ciapa Verde

Prepare the lettuce in any of the above ways, either cut into quarters or leafed, and covered with vinegar-oil mixture or vinegar-sugar mixture. Before pouring on the liquid mixture add some young and very tender scallions, or if you have a window box or earthen pot planted with a few cloves of garlic, add the garlic greens. They are simply delightful. And of course sprinkle with finely chopped parsley.

POTATO SALAD
Salata De Cartofi

This dish is very popular in Romania during the Lenten season and is prepared two or three times a week. Wash well 6 to 8 large potatoes and put to boil. When done, drain, cool very well, peel, cut into crosswise slices and put into a large salad bowl. Salt, pour on some wine vinegar, mix gently once or twice, then add pure olive oil. Again mix gently, so you will not break the potato slices, then place on individual plates or on a large serving plate. Cover with slices of onions (cut crosswise) which were first dipped in a mixture of vinegar and olive oil. Sprinkle with finely chopped green parsley.

SALADS : 189

CELERY KNOB SALAD
Salata De Telina

Wash and peel 3 or 4 large celery knobs, boil in salted water until done, but not overcooked. Cool and cut crosswise into round slices, salt a little, and pour over it wine vinegar, then olive oil. Arrange on a salad plate, slices upon slices, in layers. Decorate with green parsley and garnish with green salad or little sour pickles and ripe olives.

RED CABBAGE SALAD
Salata De Varza Rosie

Clean and rinse a head of red cabbage, drain off the water, then cut into very thin strips like fine noodles. Place in a salad bowl, salt and let stand for 15 to 20 minutes. Then squeeze out with your hands the juice which has formed and place the cabbage into another bowl. Sprinkle over with 1½ tablespoonfuls of powdered sugar, add wine vinegar and olive oil and mix together well with a wooden fork and spoon. Arrange the cabbage into the form of a mound on a serving plate and garnish with sprigs of green parsley.

RED AND GREEN PEPPER SALAD
Salata De Ardei Verde Si Rosiu

Wash and let drain a mixture of green and red peppers. Cut lengthwise into slices and clean away the seeds and membranes. Salt and let stand for 20 to 25 minutes. Pour over this slowly wine vinegar, then olive oil. Arrange the green and red slices on the serving plate into an artistic pattern. Serve with small sour pickles and decorate with sprigs of green parsley.

CUCUMBER SALAD
Salata De Castraveti

Peel 3 or 4 cucumbers, place them in very cold water and let remain there for 20 to 30 minutes. Remove from the water, let

190 : SALADS

dry in the air for a few minutes, then cut crosswise into very thin slices or use a slicer. Salt, cover with a plate and let stand for about 20 to 30 minutes. Now squeeze out the formed juice with the hands (taking care not to break the slices) and place the cucumbers in a salad bowl. Combine one small roll (or bread pulp soaked in water and the excess liquid squeezed out) with one clove of garlic which has been crushed in a small press. Add 4 tablespoonfuls of pure olive oil, mix together well, then thin with wine vinegar, adding it slowly and stirring while you add, to get a semi-liquid mixture. Pour this mixture over the cucumbers and mix well with a wooden fork and spoon. Now place on a deep serving plate, pour on a little pure olive oil, sprinkle with black pepper to taste and also with finely chopped chives (or finely chopped green peppers). Then serve it. It is a delight.

GREEN STRING BEANS SALAD
Salata De Fasole Verde

Snip the ends of one pound of very young and tender meaty green (or yellow) string beans, wash and then slice lengthwise in two. Heat water in a pot and when it is boiling fast, add salt and at the same time the string beans. This will make them retain their green color. When done, strain through a sieve, place in a casserole and let cool. In the meantime chop very fine one small onion, add it to the beans, then sprinkle with salt and pepper to taste. Pour on slowly some wine vinegar, then pure olive oil and mix together very well with a wooden spoon and fork. Sprinkle with finely chopped parsley and serve.

CAULIFLOWER SALAD
Salata De Conopida

Break up the head of a cauliflower into its flowers and boil in salted water until done. The cauliflower must not be too soft, however. Strain over a large sieve, let cool, then place on a serving plate. Mix together in a cup some tarragon vinegar (or if not obtainable use wine vinegar), pure olive oil and salt and pepper. Pour this over the cauliflower. Garnish with lobster claws and decorate with sprigs of parsley.

ASPARAGUS SALAD
Salata De Sparanghel

Clean and peel the outer covering of a bunch of asparagus, boil in salted water, strain over a large sieve, let cool and place the stalks on a large serving plate. Crush the yolks of 6 hard-boiled eggs through a press (or force through a sieve) and add to it one tablespoonful of capers, a little salt and pepper, a little finely chopped chives and some olive oil and tarragon vinegar (or if not obtainable then use wine vinegar). Mix together well, then pour this over the asparagus. Sprinkle with finely chopped parsley.

RED TOMATO SALAD
Salata De Patlagele Rosii

Wash 8 to 10 very firm large red tomatoes. Drain and cut crosswise into not too thin slices. Arrange in the center of a large serving plate. Around the tomatoes place a circle of onion slices cut crosswise. Sprinkle the tomatoes and onions with a little salt, wine vinegar and pure olive oil. Then surround the onions with sardines and black olives. Sprinkle all over with finely chopped mixed chives and parsley.

Desserts and Preserves

THE EXCITING part of every meal is the dessert. It is a feeling common to people all over the world. We all want the last course which finally remains with us and which no other flavor can intrude upon, to leave us with a glow of satisfaction. If the dessert is a success we all will remember the hostess with kind thoughts. The hostess, on her part, must plan the dessert with judgment and care. If the meal is heavy, the dessert should be light. If the main course, however, is light, then the dessert should be rich.

Although the good things produced by nature to feed our bodies and gratify our palate are used by peoples of every country, emphasis on one ingredient or imagination in combinations gives vastly different results. This is as true of desserts as it is of the substantial part of the meal. A pinch of this or that, a glass of wine or perhaps brandy, and something new is born, a new flavor and a true delight.

DOUGHS

Aluaturi

In the preparation of cakes and pancakes it is advisable to have your pans and baking dishes well cleaned and handy. Usually the ingredients can be prepared the night before, if we plan to bake next morning, with a saving of some of our energy. All dough made with yeast should be kept in a large deep pan or dish and in a warm and quiet place. Place it on a firm support

194 : DESSERTS AND PRESERVES

to avoid vibration. If you make a large quantity of dough, place the baking dish (well covered with warm towels) on a pillow which absorbs all vibrations. Be careful not to fill the dish much above the middle, as the dough will rise.

Soften the yeast with a little warm milk or water and a little flour. When it is worked into the dough and it is rising, press the dough down occasionally. Before putting the dough into the baking pan, smear it all over the bottom and sides with unmelted butter or lard with your hands (fingers) then sprinkle all over with a little flour, tilting and moving the pan so that the flour spreads evenly and thinly. Whether the dough is made with butter, lard, or yeast, it must be put in a hot oven at the beginning with a high flame, then changed to a slower heat. It is essential to use strictly fresh butter or lard. Also, when frying in deep fat as for doughnuts, we must have the fat very hot. Be careful and avoid burning, adding from time to time some cold fat. If the fat should be burned, do not continue, as your cake will have a poor taste; rather change to another dish with fresh fat. When finished with the frying, save the leftover fats for sauces and keep them in an earthenware jar or pot.

I think I will start with the much loved Romanian pancakes, *placinte* or *clatite*. This pancake is known here by its French name, Crepes Suzette. Even today, at the sound of the name, Crepes Suzette, everyone responds with "ohs" and "ahs." They would simply love to have it, but feel it is too expensive. But this is simply not so. You can, anyone can make it, and when you will ask yourself, "Now, let me see, just how much did it cost me?" you will be in for a surprise, for it will be very little indeed. But come with me and let's both make it together.

CREPES SUZETTE
Clatite

1 cup sifted flour	4 tbs. powdered sugar
salt	vanilla
1 tbs. sugar	1 orange, ½ lemon
4 eggs	rum, Marsala wine, Benedictine liqueur
milk	
butter	

DESSERTS AND PRESERVES : 195

Place one cupful of sifted flour in a deep bowl, add ⅛ teaspoonful of salt and a tablespoonful of sugar in the center of the flour and mix. Now add 4 eggs one at a time and continue to mix after adding each egg until all are mixed in. Pour in milk slowly and gradually, until you put in about one cupful, stirring constantly at the same time beating it with a spoon. Add a little water and beat well until you get a smooth thin batter. Add a little more milk and beat longer with the spoon until you get a batter that can be spread as thin as tissue. If you will add the ingredients in the order given and beat well, you can be sure there will be no lumps. This pancake mixture should be prepared 3 to 4 hours before using. While it is standing, prepare the sauce as follows.

Use a dish that could be covered very tightly. Put in 4 tablespoonfuls of powdered sugar and 8 to 10 drops of pure vanilla extract and mix well. Add the grated peel of one orange and ½ lemon and mix. Be sure to grate only the colored outer rind of the peel, not the white pulp. Now beat to a foam 4 tablespoonfuls of fresh sweet whipped butter, add it to the mixture, mix and beat together very well. Put the mixture into a double boiler and when melted add 2 tablespoonfuls of fine rum, 2 tablespoonfuls of Marsala wine and 2 tablespoonfuls of Benedictine liqueur, mixing well after each addition. Cover and keep on hand while you are frying the pancakes.

Clean the frying pan by warming it, sprinkling with salt, heating the salt a little and then wiping clean with tissue paper. Warm the clean pan, add little dabs of sweet butter and when hot, pour in just enough batter (about 2 tablespoonfuls) to cover very thinly the bottom of the pan. Quickly, before it can warm up, tilt the frying pan to the right and the left to spread the batter evenly. Then quickly run all around the edge a tablespoonful of butter or lard and fry to a nice crisp brown. Be careful not to burn by continually moving the cake in the pan. When done, turn over with a spatula, or if you dare it, flap the pancake over on its other side. When done on both sides, fold it in half in a semicircular shape, dip it in the sauce quickly and place it in a warm casserole. Continue to make pancakes until all the batter is used up (stir the batter now and then). Then pour the remaining sauce over the pancakes. The casserole should be in a warm oven. When ready to serve, pour rum over the *clatite*,

196 : DESSERTS AND PRESERVES

light it and serve immediately in the casserole. If you do not wish to use rum, serve on hot plates after pouring on the remaining sauce.

PLAIN PANCAKES
Clatite Simple

4 to 6 tbs. flour	1 tbs. powdered sugar
salt	2 eggs
vanilla	1 glass milk

If you want to make some dessert quickly, yet get a delicious result, try to make these thin pancakes. When you arrive home from work, put on an apron, wash your hands and get out a small stirring bowl (if you are preparing enough for only 2 or 3 people). Put into the bowl 4 or even 6 heaping tablespoonfuls of sifted flour, add a little salt, a few drops of pure vanilla extract and one tablespoonful of powdered sugar and mix well. Add 2 eggs and mix in well after adding each. Add one tablespoonful of water, mix, then pour in slowly and gradually one glass of milk, beating all the time, until you get a very thin batter. If you wish you may add a glass of rum, cognac or sherry, but you could do without it, as the pancakes will still be very delicious. Now let it stand, while you go about your other work, until after supper or whenever you wish to serve your hot dessert. When ready, fry the pancakes as above. Keep in the warm oven while you are finishing frying your suzettes. Serve plain with sugar sprinkled over the top, or with jam made into a roll or folded in two, or pour on a little fruit syrup to taste. Make the same batter for fritters, only a little thicker.

PANCAKES WITH CHEESE
Clatite Cu Brinza

Prepare the batter exactly as above. Get one pound of dry pot cheese (without added cream). Extract most of the liquid from the cheese by pressing through a clean napkin. Add one

DESSERTS AND PRESERVES : 197

tablespoonful of powdered sugar and one egg yolk, mix in well with the cheese and use it as a filling for the pancakes. Cover the frying pan thinly with batter, spread evenly by tilting, fry till brown, turn with a spatula and place some of the pot cheese mixture on half of the surface. Flap over the half without the cheese to make a semicircular sandwich, cover well and fry both sides to a nice brown. It must be eaten hot. You may use 2 pans for frying to finish quickly. If you use cream cheese instead of pot cheese it will be equally good.

PANCAKES WITH CASCAVAL AND DILL
Placinta Cu Cascaval Si Marar

Prepare a plain pancake batter (see PLAIN PANCAKES), but omit the rum or cognac. Make a mixture of grated Cascaval cheese, one egg yolk and one tablespoonful of finely minced fresh dill. Have it ready before you begin to fry the pancakes. In the frying pan melt enough butter to cover the bottom evenly. Fry pancakes till a nice light brown, turn with a spatula and place some of the cascaval mixture on half of the surface. Flap over the other half, press together and fry on both sides to a light brown. Serve immediately while still hot. Sprinkle with powdered sugar.

DOUGH FILLED WITH PRUNES
Aluat Umplut Cu Prune

1 lb. sifted flour	1 roll soaked in milk
½ lb. butter	salt
4 eggs	prunes

Get out a large wooden board (if you are not familiar with a board you may use a wooden bowl). Add to one pound of sifted flour ½ pound of sweet butter and work the butter into the flour with your hands. Now add one whole egg, 3 yolks, a small roll soaked in milk and pressed out, and add the necessary salt. Mix the ingredients and when you get a dough, work on it until you get it nice and smooth. Sprinkle the board with flour while you knead the dough, so it will not stick to the

198 : DESSERTS AND PRESERVES

wood. Cover the dough with a napkin and let stand in a cool place for 15 to 20 minutes.

After it is rested, sprinkle the board with flour and cut the dough in half. Roll out each to the thickness of thick noodles and cut into squares large enough to hold the prune filling. Take a square and place in the center some softened prune meat (or fresh plum), join opposite tips of the square together, then join the other two opposite tips, completely folding in the prune. Before pressing the tips together dip the corners in beaten eggs or smear the edges of the squares, so that the opposite ends will stick to each other. When finished, arrange the prune-filled pieces in a buttered baking pan. Brush them well with beaten egg and bake in a hot oven to a nice light brown. This dough can be used for other fruits such as apricots or peaches, either fresh or if dried, they must first be softened.

WINE DOUGH
Aluat De Vin

Beat together very well in a dish 8 egg yolks, ¼ pound of sugar and a little grated vanilla bark. Now add ½ pound of sifted flour, mix well and then thin very slowly with 10 to 12 tablespoonfuls of very good white wine. Pit some nice apricots (or use plums, peaches or any fresh fruit), dry, soak well in the batter and fry in very hot and deep sweet butter or fresh lard.

BUTTER DOUGH
Aluat De Unt

1 lb. flour	1 tbs. cognac
2 egg yolks	1 lb. sweet butter
salt	

Mix well on a large wooden board ½ pound of sifted flour, 2 egg yolks, a little salt and one tablespoonful of cognac. Now thin slowly with enough water to make a dough, not too soft, nor too firm. Knead on board very well. Cover and let rest.

DESSERTS AND PRESERVES : 199

Quickly make another dough as follows. Mix one pound of very fresh sweet butter into ½ pound of sifted flour, put on a board and knead very well. When done, cover and let rest.

Take the first dough and roll out a square leaf about ¼ inch thick. Now roll the second dough into a square ¼ inch thick, and about ¼ inch smaller around the sides. Place the smaller leaf over the larger one and fold over so that the smaller leaf cannot be seen. Slowly compress the two doughs into each other very well, then roll out with the rolling pin to a square leaf ¼ inch thick. Now fold this leaf lengthwise into 3 parts by making 2 folds, then fold across the width into 3 parts by making 2 folds. Cover with a towel, let stand for 10 minutes, then compress the dough and roll out with the rolling pin to a square ¼ inch thick. Fold again into 3 parts in length and in width as above, cover and let stand for 10 minutes. Repeat this procedure one more time, three in all, ending up with a leaf ¼ inch in thickness. Use this dough for meat fillings, fruit fillings, nuts, etc.

The most important thing to remember in making this butter dough is not to break the larger leaf in rolling. Also the wooden board must be spread with flour all along so that the dough will not stick to the board.

STRUDEL DOUGH
Aluat De Strudel

1 cup flour	grated nuts
lard	seedless raisins
1 egg	sugar
salt	cinnamon
butter	

Put one measuring cup of sifted flour on a board and then add a piece of chilled, solid lard the size of a large walnut, breaking and mixing it well with the flour. Mix in one whole egg and add some lukewarm salted water little by little to make a soft dough. Flour the board and knead the dough well. Beat it for ½ hour. Form it into a mound, smear all over with warm lard, then cover the dough with an overturned warmed-up dish. Let stand for 1 to 2 hours.

200 : DESSERTS AND PRESERVES

Sprinkle well a tablecloth with flour, place the dough in the center and roll it out with a rolling pin to the size of a large plate. Now start to pull the dough outward with your hands. First place the left palm under the dough, then start to pull the dough from the center with the right hand on the top. Using the fingers of both hands you pull the dough outward gently working your way all around until you have drawn out the dough to a very thin tissue. The dough must reach over the edges of the tablecloth on all sides. Tear off the thick edge of the dough.

Let the leaf of dough rest for 10 to 15 minutes, but take care it does not dry out too much. Now sprinkle the dough all over with warm butter, then with grated nuts mixed with sugar, moistened seedless raisins and a little cinnamon (use the cinnamon only if you use apple filling). Again sprinkle with some warm butter. Now turn over the overhanging dough at the 4 sides of the table onto the butter sprinkled dough on the table. Sprinkle butter on the part of the dough which has been flapped over.

Spread your ready-made filling (of apple, cherry, cheese or any filling you desire; see FILLINGS) on the half of the leaf nearest to you. Now with the help of the tablecloth roll the dough leaf until you reach the end. Place the strudel roll very carefully into a thin baking pan which has already been buttered and sprinkle with flour. Brush lightly the strudel all over with well-beaten eggs, sprinkle the top with warm butter and put into the oven to bake. Start with a high heat, then reduce it to 350° F. and bake for one hour. Serve hot.

STRUDEL SQUARE OF CHEESE
Strudel Cu Crema Brinza

Prepare the dough exactly as above, but instead of making a roll, form into 6 small mounds, each mound having enough dough when you roll it into a tissue leaf to just cover the bottom of your black baking pan. Naturally you will need more ingredients according to the size of the baking dish. Butter and

DESSERTS AND PRESERVES : 201

sprinkle with flour the bottom of the pan. Add a leaf of dough to cover the bottom. Sprinkle over with warm butter, a little grated lemon peel mixed with sugar and a little grated vanilla bark. Repeat this two more times, first the leaf of dough and then topped with the butter, peel, sugar and vanilla. Add your filling (cheese, fruits, nuts or meats) and spread evenly. Now add the 3 layers of dough on top as you did on the bottom. On top of the filling put the butter, peel, sugar and vanilla and cover with a leaf of dough. Repeat this 3 times. Smear the top with beaten egg and sprinkle with warm butter. Bake, cut into squares and serve hot. If needed the next day, warm in the oven. Instead of 6 leaves of dough, you may use 12, even up to 20.

CREAM CHEESE STRUDEL
Strudel Cu Crema Brinza

Prepare exactly as above but use 10 or 12 dough leaves, half on the bottom, half on top. Make the filling by combining cream cheese with one egg yolk, sugar to taste, softened seedless raisins and a little grated vanilla bark. Bake and cut into squares. Serve hot. When served next day, reheat slowly in the oven. Try it, you will just love it. If you will replace the cream cheese with apricots, you will get an unusual and delectable dessert.

NUT SQUARES WITH SYRUP
Aluat Cu Nuci Si Sirop

Prepare exactly as above, using 10 leaves of dough. Between the leaves sprinkle with butter and grated lemon peel. Fill with a nut filling (see NUT FILLING). When baked pour on a fruit syrup, put back in the oven for a few minutes, then cut into squares and serve hot. The syrup will swell the dough and moisten the nuts. Cover the squares with the syrup remaining in the pan.

202 : DESSERTS AND PRESERVES

DRY LIES
Uscatele Mincuni

8 egg yolks	flour
powdered sugar	lard
salt	cinnamon
1 glass rum	

Mix in a dish 8 egg yolks, one tablespoonful of powdered sugar, a little salt and one glass of rum. If rum is not at hand use cognac, but rum is preferred. Mix very well, then add slowly, with constant stirring or beating, enough flour to make a rather soft dough. Knead it very well until the dough is firm, cut into 6 to 8 portions, form them into the shape of a mound, cover with a clean towel or tablecloth and let rest for 20 to 25 minutes. Now roll out each mound with a rolling pin on a board sprinkled with flour, to ⅛ inch thickness. Cut with different cake forms.

Prepare a large deep frying pan and fill to a little more than half with lard. You may use butter, but lard is preferred. When the fat is very hot fry the pieces of dough to a nice light brown. When done, lift them out with a large spatula, but be very careful not to break them as they are very fragile. When removed from the fat, keep the spatula over the pan for a little while until the excess fat has a chance to run off. Place them on a large serving plate and sprinkle with powdered sugar and cinnamon. Keep in a warm place until ready to serve. They can be kept for later use, but are too delicious to perish from old age. And why are they called dry lies? Because it is hard to believe that a great big plate of this delicacy can disappear so quickly, as it always does.

DOUGHNUTS WITH CHERRIES
Gogosi Cu Cirese

1 to 2 cakes of yeast	salt
milk	½ lb. melted butter
flour	vanilla bark
8 egg yolks	cherries
2 tbs. powdered sugar	lard

DESSERTS AND PRESERVES : 203

Soften 1 to 2 cakes of yeast with a little warm milk, mix well, then add enough flour with constant stirring to make a soft batter. Cover and let stand to ferment.

Put 8 egg yolks in a mixing bowl and beat to a foam together with 2 tablespoonfuls of powdered sugar, a little salt, ⅓ pound of melted sweet butter, 10 to 12 tablespoonfuls of warm milk, 2 tablespoonfuls of lukewarm water and a little grated vanilla bark. Add the fermenting batter and stir. Add slowly, with constant stirring, enough sifted flour to make a rather soft dough. Keep on beating until the dough starts to form bubbles. Cover and let stand in a warm place. Spinkle a large wooden board with flour, place the dough on it and roll out to ½ inch thickness. Cut into circular pieces with a tin form or use a glass.

Place a pitted cherry in the center of a circular piece, cover with another piece and press the edges together with the fingers. Repeat until all the pieces have been used up. Place the doughnuts on a warm wooden board sprinkled with flour, leaving enough space between them to take care of their growth in size. Sprinkle lightly with flour, cover with a towel and let stand until the doughnuts have grown to twice their original size.

Fill a casserole half full of lard, and when very hot, fry the doughnuts to a light brown. Keep turning the doughnuts and see that they do not touch each other. When done, remove from the casserole with a slotted spoon, let the excess fat run off, then place on a plate covered with absorbing paper. Arrange the doughnuts on a hot serving plate, sprinkled with powdered sugar.

Serve hot, but they are equally delicious when cold.

PLAIN DOUGHNUTS
Gogoase Simpli

Prepare exactly as above, but roll out the dough thicker. Serve hot sprinkled with powdered sugar. If you want to try something new, replace the vanilla in the above recipe with some grated lemon peel and a very little pure maple syrup extract. Serve either hot or cold.

204 : DESSERTS AND PRESERVES

FILLINGS

POT OR FARMER CHEESE FILLING
Brinza or Urda Pentru Umplatura

Any kind of cheese makes a delicious filling for dough. Here is one such mixture. Combine one pound of pot (or farmer) cheese, 2 eggs, 2 tablespoonfuls of heavy sweet cream, a little salt to taste, one tablespoonful of sugar and a little grated vanilla bark. When well mixed, add one tablespoonful of finely chopped fresh dill and mix.

POT CHEESE FOR STRUDEL
Brinza De Vaca Pentru Umplatura

Put in one tablespoonful of sweet butter in a mixing bowl and beat to a foam. Add 3 tablespoonfuls of powdered sugar, mix well, then mix in 4 egg yolks, one at a time. Add one grated lemon peel and mix for 10 to 12 minutes. Combine with 2 pounds of dry pot cheese (without cream in it). Add a little salt to taste and 3 tablespoonfuls of heavy sweet cream and again mix well. Beat the 4 eggs whites to stiffness, add to the cheese mixture and mix gently. Use this filling for strudels or other cakes.

SWEET CREAM FILLING
Umplatura De Smantana

Beat 1½ tablespoonfuls of fresh sweet butter to a foam in a mixing bowl. Add 8 egg yolks, mix, then add 2 tablespoonfuls of powdered sugar and a little grated vanilla bark. Mix well for 15 to 20 minutes, then add ½ pint of heavy sweet cream and 1½ tablespoonfuls of very fine (or pulverized) rolls or bread crumbs. Mix well. Now beat to stiffness only 6 of the eggs whites and mix into the mixture very gently. Use as a filling for strudel, pancakes or other pastries.

DESSERTS AND PRESERVES : 205

APPLE FILLING
Umplutura De Mere

Peel 3 to 4 pounds of apples, cut lengthwise into very thin slices and place in a large pan. Sprinkle with 8 tablespoonfuls of powdered sugar and one teaspoonful of powdered cinnamon. Let stand for 10 to 15 minutes.

For making apple strudel, sprinkle the strudel dough leaf with warm butter or lard and spread on evenly the apple filling above (after first having drained away the liquid formed) on half of the leaf. Sprinkle the apple with a handful of seedless raisins, then with a little warm butter, roll and bake. Use the same filling to make apple cake squares or strudel squares.

FILLING OF NUTS
Umplutura De Nuci

Finely grate ½ to 1 pound of nuts and mix with ½ pound of sugar, one teaspoonful of powdered cinnamon, a few powdered cloves and ½ pound of seedless raisins. You may replace the cloves in the mixture with a little grated lemon peel and grated vanilla bark. Use as a filling for strudel or cake. When baked, pour on some strawberry syrup, put back in the oven for a few minutes. Serve hot.

APRICOT FILLING
Umplutura De Caise

Pit the apricots, boil in very little water with sugar and a little vanilla bark. Press through a sieve and use.

RAW CABBAGE FILLING
Umplutura De Varza Dulce

Cut one large raw cabbage into slices made as thin as possible, put into a large bowl, sprinkle with salt, but do not oversalt, and let stand for a little while. Heat 3 level tablespoonfuls of

206 : DESSERTS AND PRESERVES

lard and when very hot squeeze out the cabbage with your hands, add to the fat and stir until the cabbage is very hot throughout. Now add a tablespoonful of powdered sugar and with occasional stirring to prevent burning, fry until it is done. Add some pepper, enough to feel the taste of it, then let cool and use for strudel or the making of squares.

MEAT FILLINGS
Umplutura De Carne

Prepare them the same as the strudel or cake fillings. See MEAT FILLINGS.

SOUR CHERRY FILLING

Prepare exactly as the POT CHEESE FOR STRUDEL, replacing cheese with pitted sour cherries. Use powdered sugar generously.

FRIED RIPE FRUIT DESSERT
Desert De Fructe Prajite

Peel 1 to 2 dozen ripe apricots, cut in half, pit and place on a large dish. Spinkle over with vanilla mixed with powdered sugar. Let stand for 35 to 45 minutes. In the meantime prepare a wine paste (see WINE DOUGH). Soak the apricots well in the paste, then fry quickly in deep boiling lard to a light brown. Remove from the pan with a pierced blade pastry spoon and allow the excess fat to run off before placing on a large serving plate. Sprinkle with sugar mixed with vanilla. Serve hot.

PRUNES OR PLUM DESSERT
Desert De Prune

Prepare exactly as above, using plums, but replacing the vanilla with cinnamon. Also after being fried, drain the fat on absorbing paper, then dredge in finely grated nuts mixed with

DESSERTS AND PRESERVES : 207

vanilla and sugar or in grated sweet chocolate. Arrange nicely
on a serving plate. Serve hot.

If you use prunes instead of fresh plums, stew them in a
little water, strain, pit, let dry, then proceed as with the plums.

GAY HORNS WITH WINE
Cornuri Fericite in Vin

Butter horns which have been given good old wine to drink.
No wonder they are gay, and you will be too, after enjoying
this unusual dessert.

Get 12 to 16 butter horns from the bakery (or make them
yourself if you love to bake). Slice them crosswise in half.
Warm good white wine, enough to be able to soak the cut
butter horns, add 2 to 3 tablespoonfuls of water, sugar to taste
and one tablespoonful of ground cinnamon, and mix together
well. Immerse the horns in the wine mixture, turn over on both
sides, but be careful they do not become too soft. Soak them
just enough so that they can be handled without breaking. Remove from the wine, dredge in beaten eggs, then fry quickly in
deep hot lard on both sides to a light brown. Drain off fat,
place on a serving plate and serve hot.

TORTES

To know how to make a good torte is the duty of every home-
maker in Romania. Even though it will be made only once or
twice each year by the poorest family due to the cost of the
ingredients, they still will produce a wonderful torte. It will
mean, of course, that they will have to save up the necessary
eggs, instead of selling or bartering them at the village market
place.

The preparation of the torte by the young girls of the villages
and the towns is a Romanian custom. Usually on a Sunday
afternoon the village girls will meet at the home of one who
can afford more of the torte ingredients, but each will bring
something along. The kind of torte they will make is decided

208 : DESSERTS AND PRESERVES

by all the girls and most of the time it will be something complicated. If successful, their accomplishment will be all the greater and they will glow with pride. Oh, how they pray that it will come out all right. Then the news will quickly spread around that the girls of this or that school made a heavenly torte, oh, what a torte! And so they not only spend an interesting and pleasant Sunday, but have learned something of value to them in their future life, too.

Of course, the lady of the house (*Lelea Ancuta*) will let the goose out of the bag to some boys, who will arrive just about the time the torte will be ready. Just in case the girls are not successful, *Lelea Ancuta* will have prepared her own torte on Saturday evening, to bring out to the table, to shield the girls from a horrible embarrassment. *Lelea Ancuta*, her good soul showing on her smiling face, will appear at the threshold, followed by the boys, and will set a nice table with hot chocolate and whipped cream, *Chocolata cu Frisca*, where half the cup is filled with whipped cream to which a little vanilla has been added. If the girls' torte is successful, then so much the better, as *Lelea Ancuta* and the boys will help to eat it, while showering the girls with praise.

They make a pretty picture around the table. Someone will begin to sing a folk song and soon all join in and this gayety will continue for some time. Then thanking the hostess nicely, they will run home before the sun sets, as it is not considered proper for a girl to be out after nightfall. And so they have ended a gay afternoon, but not before they have made a date for the following Sunday, naturally in a different home. Now, wouldn't it be nice if our young girls started cooking and baking parties like this, right in their own homes?

There are a few directions which must always be followed when making tortes. Stirring and beating must be in one direction only and with a rhythmic stroke, not fast at one time and slow at another, but with the same speed. If this is not done, the torte will not rise equally. The torte baking form must be buttered well and sprinkled with flour. When making tortes containing butter always work in a cool place. Never use lard, only butter. The butter should be strictly fresh, chilled and solid.

DESSERTS AND PRESERVES : 209

Have all your ingredients already prepared and close at hand, as you must work fast when you start the beating. The eggs and cream must be beaten quickly and in one direction to stiffness. When it is so stiff that it will not run out of the dish when turned on its side, it is done. Use immediately. The eggs must be strictly fresh and kept in a cool place. Sift the powdered sugar and the flour before using. All nuts used must be grated; if possible do this by machine. Finely grated bread crumbs must be sprinkled in slowly, until the mixture is the consistency of a thick batter.

In the making of every torte use the juice of one lemon. In the baking start with a low flame. As the torte grows increase the flame. When turning the baking form, be careful not to shake the torte, as shaking will cause it to fall. On the chocolate torte and those made with almonds, filberts and walnuts, pour on as soon as they come from the oven sugared wine or syrup of any kind you like. When the torte is baked, leave to cool in the dish.

TORTES WITHOUT BUTTER
Torta Fara Unt

CHOCOLATE TORTE
Torta Cu Ciocolata

12 eggs	½ lb. almonds
½ lb. powdered sugar	3 bars chocolate
vanilla	bread crumbs

Mix in a casserole 12 egg yolks and beat in one direction only after having added ½ pound powdered sugar and a little vanilla. Beat ½ hour. Then add ½ pound of finely grated almonds and 3 bars of scraped chocolate and mix well. Beat to stiffness the 12 egg whites and add to the mixture. Now add finely grated bread crumbs, sprinkling them on slowly until the mixture is the consistency of thick batter, and mix in very gently.

Butter well your torte form, put in the whole mixture and bake slowly for one hour. When it is done and after cooling, you may glaze it if you wish.

LEMON TORTE
Torta De Lamaie

14 eggs	1 lemon
¾ lb. powdered sugar	8 egg whites
½ lb. almonds	bread crumbs

Mix in a casserole 14 egg yolks and ¾ pound of powdered sugar. Beat in one direction only for ½ hour. Now add ½ pound grated almonds and the grated peel and juice of one lemon. Mix well. Beat to stiffness the whites of 8 eggs and add to the mixture. Now add finely grated bread crumbs, sprinkling them on slowly, and mix in gently.

Butter well the tin torte form, put in the whole mixture and bake slowly for ¾ hour. When it is done and cooled, you may glaze it if you wish.

TORTE WITH NUTS
Torta Cu Nuci.

12 eggs	grated cloves
½ lb. powdered sugar	½ tsp. nutmeg
1 lemon	3 tbs. bread crumbs
½ lb. grated nuts	1 pt. white wine
1 tsp. cinnamon	½ lb. sugar

Put in 12 whole eggs and ½ pound of powdered sugar into a deep casserole. Beat constantly with an egg beater for one hour until it is thick. Add the grated peel and the juice of one lemon, beat a little, then add ½ pound of grated nuts, a teaspoonful of powdered cinnamon, a few grated cloves, ½ tablespoonful of scraped nutmeg and 3 tablespoonfuls of fine bread crumbs. All of these ingredients are to be sprinkled in slowly, a little at a time, then gently mixed.

Butter well in the torte form, put in the whole mixture and bake slowly for one hour. Remove from the form and before it has cooled pour on a warm wine syrup. The wine syrup is prepared by boiling one pint of good white wine with ½ pound of sugar for 15 to 20 minutes.

DESSERTS AND PRESERVES : 211

TORTES WITH BUTTER
Torta Cu Unt

ROMANIAN TORTE
Torta Romaneasca

⅓ lb. sweet butter   1 lemon
8 egg yolks   4 tbs. rum
⅓ lb. powdered sugar   2 tbs. bread crumbs

Beat ⅓ pound of sweet butter to a foam, add 8 egg yolks
and ⅓ pound of powdered sugar and mix together well for
½ hour. Now add the grated peel and juice of one lemon and
4 tablespoonfuls of good rum and mix well again. Beat to
stiffness the 8 egg whites and add it to the mixture. Add 2
tablespoonfuls of grated bread crumbs, sprinkling in slowly and
mixing very gently.

Butter the torte form, put in the mixture and bake slowly
for ¾ hour. If you want to top with a glaze of frozen lemon
when the torte is done, return it back to the oven to be dried.

TORTE WITH ALMOND
Torta Cu Migdale

¾ lb. butter   12 eggs
¾ lb. powdered sugar   ⅓ lb. almonds
1 lemon   ⅓ lb. flour

Beat ¾ pound of fresh sweet butter and ¾ pound of powdered
sugar to a foam. Add the grated peel and juice of one lemon
and 12 egg yolks. Add one yolk at a time and mix well after
each addition. Put in ⅓ pound of grated almonds and mix well
again. Beat to stiffness 8 egg whites and combine with the
mixture. Now add ⅓ pound of sifted flour, sprinkle in slowly,
a little at a time, and mix gently.

Divide the mixture into 2 equal portions. Get 2 equal sized
torte dishes, butter them, and bake the tortes to a nice brown.
Remove from the fire and let cool. Cover one torte with strawberry jam and place the other torte on top of the jam. If you

212 : DESSERTS AND PRESERVES

wish you may glaze the top of the double torte with fruits from compote, but well drained of its liquid.

TORTE OF BUTTER LEAVES
Torta De Foi Cu Unt

Place on a large wooden board ½ pound powdered sugar, ½ pound grated almonds and ½ pound strictly fresh sweet butter. Mix all these well together to make a dough and knead it well. Divide into 6 parts and roll out each with the rolling pin to the exact size of the torte form. Bake each leaf of dough separately.

When they are all baked, take a leaf, spread with apricot (or any other fruit) preserve, cover with another leaf, again spread with preserve and continue adding these alternate layers and finish with a baked leaf on top. Now decorate the top of the torte with the pieces of fruit taken out of the preserve.

CHATEAUX

To be successful in the making of a good chateaux you must always stir in one direction only, whether you are mixing in the ingredients or stirring while cooking. If you should reverse the direction only once, the chateaux will be ruined. Neither must the mixing be interrupted. The mixture must be heated on a high flame quickly in a double boiler and just as soon as it starts to boil immediately removed from the fire. Continue to mix steadily and in one direction until cool and calm.

All of the chateaux are to be used to top cakes, puddings and pastries of all kinds.

CHATEAUX
Satou

16 egg yolks	1 lemon
8 tbs. powdered sugar	1 pt. white wine

Add to a deep casserole 16 egg yolks, 8 tablespoonfuls of sifted powdered sugar and the grated peel of one lemon. Mix well in one direction only for 30 to 40 minutes. Bring one pint of good white wine to a boil. Now with the left hand pour the wine into the egg yolk mixture, a little at a time, while with the right hand stir constantly in one direction until all the wine has been added. Quickly place the casserole in a double boiler over a high flame, and stir constantly in one direction while the mixture is getting thicker. When it comes to a boil, remove from the heat quickly. Continue the stirring, always in one direction until calm and cool. Use as a topping for cakes, puddings or over anything you wish. I prepare my chateaux in a double boiler and so far I have never failed.

WINE CHATEAUX
Satou De Vin

1 lemon	10 egg yolks
1 navel orange	1 pt. white wine
½ lb. powdered sugar	

Grate the rind of one lemon and one navel orange. Do not grate any of the white pulp in the peel, only the colored, oily outer layer. Have ready ½ pound of powdered sugar. Put some of this sugar into a mortar, add the grated rind and pound with a pestle until the rind is well mixed in and ground up. Now put this mixture together with the rest of the sugar into a glass bottle, close tightly and let stand for 2 days to have the flavor permeate throughout. When ready to use combine with 10 egg yolks. Mix well in only one direction for about ½ hour. Bring one pint of good white wine to a boil. Now with the left hand pour the wine into the egg yolk mixture, a little at a time, while with the right hand stir constantly in one direction until all the wine has been added. Quickly place the casserole in a double boiler over a high flame and stir constantly in one direction while the mixture is getting thicker. When it comes to a boil, remove from the heat quickly. Continue the stirring, always in one direction, until calm, but not too cold. Pour over cakes and puddings or serve in a sauce dish. It is very delicious. Will you please try it?

214 : DESSERTS AND PRESERVES

CHATEAUX OF RASPBERRY
Satou De Smeura

Clean some ripe raspberries, press through a clean white cloth, then strain the juice through a very fine sieve into a casserole. The liquid should be clear. Use enough raspberries to make ½ pint of juice. Put this into a deep pot, add 10 tablespoonfuls of good white wine, 10 egg yolks and 10 tablespoonfuls of powdered sugar and mix well. Put into a double boiler and during all the time it is heating beat with an egg beater until the liquid starts to rise in the pot. Then remove from the heat and pour over cakes or puddings. It is especially delicious with sponge cake. In the winter use syrup of raspberry.

CHATEAUX OF STRAWBERRY
Satou De Fragi

Prepare as the WINE CHATEAUX above, but add to the wine while it is on the stove and before it has come to a boil 5 tablespoonfuls of fresh strawberries which have been pressed through a sieve.

Soak a handful of strawberries in a glass of rum or liquor for some time. Then pour this mixture over the chateaux before serving. Use on cakes or puddings. In the winter instead of fresh strawberries use strawberry preserves.

CHATEAUX OF CURRANTS
Satou De Coacaze

Take one pound of ripe currants and get the clear juice from them, as was done with the raspberries in the above recipe. Combine the juice in a deep pot with 10 egg yolks and ½ pound of powdered sugar, mix and put to heat in a double boiler. While heating, beat continuously with an egg beater until the liquid thickens and starts to rise in the pot. Remove quickly when this happens and serve immediately.

DESSERTS AND PRESERVES : 215

CHATEAUX OF ORANGE
Satou De Portocale

Prepare sugar and grated orange rind as is done in the WINE CHATEAUX recipe above. Now put 10 tablespoonfuls of this flavored sugar into a deep pot and add 12 egg yolks, 10 table-spoonfuls of orange juice (preferably from navel oranges) and 10 tablespoonfuls of good white wine. Heat in a double boiler and in the meantime keep beating with an egg beater until it begins to boil, then remove immediately and use.

CHATEAUX OF LEMON
Satou De Lamaie

Prepare exactly as above, but use lemon flavored sugar instead of orange. Also replace the orange juice with lemon juice.

FOAM OF SYRUP
Spuma Cu Sirop

Beat 10 egg whites to a stiff foam. While you are beating the whites bring 20 tablespoonfuls of any fruit syrup you desire up to the boiling point but do not boil. Now with the left hand add the syrup to the egg whites slowly, a little at a time, and with the right hand beat continuously with the egg beater until all the syrup has been added. Use over puddings, cakes and pastries.

VANILLA CHATEAUX
Satou De Vanilie

12 egg yolks	vanilla
8 tbs. powdered sugar	1 pt. milk

Combine in a pot 12 eggs yolks, 8 tablespoonfuls of powdered sugar and plenty of ground vanilla or vanilla extract to suit your taste. Mix well for ½ hour and in one direction only. Bring one pint of milk up to the boiling point, but do not boil.

216 : DESSERTS AND PRESERVES

Now with the left hand pour the milk into the yolk mixture, a little at a time, while with the right hand stir constantly in one direction until all the milk has been added. Quickly place the casserole in a double boiler over a high flame, and stir constantly in one direction while the mixture is getting thicker. When it comes to a boil, remove from the heat quickly. Continue the stirring until calm and cool.

CHOCOLATE CHATEAUX
Satou De Ciocolata

Prepare exactly like the VANILLA CHATEAUX above, but use 10 egg yolks instead of 12. Also add 3 or 4 small bars of scraped chocolate to the milk and bring to a boil. Use this instead of the milk in the above recipe.

CHAMPAGNE CHATEAUX
Satou De Champagne

Combine in a pot 10 egg yolks, 5 whole eggs, ¾ pound of sugar impregnated with lemon rind (see WINE CHATEAUX above), the juice of 2½ lemons and one pint of good white wine. Put in a double boiler and keep beating constantly with an egg beater until the mixture starts to thicken. Then add 3 glasses of champagne, a little at a time, stirring all the time. Serve immediately.

BIRD MILK OR FLOATING ISLAND
Lapte De Pasere

1 qt. milk	10 eggs
7 or 8 lumps sugar	5 tbs. powdered sugar
vanilla bark and extract	

Heat in a casserole one quart of milk together with 7 or 8 lumps of sugar and ½ piece of vanilla bark broken into small pieces. Beat 10 egg whites to stiffness, then when the milk begins to boil add the whites to the slowly boiling milk with a tablespoon. Boil about 1 to 2 minutes, then gently with a spatula turn the foam over, but be careful not to break it. When nice and

DESSERTS AND PRESERVES : 217

firm on both sides lift out carefully and place on a large serving plate.

In another pot combine 10 egg yolks, 5 tablespoonfuls of powdered sugar and a few drops of vanilla extract. Beat very well in only one direction for 15 to 20 minutes. Place the pot on the fire and while constantly stirring in one direction with the left hand, add the milk in which the whites have been boiled. Continue to stir in one direction until the mixture gets thicker. As soon as the mixture comes to a boil, immediately remove from the fire, but continue the stirring until it is cool. Put this mixture into a large glass dish, then add the egg white foam. Decorate with seedless raisins or with fresh cherries, strawberries or raspberries. If these fruits are not in season, use instead the fruit taken out of preserves. Place in the refrigerator. Serve cold.

PRESERVES OF FRUITS
Dulceturi De Fructe

In Romania the country women and even women in towns and cities are busy from early spring to late autumn with the preservation of the fruits of the fields and orchards. Every free moment they devote to this labor of love. I remember clearly the long, long ago of 1914, before the first World War. I had my share and my extreme youth did not spare me from the horrors which aged me practically overnight. But how can I ever forget the sweet days of my childhood, carefree, close to the beauties of nature and filled with the color of native song and dance? And what child in Romania has not been enchanted with the aromas coming from the kitchen, nor deeply impressed with the love of cooking and skill that even the poorest housewife had in great abundance? And what child could ever forget the famous pantries, which were the pride of every Romanian housewife? There were rows and rows of jars of *dulceata*, compote, marmalade and syrups. The fruits were picked at full ripeness and the flavors couldn't be improved upon. And the colors of the jars seemed to blend in a harmony, like the colors of their beautiful and graceful costumes that they create from a rich imagination and then make with their own hands.

218 : DESSERTS AND PRESERVES

It is a custom in every Romanian home, whether it be rich or humble, to serve the sweet *dulceata* (preserves) to anyone who comes to visit them. As soon as the guest is seated some one will appear with a nice handmade tray, covered with a colorful doily. On it there will be a glass of ice cold spring water and a beautiful little plate with about a heaping teaspoonful of the patriarchal *dulceata*. This is then graciously offered to the guest and to all the other people who are present. The spring water serves to cool the visitor and the sweet offering is a symbol of the sweet hospitality extended to him. Besides, he is welcomed with the words, *Bineati Venit*, implying it is an honor for him to have come to their home. And while partaking of the *dulceata* it gives time to the guest to cool off, rest himself and collect his thoughts.

This wonderful tradition has been passed along from mother to daughter from ancient times. It is carried out with dignity and sincerity. To serve or partake of the *dulceata* is a duty having religious overtones.

The fruits used in making the *dulceata* are green grapes, wild red cherries, citron, black cherries, wild strawberries, apricots, raspberries, green plums, green hazel nuts, oranges, rose petals, currants, gooseberries, etc.

In the writing of this book I have naturally relived the innocent and beautiful days of my youth in the old country, where I first learned to love cooking. And because those days were full of sweetness I feel it is fitting that I end with those wonderful Romanian *dulceatas*, full of sweetness and goodness. And in offering to you some of these dishes, I say to you "Thank you nicely," and "*Pofta Buna*," good appetite.

DULCEATA OF ROSE PETALS
Dulceata De Trandafir

½ lb. rose petals
1 tsp. sour salt
2 lbs. sugar

1 tbs. powdered sugar
1 lemon

Get ½ pound of nice rose petals with a fine aroma and very red in color. Cut off the white part of the petals at the stem end

DESSERTS AND PRESERVES : 219

and place in a pot with those petals which are already wilted. Add one quart of water, boil for 3 minutes, then remove from the fire. Add one tablespoonful of powdered sour salt, let stand for 15 minutes, then strain. Let it settle. When the liquid is clear, pour this liquid into a pot, add 2 pounds of sugar and boil until it is dissolved. Remove the foam from the top during the boiling.

While the sugar is boiling, sprinkle the bunch of red petals with one tablespoonful of powdered sugar and the juice of one lemon. Knead well with the hands, then put them into the hot sugar syrup and boil until done. Remove from the fire. Put the *dulceata* in a porcelain saucepan, cover with a wet towel and let cool in a cool place, then put into jars. In the summer it makes a delightful soft drink if it is dissolved in cold water or seltzer. It can also be used on toast, french toast and butter rolls, but sparingly.

GREEN HAZEL NUT PRESERVE
Dulceata De Nuci Verzi

2 lbs. green hazel nuts	½ lemon
2 lbs. sugar	vanilla bark

Get 2 pounds of small young green hazel nuts (before the hard shell has been formed). They should be just a trifle larger than filbert nuts. Remove the green shell, place them in cold water and boil for 10 minutes. Wash very well in 6 or 7 changes of water. Now when this is done, let soak in cold water for 10 to 12 minutes, discard the water, add fresh water and let soak for another 10 to 12 minutes. Continue this for 6 soakings, then let the water drain off.

Boil 2 pounds of sugar with 2 quarts of water to make a thick syrup. Just before the syrup is done add the nuts and ½ lemon cut into very thin slices. When the green nuts are nearly cooked, add ½ piece of vanilla bark cut into very small pieces. Remove from the fire, place in a saucepan, cover with a wet towel and let cool. Then put up in jars and away to the pantry with them.

WILD CHERRY PRESERVE
Dulceata De Visine

Get 2 pounds of wild cherries, remove stems and pit with a needle. Proceed exactly as above, using one pound of sugar for each pound of fruit.

APRICOT PRESERVE
Dulceata De Caisa

2 lbs. green apricots	½ lemon
2 lbs. sugar	vanilla bark

Get 2 pounds of very young green apricots, before the pits have become hard. Prick the surface in 2 or 3 places. Wash them in a few changes of cold water. Place the apricots in parchment and heat in boiling water until soft. Remove the fruit from the parchment and scatter on a sieve to drain out well all the water.

Boil 2 pounds of sugar with 2 quarts of water to make a thick syrup. Skim off the scum formed. Just before the syrup is done add the apricots and ½ lemon cut into very thin slices. Continue the boiling until done, then add a piece of vanilla bark cut into very small pieces. Put the apricots into a saucepan, cover with a wet towel and let cool in a cool place. Then put up in jars.

Index

Almond Sauce with Horse-radish, 178
Almond Torte, 211
Anise Sauce for Fish, 178
Appetizers 7–11
Apple Filling (Strudel), 205
Apple Sauce, 180
  Game, 180
  with Horse-radish, 185
Apricot Filling (Strudel), 205
Apricot Preserve, 220
Artichokes, Fried, 49
Asparagus, Braised, 50
  in Cream, 50
  Salad, 191

Bean Puree, 21
Beans, Dried, Soup, 19
  Mashed, 51
  with Oil, 50
  with Pork, 51
  with Sausages, 51
Beans, String, Green, 69
  in Oil for Lent, 69
  with Meat, 68
  Peasant Style, 68
Beef, 99, 104–12, 133–6, 149
  Boiled, 110
  Boiled, Roasted, 110
  Brains, 111
  Chops, Grilled, 105

Beef, Cutlets in Cream, 106
  Cutlets with Onions, 105
  Fillets, Grilled, 105
  Flanken, Grilled, 105
  Leftovers, 111
  Meat Balls, 133–6
  Mititei, 99
  Roast, 106
  Roast ala Bucuresti, 108
  Roast, Stuffed, 107
  Steak ala Sinaia, 108
  Steak, Grilled, 104
  Steak, Raw, 109
  Steak, Rib, Grilled, 105
  Stew, 149
  Stew in Ale, 149
  Stew with Potatoes, 150
  Stock, 15
  Tongue, 111
  Tongue, Smoked, 112
  Tongue, Smoked, with To-matoes and Olives, 112
Beer Soup, 22
Beets, 51
Bird Milk or Floating Island (Dessert), 216
Brains, Balls, 134
  with Cream or Wine Sauce, 119
  with Mushrooms (Stuffed), 74
Briar Sauce, 180
Brown Sauce, 173

221

222 : INDEX

Butter Dough, 198
Butter Dumplings, 166
Butter Sauce, 174

Cabbage, ala Cluj, 52
  Filling (Strudel), 205
  Fried, sweet, 56
  Raw (Red), 55
  Salad (Red), 189
  Shredded, 55
Cabbage, Stuffed with Meat, 42
  with Rice, 40
Cabbage (Turnip) with Cream, 55
Cabbage, with Meat (Savoy), 56
Caper Sauce, 181
Caraway Seed Soup with Dumplings, 20
Carp, ala Macedon, 83
  Marinated, 81
  ala Ovidiu, 80
  in Beer, 83
  Roe, Paste of, 8
  Stuffed, 82
  with Vegetables, 82
Carrots, Roasted, 56
Cauliflower, Braised, 57
  in Cream, 57
  Salad, 190
Celery, Musaca, 39
Celery Knob, Salad, 189
  Sauce, 182
Champagne Chateaux, 216
Chateaux, 212-16
  Champagne, 216
  Chocolate, 216
  Currant, 214
  Lemon, 215

Chateaux, Orange, 215
  Raspberry, 214
  Strawberry, 214
  Vanilla, 215
  Wine, 213
Cheese Dumplings, 167
Cheese Fillings (Strudel), 204
Cheese, White Goat, 7
Cherry Doughnuts, 202
Cherry Filling (Strudel), 206
Cherry Preserve (Wild), 220
Cherry Sauce, 179
Chicken, 87-92
  Breaded, 90
  with Cream, 92
  Fillings for, 131
  with Garlic and Butter Sauce, 91
  with Lemon, 92
  Livers with Mushrooms, 74
  Livers, Stew, 141
  Livers, Stew with Onions, 141
  with Okra, 60
  with Onions, 91
  Peasant Style, 89
  Piquant (Leftovers), 89
  Roast, in Casserole, 87
  Roast, with Oranges, 87
  Roast, with Rice, 88
  Sauce for, 178
  Soup, 13
  Stew, in Cream, 144
  Stew, Peasant Style, 142
  Stew, with Tarragon, 143
  Stew, with Tomatoes, 143
Chocolate Chateaux, 216
Chocolate Torte, 209
Chopped Meat Dishes and Fillings, 127–38
Ciorbas, 23–32
  Fish, 29

INDEX : 223

Ciorbas, Fish, for Hangover, 30
  Fish with Sour Cream, 29
  Lamb (Spring), 26
  Leek, 31
  with Meat Balls, 24
  with Mushrooms, 32
  Rabbit, 27
  Summer Squash, 30
  Tripe, 28
  Veal, 27
Cod with Onions, 83
Cream Sauce, 173
  with Horse-radish, 178
Crepes Suzette, 194
Cucumber, Salad, 189
  Sauce, 183
Currant Chateaux, 214
Currant Sauce, 179
  for Game, 179

Desserts and Preserves, 193–
  220
Dill (Green) Sauce, 183
Doughnuts, Plain, 203
  with Cherries, 202
Doughs, 193
  Butter, 198
  Strudel, 198
  Wine, 198
Dry Lies (Dessert), 202
Duck, ala Roumaine, 94
  with Gherkins, 95
  with Olives, 95
  Roasted, with Olives and
    Beer, 94
Dulceata of Rose Petals, 218
Dumplings, 165–9
  Butter, 166
  Cheese, 167
  Farina, 165

Dumplings, Flour, 166
  Liver, 168
  with Olive Oil, 167
  Pot Cheese, 168

Eggplant, 1–6
  Baked in Butter, 3
  Baked Stew with Meat, 5
  ala Bucharest, 4
  Cheese, 5
  Fried, 2
  ala Garlic, 6
  Garnishing, 4
  Lenten, 2, 3
  Musaca, 36
  Paste, 1
  Stuffed, 2, 3
Eggs,
  Omelet with Cascaval, 158
  Omelet with Mushrooms, 74
  see also Omelets, 153–8
  Romanian Eyes, 158
  Sauce, 186
  Scrambled, 156–7

Farina Dumplings, 165
Fillings, 127–38
  for Strudel, 204–6
Fish, 79–85
  Baked in brown paper, 85
  Broiled, 79
  Ciorba, 29–38
  Filling for, 132
  Ghivetch, 35
  Roe, 9
  Roe in Jelly, 9
  Roe (Pike), Paste of, 8
  Sauce, 177

224 : INDEX

Fish, Sauce with Anise, 178
  Stew, 80
  see also names of Fish
Floating Island (Dessert), 216
Flour Dumplings, 166
Foam of Syrup, 215

Garlic, Sauce, 175
  Soup, 20
Gay Horns with Wine, 207
Ghivetch, 33–35
  with Fish, 35
  with Meat, 35
  Vegetable, 34
Goose, Roast, 93
  with Sauerkraut, 95
Goose Liver, 96
  Breaded, 96
  Stew Peasant Style, 142
  Stuffed, 96
Gooseberry Sauce, 180
  Soup, 18
Grape Sauce, 181
Grapevine Leaves Stuffed with
  Lamb, 138

Ham, Filling, 131
  in Pudding with Potatoes,
  127
Hazel Nut (Green) Preserve,
  219
Herring, 9–11
  Creamed, 9
  Gourmet, 11
  Marinated, 9
  Paste, 10
  with Vegetables, 10
  in Vinegar, 10

Hors D'Oeuvres, 7–11
Horse-Radish Sauce, 186
  with Almonds, 178
  with Apple Sauce, 185
  with Cream Sauce, 178

Kohlrabi,
  with Noodles, 57
  as a Side Dish, 58
  Stuffed, 42

Lamb,
  Chops, 122, 123
  Ciorba, 26
  Extras, 121
  Fillings for, 131
  for Fillings, 130, 131, 136
  with Okra, 59
  Sauce for, 177
  Schnitzel, 122
  Spring, 120
  Stew, 151
  Stew with Green Herbs, 151
  Stew with Green Peppers
    and Carrots, 152
  Stew with Okra, 152
  Stuffed Grapevine Leaves,
    138
  see also Mutton
Leeks, Ciorba, 31
  Stew, with Meat, 58
  Stuffed with Meat, 43
  Stuffed with Rice, 42
Lemon Chateaux, 215
  Sauce, 172
  Torte, 210
Lenten Eggplant with Toma-
  toes and Olives, 2, 3

INDEX : 225

Lenten Mushrooms in Wine, 75
Lettuce Salad, 187
 with Eggs, 187
 with Scallions, 188
 with Sugar, 188
Lettuce Soup, 17
Liver, Balls, 133
 Dumplings, 168
 Pudding, 126

Mamaliga Dishes, 159–63
 Modern Method, 161
 Traditional Method, 160
 with Butter, 162
 Cold, Peasant Style, 163
 with Cream, 163
 Dumplings with Cheese, 162
 Fried Slices, 162
 Layer with Cheese, 161
 with Milk, 163
 with Sauerkraut, 163
 Stuffed, 162
Meat Dishes, 97–138
 Broiled, 97
 Chopped, 127–38
 Ciorbas, 24
 Fillings, 127–38
 Ghivetch, 35
 Loaf, 137
 Puddings, 125–7
 Soups, 14, 15
 Stews, 144–52
 see also names of meats
Mititei, 99
Musaca, 35–40
 with Celery, 39
 with Eggplant, 36
 with Noodles, 38

Musaca with Potatoes, 38
 with Wine, 37
Mushrooms, 71–7
 with Brown Sauce, 76
 with Butter Sauce, 76
 with Chicken Livers, 74
 Ciorba, 32
 Filling, 132
 Garnish, 77
 with Lemon, 77
 Lenten, in Wine, 75
 with Omelet, 74
 Plain, 77
 Roumaine, 71
 Sauces, 184–5
 Stew, 73
 Stuffed with Brains, 74
 Stuffed with Chicken Livers, 74
 Stuffed, Grilled, 73
 in Wine, 75
Mutton,
 with Garlic, 123
 Leg ala Flora, 124

Noodles, Musaca, 38
 with Kohlrabi, 57
Nut Filling for Fish, 132
 for Strudel, 205
Nut Squares with Syrup, 201
Nut Torte, 210

Okra, 59–60
 with Chicken, 60
 with Young Lamb, 59
 with Oil, 60
 with Veal, 60
Olive Oil Sauce, 186

226 : INDEX

Olives, paste, 7
Omelets, 153–8
  with Cascaval, 158
  with Cherries, 154
  with Mushrooms, 74
  with Pot Cheese, 155
  Soup, 14
  with Sour Cream, 156
  with Strawberries, 154
  with Strawberry Jam, 155
  with various Whole Fruit
    Jams, 156
Onion Sauce, 175
Orange Chateaux, 215
Orange Sauce, 181

Pancakes, Plain, 196
  with Cascaval and Dill, 197
  with Cheese, 196
Parsley (Green) Sauce, 183
Paste, Carp Roe, 8
  Eggplant, 1
  Herring, 10
  Olives, 7
  Pike Roe, 8
  White Goat Cheese of
    Braila, 7
Peas, Green, 60
Peppers, 61–3
  ala Sinaia, 62
  Baked Romanian, 62
  in Oil, 61
  Salad, 189
  Stuffed with Meat, 43
  Stuffed with Rice, 44
  Stuffed with Vegetables, 45
Pike Roe, Paste of, 8
Plum Dessert, 206
Pork, 100–4
  ala Anisoara, 104

Pork and Beef Sausage, 101
  Brains, Grilled, 101
  Chops, Grilled, 100
  Chops in Sauce, 102
  Chops in Beer, 102
  Fillet, Grilled, 100
  Kidney, 100
  Liver, Grilled, 101
  Loin, Grilled, 101
  Roasted Suckling Pig, 103
  Sausage, 101
  Sausage, Grilled, 101
  Stew, 147
  Stew Peasant Style, 148
  Stew with Potatoes, 148
  Tongue (Fresh), 112
  Tongue (Fresh) with Sauce,
    113
Potato Soup, 16
  Soup with Smoked Pork,
    17
Potatoes, 63–6
  Breaded, 65
  Breaded Patties, 66
  with Cheese, 64
  with Eggs, 63
  Fried with Onions, 65
  Fried, New, 66
  Musaca, 38
  Peasant Style, 63
  in Pudding with Ham, 127
  Roasted, 65
  with Sausage, 65
  Stew, 64
  Stuffed with Ham, 45
  Stuffed with Liver, 46
  Stuffed with Mushrooms, 46
Preserves of Fruits, 217–20
Prunes or Plum Dessert, 206
Pudding, with Potatoes and
    Ham, 127
  with Rice and Tongue, 127

INDEX : 227

Rabbit Ciorba, 27
Raspberry Chateaux, 214
Rice, Fried, 66
  Pilaf, 67
Rose Petals, Dulceata, 218

Salads, 187–91
  Asparagus, 191
  Cabbage (Red), 189
  Cauliflower, 190
  Celery Knob, 189
  Cucumber, 189
  Leaf Lettuce, 188
  Lettuce, 187
  Lettuce with Eggs, 187
  Lettuce and Scallions, 188
  Lettuce with Sugar, 188
  Peppers, Red and Green, 189
  Potato, 188
  String Bean, 190
  Tomato, 191
Salmon, Marinated, 81
  with Garlic, 84
  with Onions, 84
Sauces, cold, 185–6
  Apple, with Horse-radish, 185
  Eggs, Hard-Boiled, 186
  Horse-radish, 186
  Olive Oil, 186
Sauces, hot, 171–85
  Almond with Horse-radish, 178
  Anise, for Fish, 178
  Apple, 180
  Apple (Game), 180
  Briar, 180
  Brown, 173
  Butter, 174
  Caper, 181

Sauces, Celery Knob, 182
  Cherry, 179
  for Chicken or Veal, 178
  Cream, 173
  Cream with Horse-radish, 178
  Cucumber, 183
  Currant, 179
  Currant, for Game, 179
  Dill, Green, 183
  for Fish, 177
  for Fish, Anise, 178
  for Game Meats, 176, 179, 180
  Garlic, 175
  Gooseberry, 180
  Grape (Sour), 181
  Horse-radish, with Almond, 178
  Horse-radish, with Cream, 178
  for Lamb and Mutton, 177
  Lemon, 172
  Mushroom, 184–5
  Mushroom with Wine, 18
  Onion, 175
  Orange, 181
  Parsley, Green, 183
  for Roast Meats, 176
  Sorrel, Green, 182
  Tarragon, 182
  Tomato, 183, 184
  for Veal, 178
  White, 174
  Wine, 172
Sauerkraut, Fried, 55
  with Mamaliga, 163
  Stew (Shepherd's), 54
Sausage, Beef and Pork, 101
  Mititei, 99
  Pork, Grilled, 101
  with Potatoes, 65

228 : INDEX

Shepherd's Sauerkraut Stew, 54
Sorrel, Green, Sauce, 182
Soups, 13–22
    Bean (Dried), 19
    Beef Stock, 15
    Beer, 22
    Caraway Seed with Dumplings, 20
    Chicken, 13
    Garlic, 20
    Gooseberry, 18
    Lettuce (Green), 17
    Meat, 14
    Omelet, 14
    Potato, 16
    Potato with Smoked Pork, 17
    Stock, 15
    String Bean, 17
    see also Ciorbas
Squash, Breaded, 67
    with Cheese, 68
    Ciorba, 30
    with Oil, 67
    Stuffed, 46
Stews, 139–52
    Beef, 149
    Beef in Ale, 149
    Beef with Potatoes, 150
    Chicken, 92
    Chicken in Cream, 144
    Chicken Liver, 141
    Chicken Liver with Onions, 141
    Chicken Peasant Style, 142
    Chicken with Tarragon, 143
    Chicken with Tomatoes, 143
    Eggplant with Meat (Baked), 5
    Fish, 80
    Goose Liver Peasant Style, 142
    Lamb, 151

Stews, Lamb with Green Herbs, 151
    Lamb with Okra, 152
    Lamb with Green Peppers and Carrots, 152
    Leek with Meat, 58
    Mixed Meat, 150
    Mushroom, 73
    Pork, 147
    Pork Peasant Style, 148
    Pork with Potatoes, 148
    Potato, 64
    Veal, 144
    Veal with Mushrooms, 147
    Veal from the Neck, 146
    Veal from the Shoulder, 146
    Veal with Vegetables, 146
    Veal in Wine, 145
Strawberry Chateaux, 214
String Beans, Salad, 190
    Soup, 17
    Green, 69
String Beans, with Meat, 68
    in Oil for Lent, 69
    Peasant Style, 68
Strudel, 199–201
    Cheese Square, 200
    Cream Cheese, 201
    Dough, 199
    Nut Squares with Syrup, 201
Strudel Fillings, 204–6
    Apple, 205
    Apricot, 205
    Cabbage, Raw, 205
    Cheese, Pot, 204
    Cherry, Sour, 206
    Cream, Sweet, 204
    Meat, see Meat Fillings,
Sturgeon, with Herbs, 84
    Marinated, 81
    with Onions, 84

INDEX : 229

Tarragon Sauce, 182
Tomato, Salad, 191
  Sauce, 183, 184
Tomatoes, Stuffed, 47–9
  Green, 47
  Red, 47
  with Chicken, 48
  with Eggs, 49
  with Ham, 48
  with Pot Cheese, 49
  with Rice, 47
Tongue, 111–3
  Beef, Smoked, 112
  Boiled (Smoked) with
    Tomatoes and Olives, 112
  Fresh Pork, 112
  Fresh Pork with Sauce, 112
  Fresh with Sauce (Cold),
    113
  in Pudding with Rice, 127
Tortes, 207–12
Tripe Ciorba, 28
Turkey Leftovers, 89
Turnips, Roasted, 69

Vanilla Chateaux, 215
Veal, 113–20
  ala Anisoara, 114
  Brains with Cream or Wine
    Sauce, 119
  Brains, Fried, 119
  Chops, Fried, 116

Veal, Chops Natural, 116
  Ciorba, 27
  Extras, 119
  for Fillings, 129
  with Garlic, 116
  Leg, ala Cluj, 113
  Liver, 120
  Liver Flora, 118
  Liver Stuffed, 117
  with Mushrooms, 117
  with Okra, 60
  Peasant Style, 115
  Roast, 113
  Sauce, 178
  Stew, 144
  Stew with Mushrooms, 147
  Stew from the Neck, 146
  Stew from the Shoulder,
    146
  Stew with Vegetables, 146
  Stew in Wine, 145
Vegetables, 33–69
  Ciorbas, 30–1
  Ghivetch, 34
  Musaca, 35–40
  Stuffed, 40–9
  see also names of vegetables

White Sauce, 174
Wine Chateaux, 213
Wine Dough, 198
Wine Sauce, 172

Manufactured by Amazon.ca
Bolton, ON